Otto Rahn
Grail Hunter

"Richard Stanley takes us on a fascinating hike through past and present, with rich scenery that is equal parts personal journey and fascinating occult history. From the Cathar castles to following the quest of occult-minded Nazis, Stanley quenches our thirst with a drink from the Grail in a literary journey you will want to take."

CHRIS BENNETT, HISTORIAN OF SPIRITUAL ENTHEOGEN USE, AUTHOR OF *LIBER 420: CANNABIS, MAGICKAL HERBS AND THE OCCULT*, AND COAUTHOR OF *GREEN GOLD THE TREE OF LIFE* AND *SEX, DRUGS, VIOLENCE AND THE BIBLE*

"At once a carefully researched, multi-layered historical analysis that includes important interviews with surviving witnesses as well as a deeply personal engagement with the material, this will be the definitive text on what we know and what we can know about the enigmatic and ultimately tragic figure of Otto Rahn—seeker of the Holy Grail and SS officer on Himmler's personal staff whose career spanned archaeological investigations at the Cathar fortress of Montségur and a stint as a prison guard at Dachau. This is the story not only of Rahn's struggle to unravel the Cathar secret, but also of what would become Richard Stanley's own quest to understand this tortured, lonely German scholar and to follow in his footsteps into a startling, luminous reality. Well written, engrossing, and indispensable for seekers of Grail history and its mysteries"

PETER LEVENDA, AUTHOR OF *THE SECRET TEMPLE* AND *UNHOLY ALLIANCE*

"*Otto Rahn, Grail Hunter* is the story of one flawed man's quest for the ultimate and redeeming treasure. Based on decades of firsthand research, this book sheds much-needed light on a shadowy, fateful figure but also relates to a perennial theme of the European spiritual tradition: the perilous quest for the greatest of all non-earthly treasures, the ever-elusive and transcendent Grail. Richard Stanley is a natural-born storyteller who draws the reader into his intriguing, strange, and darkly humorous tale of wonder and tragedy, where the threads of his own life and those of his subject become irrevocably interwoven. Those who who follow in the footsteps of the Grail hunters may soon find themselves transformed from skeptics into seekers, sharing in the triumphs and trials of the quest."

AKI CEDERBERG, AUTHOR OF *HOLY EUROPE* AND *JOURNEYS IN THE KALI YUGA*

"Richard Stanley's research on Otto Rahn is unique. He has immersed himself in Rahn's life for many years and is a leading authority on the subject. He is also a wonderful storyteller, and I highly recommend his book."

JOY MILLAR, COFOUNDER OF THE SAUNIÈRE SOCIETY

Otto Rahn
Grail Hunter

The Secret of the Cathars and the Return of the White Lady

RICHARD STANLEY

Inner Traditions
Rochester, Vermont

Inner Traditions
One Park Street
Rochester, Vermont 05767
www.InnerTraditions.com

Copyright © 2025 by Richard Stanley

All rights reserved. No part of this book may be reproduced or utilized in any form or by any means, electronic or mechanical, including photocopying, recording, or any information storage and retrieval system, without permission in writing from the publisher. No part of this book may be used or reproduced to train artificial intelligence technologies or systems.

Cataloging-in-Publication Data for this title is available from the Library of Congress

ISBN 979-8-88850-155-9 (print)
ISBN 979-8-88850-156-6 (ebook)

Printed and bound in India by Nutech Print Services

10 9 8 7 6 5 4 3 2 1

Text design and layout by Debbie Glogover
This book was typeset in Garamond Premier Pro with Cabazon, Gill Sans MT Pro, Gitan Latin, and Kepler Std used as display fonts

Creative Commons Agreements: fig. 1.3 (CC-BY-SA 3.0); fig. 4.13 (CC BY-SA 4.0). Figs. I.1, 1.2, 2.2, 3.4, 4.1, 4.3, 4.5, 4.6, 4.7, 4.8, 4.9, 4.14a, 4.14b, 4.20, 6.1, 6.5, 6.6, 6.10, 6.11, 6.13, 6.20, 6.21, 6.23, 7.1, 8.1, 8.8, 8.9, 8.10, 10.10, 13.13, 14.2, 16.1, 16.3, and 18.10 are courtesy of the Otto Rahn Memorial Website.

To send correspondence to the author of this book, mail a first-class letter to the author c/o Inner Traditions • Bear & Company, One Park Street, Rochester, VT 05767, and we will forward the communication.

Scan the QR code and save 25% at InnerTraditions.com. Browse over 2,000 titles on spirituality, the occult, ancient mysteries, new science, holistic health, and natural medicine.

For Madame Aimeé Couquet
(?–2021)
Keeper of Maison Couquet and
the Auberge d'Montségur.
Happy trails til we meet again.

**Hamilton White, Aimeé Couquet, and Richard Stanley, autumn 2019.
Photo by James "JB" Bourne.**

Contents

Foreword by Hamilton White	xi
INTRODUCTION To Know Is to Die	1
A Note on the Terminology Used in This Book	5
1 Close Encounters with the Ancient World	8
2 A History of the Cathars	23
3 Who Was Otto Rahn?	60
4 Otto's Quest for the Grail *The Crown of Lucifer*	73
5 A Visit to the Devil's Lake *Summer 1998*	108
6 Into the Labyrinth of the Pyrenees	120
7 Infiltrating the Order of the Polaires	154

8 The Methodology of Information
and Disinformation 190
Europe Hypnotized

9 Pagan Imperialism 203
Europe 1932–1938

10 Dark Camelot 214
Castle of the SS Order

11 The Fear 230
Germany 1938–1939 and Geneva 1998

12 Summer Solstice at Montségur 244
Midsummer 1998

13 The Stones from the Sky 256

14 The Face in the Pentagram 292
Autumn 1998

15 Searching the Ends of the Earth 302
Iceland 2005

16 The Death and Transfiguration of Otto Rahn 310
Germany 1938–1939

17 Aftermath 324

18 The Three Mothers	**328**
19 The Coming of the White Lady	**349**

EPILOGUE
Portal into Summer   371
Montségur June 21, 2015

APPENDIX 1
Otto Rahn   383
Life of the Grail Hunter

APPENDIX 2
Chronology of the Last Crusade   386

APPENDIX 3
Cathars of Montségur   408
The Martyred and Their Legacy

APPENDIX 4
The Holy Grail in the *Nottingham Evening Post*   415

Bibliography   418

Index   421

Foreword

Hamilton White

Ach, Mutter, was ist Gott?
[Oh, Mother, what is God?]
Wolfram von Eschenbach

While sat among the ruins of a twelfth-century Templar castle, I received the sad news that Madame Aimeé Couquet had departed this mortal coil, a sprightly old lady whom I met a couple of times and the very last surviving link to the intriguing character of the so-called Nazi Grail hunter, Otto Rahn.

For a moment I paused to contemplate my own mortality and reflect on the last few years since I happened, quite by accident, onto a large cache of Knights Templar relics, missing since the order fell from grace. This discovery had taken me across Europe, through the old Byzantine Empire, to Temple Mount in Jerusalem, and down to Occitania where so many paths seemed to merge: Templars, Cathars, crusaders, esoterics, Rahn, the Nazis, and now Richard Stanley, a Hollywood director! We have all walked the same pathways over the last 800 years or so. It is curious how so many disparate elements blend all our journeys together in the madness that is the "Zone," an area in the French Pyrenees of approximately 150 square kilometers renowned for its many present-day mysteries and aberrant belief systems, a region that was once the mountainous cradle of the Cathar faith.

I have walked with Richard up the ancient track to Montségur. We stood where Esclarmonde stood, looked down over the field where the unrepentant Cathars burned, sat on the stones Rahn sat upon when he contemplated the Grail and its meaning. What thoughts were going through his mind as he explored the initiatory mountain—the rock formation known as "the pog," as it is called in Occitan, upon which the Chateau de Montségur sits—and its environs? It is known that he was well versed in the works of Crétiené de Troyes and Wolfram von Eschenbach, two of the earliest writers on Grail mythology—stories made popular by the traveling band of troubadours that frequented Europe in the early Middle Ages.

Was Rahn seeking a physical object—a cup or platter as described in these epics? Could he have been on a different pathway, to locate the mythical Cathar Grail, a magical stone sent down from the heavens? Maybe he believed that the Grail was more of a spiritual concept—something within each and every one of us that leads to enlightenment?

Fig. F.1. Montségur castle sitting atop the pog rock formation. In old Occitan the word *pog* indicated something larger than a hill, yet smaller than a mountain (*puig*). It is not hard to believe the cliffs and forests of Montségur hide a secret, a mystery that lingers until the present day. Photo by Richard Stanley.

Foreword **xiii**

Fig. F.2. Hamilton White in the grotto of Ornolac, May 2022. Commonly known as the *eglise*, or cathedral, the grotto was used as a place of worship in ancient times and provided sanctuary to the fleeing heretics. In the initiatory journey outlined by neo-Cathar patriarch Antonin Gadal, it is the place where you leave your old life behind and step into the unknown.
Photo by Richard Stanley.

With Richard, I followed the Rahn trail over the Pyrenees to Montserrat and gazed at the same Black Madonna he cast his eyes over nine decades ago.

What is the enduring fascination with Rahn? Of Jewish heritage, he answered directly to Reichsführer Heinrich Himmler; his first book *Crusade against the Grail* becoming mandatory reading for those joining the SS. How did this lead to his eventual demise alone on a Tyrollean mountain in 1939?

Richard's own quest over the last thirty years has been his attempt to answer all these questions. Brilliantly researched, Richard contacted every surviving associate of Rahn from those pre-World War II days. The result is undoubtedly the definitive work on the short life of a gentle, fascinating, and much misunderstood man who strolled through the Occitan Valleys chasing his dreams all those years ago.

HAMILTON WHITE, PORTUGAL

HAMILTON WHITE is an author, collector, and dealer in antiquities, with a particular interest in weapons and artifacts of the crusader period. He is custodian of the Tomar Hoard, a unique collection of Knights Templar relics first discovered in Portugal in 1960. He spent many years exploring the islands of the Caribbean and has loaned his large collection of items relating to slavery, piracy, and the colonial era to what is now The Heritage Museum of the Bahamas in Nassau. He is the author of several history books.

INTRODUCTION

To Know Is to Die

Fig. I.1. Otto Wilhelm Rahn, 1904–1939.

It is not by chance I have come to be the caretaker of SS Obersturmführer Otto Wilhelm Rahn's memory, for if his story was ultimately an initiatory journey, then so is my own.

In the two decades I spent searching for Otto Rahn, I found something I can scarcely contain in words, a privileged glimpse beyond the mirror into a shadowland that exists one step from the world we think we know. Otto's work opened my eyes to that otherworld and despite his many shortcomings as a human being, I owe him much. He blazed the pathless trail for me and all those who will surely come after us. In the twilight years before World War II, Otto Rahn may have come closer than anyone in our modern era to comprehending the secret of the most sacred relic in Christendom, the high Holy Grail. Some believe he paid for that knowledge with his life. For Otto Rahn the initiatory journey ended in a precipice, yet he was prepared to make that final leap of faith.

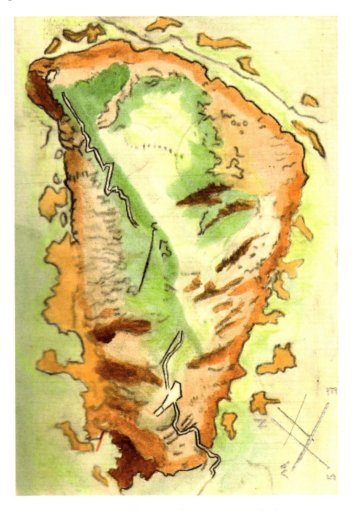

Fig. I.2. The pog of Montségur—a map of the quest.

Fig. I.3. The author pictured with ballista ammunition found on the east face of the pog, circa 1998.
Photo by James "JB" Bourne.

What follows is not a work of fantasy or speculative fiction. It is a faithful account drawn from firsthand testimony, letters, and journal entries. Whenever possible I have left the original texts unaltered, other than changing a few names to protect my informants.

As for the merits of Otto Rahn's case, I humbly lay my field notes before you so you may be the judge.

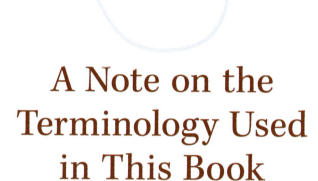

A Note on the Terminology Used in This Book

Throughout the text I have used the word *Cathar* to describe the dualist "heretics" who lived and died in southern Europe between the twelfth and fourteenth centuries and in some instances refer to their all but vanished faith as Catharism. It has become fashionable for modern historians, snippy archaeologists, and internet pedants to insist the Cathars never existed, given the accused heretics never identified as such, at least not in any of the documents that have come down to us. These humble, self-effacing souls referred to each other simply as good folk, good men, and good women—sometimes as the old, good beards, or good Christians, although this too can be deceptive given their nameless belief system incorporates elements of Buddhism and pagan animism.

It was largely the crusaders and Inquisitors who followed in their steps who used this term to define their enemy and the epithet has been adopted by subsequent researchers, given the tendency of history to be written by the victors. In truth the term *Cathar* was a loose definition, covering a broad tranche of individuals who expressed views or practiced rites and beliefs that existed outside or directly at odds with the straight and narrow of Holy Roman dogma. I will leave it to other better-informed scholars to split hairs over the differences between a deaconess, a perfecta, a priestess, an enchantress, a wise woman, and a witch—all faced the stake just the same.

The word *Cathar* is widely believed to be derived from the Greek *katharoi*, literally the "pure ones," although historically the term seems to have largely been used as a pejorative. In a subliterate premedieval world it is impossible to ignore the phonetic resemblance to other calumnies commonly used by the crusaders to belittle their victims, the Arabic term *kafir*, or unbeliever, generally applied to pagans and Black Africans, or the Teutonic *ketzer* or *ketter*, literally "black cat," used to decry witches.

In the latter part of the twentieth century, the term *Pays Cathar*, quite literally the "land of the Cathars" or "Cathar country" was widely promoted by French tourism as a rebranding exercise in the former departments of Languedoc-Roussillon and the Midi-Pyrénées, an initiative central Parisian authority later came to regret when fears grew that the promotional gimmick had inadvertently encouraged regionalism and Occitan separatism. These tensions came to a head in 2016 when inhabitants of the region voted overwhelmingly to revert to their former boundaries, bringing the geographic entity of Occitania back onto the map after an absence of more than seven centuries.

In the far-off days before the crusade, the north and the south of France spoke two completely different languages. Those in the north spoke Lenga d'Or while in the south, the language of the troubadours, Lenga d'Oc was the native tongue, named after the positive particle *Oc*—the Occitan word for "yes," derived from the Latin *hoch*. There was never a single standard spoken or written version of this language. The oldest surviving example dates from the tenth century, a manuscript transcribed in a mixture of Latin and d'Oc. The belief system known to modern historians as Catharism emerged in the Languedoc region in the eleventh century. Adherents to this essentially gnostic dualist tradition were commonly referred to as Albigensians, after the city of Albi where the faith took hold—from the Roman *Civitas Albigensium*—literally the "white city" or the "white people."

The faithful of this nameless religion were known as credentes and initiates as perfecti—*parfait* in French or *perfectus* in Latin. The central rite of their faith was a sacrament known as the consolamentum—a mysterious ceremony involving the laying on of hands that most credentes received on their deathbeds as an extreme unction, a form of anamnesis otherwise available only to adepts who had passed through all the stages of initiation.

It is said those who received the consolamentum were liberated from the cycles of time and material incarnation and came to remember their true nature as spiritual beings whose lives extended beyond their apparent births and deaths. Should any of these pure souls exist, may they give my thoughts consideration and lend strength to my words.

1
Close Encounters with the Ancient World

In a distant land, unreachable by your strides, a castle by the name of Mont Salvat exists.

WOLFRAM VON ESCHENBACH

I first came to the remote Pyrenean settlement of Montségur and scaled the mountain overlooking the village in the dog days of the summer of '92. Britain's Channel Four television had recently broadcast a hit show entitled *The Real Jurassic Park*, concerning efforts to extract dinosaur DNA from amber and were looking at a potential follow-up, provisionally entitled *The Real Raiders of the Lost Ark*, for a similar child-friendly, early evening slot. They say the devil makes work for idle hands and when the religion department offered me a healthy advance to research the story I jumped at the chance, being shy of a few pence at the time.

My initial companions on this ill-advised venture were a young researcher and occasional contributor to Britain's leading paranormal journal *The Fortean Times*, Mike Dee, and my then partner, artist, and designer Cat Knightly.

Fig. 1.1. The castle of Montségur.
Photo by Richard Stanley.

Given the European war had been over for forty-seven years and I had no great faith in the stories that Adolf Hitler was secretly alive and living in Argentina or Antarctica, I had no reason to believe I might be putting Cat in danger by bringing her with me. None of us had the slightest inkling of the rabbit hole we were about to fall into or just how deep that hole would be, a black hole in consensus reality lined with jagged, inconvenient data that would tear apart everything I thought I knew about modern Europe and give me an unwanted insight into the dark forces that brood over our fragile civilization. Certainly the meridional sun shone brightly enough and the day was warm as we steered our rental car up the winding road, threading its way ever deeper into the mountainous heart of the Ariège, a region described by the *Guardian* newspaper as "western Europe's last great wilderness area" but they do say that about the Pyrenees, "warm in the sunshine and cold in the shadows."

The Hitler survival myth and the so-called Nazi mysteries began to take root in the popular psyche shortly after the last round of the war was spent and the National Socialist German Workers' Party officially ceased to exist as a political entity, setting in motion a determined effort to define an esoteric aspect to National Socialism and reposition *Mein Kampf* as a mystical or quasi-religious text. Thousands of SS men and ordinary Wehrmacht confined to detention camps or facing ruin in postwar Germany sought an ideal they could cling to that was beyond the reach of the conquering Allies and unsullied by the criminal actions of their vanquished leadership. Some retreated into denial, while others found reassurance in viewing defeat as an inevitable phase in a millennial struggle that would eventually see their errant beliefs exonerated and the greater Aryan race triumph over its imaginary oppressors.

The earliest accounts of these Nazi mysteries surface in Pauwels and Bergier's rambling occult exegesis *The Dawn of Magic*, also published as *The Morning of the Magicians* (1960), and *Hitler et la Tradition Cathare*, also published as *The Occult and the Third Reich* (U.S. paperback edition, 1971), by Jean-Michel Angebert, a joint pseudonym for Michel Bertrand and Jean Angelini. These two books raised the specter of nebulous occult forces lurking behind the banal facade of the Third Reich. This largely mendacious mythology was codified and compounded in Trevor Ravenscroft's *The Spear of Destiny* (1972), a book the author later admitted was based on channeled information achieved through his alleged astral communion with the spirit of late theosophist Walter Johannes Stein, erroneously positioning this mild mannered literary historian as Hitler's occult initiator.

Despite the wildly contentious nature of his material, Ravenscroft's popular bestseller successfully promulgated the unsubstantiated notion that the Reich had deliberately sought to gain control over a series of talismanic power objects including the Ark of the Covenant, the Holy Grail, and the Spear of Longinus, a spear literally believed to have pierced Christ's side on the cross, a shopping list of lost relics that got longer as the tales grew taller. Ravenscroft's opus doubtless served to fuel Lawrence Kasdan's screenplay for *Raiders of the Lost Ark* (1981), leaving us with the sticky problem of trying to determine whether there was any truth to the murky backstory behind Spielberg's beloved classic.

I don't know why Channel Four television picked me for the job. Perhaps it was just the hat. My field of study had been anthropology, and I had no real background as a military or medieval historian, despite considering myself widely read.

During the early phases of our research, Mike Dee had drawn my attention to a curious, pseudo-autobiographical memoir written by a retired Texan army officer and chili cook-off champion, Colonel Howard Buechner, a self-published book entitled *Emerald Cup, Ark of Gold* (1991). Buechner's main claim to fame, that he was the "first Allied doctor to enter Dachau," has gone largely unchallenged, but these events take up less than a chapter of his very strange autobiographic account. Instead the former U.S. army surgeon unpacks an unlikely yarn concerning an obscure sect of heretical Christians, commonly known as the Cathars, who flourished in the south of France in the twelfth century and were said to have counted among their treasures the most high Holy Grail, a relic believed by Buechner to have been the literal emerald cup of Abraham.

According to Buechner's claims, based on unsubstantiated oral testimony allegedly drawn from captured Nazis after the war, the Reich had dispatched their very own Grail hunter, a mysterious occult scholar and medievalist named Otto Rahn who succeeded in locating

Fig. 1.2. Colonel Howard Buechner.

the sacred treasure in the French Pyrenees but died before it could be secured. Buechner was crucially unclear about quite how or when Rahn was supposed to have died, hinting that he had turned against his Nazi masters and either committed suicide or perished in the camps, suggesting he was held in Dachau until the latter stages of the war, only to be executed shortly before the arrival of the U.S. first army. The Holy Grail, Buechner insisted, was retrieved from the castle of Montségur in a daring commando raid, led by none other than elite paratrooper Otto Skorzeny.

At this stage, I was pretty much ready to throw Buechner's book at the wall, given Skorzeny's name tends to crop up in connection with every Nazi conspiracy theory, from dinosaur survivals to the Hollow Earth. It was true Skorzeny had rescued Benito Mussolini from the Allies in an extraordinary glider assault on the mountaintop fortress that held the fascist dictator in the fall of 1943, but virtually everything else written about the colorful commando leader usually turned out to be an exaggeration, if not outright fabrication. I suspected this tale would prove to be little more than another wild fiction. It certainly had all the elements of a pulp fantasy. It was all but impossible to believe in the existence of the Holy Grail as a physical relic and if this suggestion was not already far-fetched enough, Buechner went on to claim the "emerald cup" had been spirited to Antarctica in a secret U-boat convoy at the end of the war, apparently along with the "real Adolf Hitler."

In a psychotic variant on the myth of the eternal return, embroidered over the years by countless pseudohistorians and right-wing mythomaniacs, the führer was rumored to have survived the fall of Berlin, safe in the protective womb of a secret Nazi base hidden deep within the permafrost, presiding over the continuing esoteric struggle against the war's exoteric victors from his lair within the Hollow Earth, apparently waiting for the stars to come round before rising like Cthulhu to conjure a victorious Fourth Reich from the frozen embers, a second coming symbolized by the black sun, the twelve-armed Merovingian rune wheel

Fig. 1.3. Otto Skorzeny (1908–1975). German Bundesarchiv, Bild 183-R81453.

inlaid on the floor of the Hall of the Supreme Leadership in the SS order castle, the Schloss Wewelsburg, whose twelve radiant lightning bolts are believed by some to literally represent the dark light of the world within.

While entertaining enough in a *Boys Own Adventure* kind of way, I was only too aware that Buechner's fantasy had a potentially dangerous downside. Since the assassination of their leader George Lincoln Rockwell in the sixties, the American Nazi Party had taken a subtle and insidious approach to the media, adopting the neo-Trotskyite policy of entryism, infiltrating pop cultural movements such as the UFO community or the New Age movement (via intermediaries such as David Icke and *Nexus* magazine) to sow the seeds of militant pan-Aryanism without drawing attention to their racist agenda. The so-called Nazi mysteries (i.e., Ravencroft's spear, Kasdan's ark, and Buechner's emerald cup) had been adopted into the canon of these toxic beliefs and there is no doubt modern white supremacists have reaped some small benefit from old Indiana Jones in the process, something Steven Spielberg definitely wouldn't like to consciously consider. All publicity is good publicity, after all. It was possible these seemingly harmless fantasies could inadvertently prick the curiosity of young minds, while simultaneously distracting from the cruel memory of the Reich itself by erroneously suggesting the Nazis were an interesting, potentially spiritual people with something to say rather than just a bunch of murderous common thugs.

Accordingly, I approached Buechner's yarn with trepidation, setting aside just twenty-four hours in our itinerary to familiarize ourselves with the ruins of the Cathar citadel of Montségur, identified in his poorly copyedited text as the mythical "castle of the Grail." We arrived in the village at the base of the castle crag late in the day and were immediately impressed by the age of its narrow streets and the dilapidated stone-walled houses that seemed preserved from an earlier epoch. The densely forested mountains surrounding the settlement had isolated the village of Montségur from the tidal flow of European history until the first tar road, the D9, was cut into the valley in the mid 1960s. The very names of the surrounding topography clearly indicated the superstitious terror the conquering Roman Catholic crusaders must have felt for this remote, sparsely populated region, a district repeatedly anathematized by successive papacies. On three sides of the tiny ham-

Fig. 1.4. The village of Montségur.
Photo by James "JB" Bourne.

let rose the somber cliffs of the Rock of Shadows (Roc de la Mousse), the Rock of the Witches, and the Mountain of Fear (Montagne de la Frau)—and it was impossible not to notice that the local river rose from a topographic feature known as the Lac du Diable, or Lake of the Devil, just as Montségur itself had been referred to in times gone by as the Serpent's Head or the Synagogue of Satan.

On the day I first set foot in the village, the settlement was almost a ghost town, the original population having largely drained away with the coming of the road. Certainly you'd have to be crazy to live in a place like this, I told myself, utterly remote from the world and haunted by such a dire history. The ruins on the summit of the oddly shaped mountain overshadowing the village fired my imagination and we resolved to hike up to the abandoned castle to watch the sun go down. We were due to make an early start, so this would be our one and only chance to take in the remains of the twelfth-century citadel that had inspired Buechner's fanciful tale.

The white-walled fortress of Montségur clings to a spur of rock, 1,207 meters (3,960 feet) above the hills of Plantaurel on the northern face of a great massif known as the Tabor, or Throne of the Gods. Thanks largely to its inaccessible location, Montségur was among the very last of the so-called Cathar castles to fall to the Holy Roman crusaders. During a ten-month siege, the castle's defenders, a core group of little more than 300 knights and men-at-arms, took advantage of this all but unassailable position to hold at bay an army of up to 10,000 battle-hardened dogs of war. Despite the individual heroism (some might say fanaticism) of the defenders, the siege's outcome was inevitable.

The beleaguered garrison capitulated in the spring of 1244, and the survivors were granted surprisingly lenient terms. All who recanted and chose to return to the bosom of the mother church were spared while those who insisted on clinging to their heretical beliefs went to the stake. Such was their faith that, rather than recant, a great many of those who fought alongside the "heretics" chose to convert to their nameless religion at the final hour and go with them to their doom.

16   Close Encounters with the Ancient World

Fig. 1.5. The author on the battlement of Montségur.
Photo by James "JB" Bourne.

After a brief ceasefire to allow the castle's occupants to celebrate the spring equinox, a date synonymous with the Manichaean feast day of Bema, some 225 martyrs allegedly perished in the flames on the *Camp de Cremat*, or the field of the stake, at the base of the mountain. This action marked the end of any real political resistance to the patriarchal rule of the Holy Roman Church and rang the death knell for the mysterious dualist faith of old Occitania.

The trees arched above our heads, crowding in around the narrow path, and as we climbed higher Mike grew visibly apprehensive. Perhaps it was simply his fear of the coming dark, which was already creeping up from the ravines below but, for whatever reason, by the time we came in sight of the walls of the keep, Mike was feeling too uncomfortable to take another step. When he realized I had no intention of turning back he rounded on Cat.

"Are you coming with me or staying with him?"

Cat cast me an uneasy sidelong glance, confused by the change that had come over our companion.

"Staying with him, I guess . . ."

"Then give me the car keys."

Mike thrust out his hand and with the slightest of frowns. Cat did as he asked. Then, turning wordlessly, Mike hurried away down the mountain. We watched him go, confused and slightly unnerved, wondering what it was about this place that could have alarmed him. Shrugging it off we found our way to the highest point in the castle, the broad white battlement overlooking the gorge far below.

Even then it occurred to me there was something a little strange about the castle's architecture, but there was so little left of it other than its battered outer walls, that it offered scant clues as to the true purpose of its creation. While immediately impressed by the fact anyone could have built such a beautiful and complex construction at this altitude, I nonetheless suffered from the typically smug twenty-first-century assumption that the inhabitants of twelfth-century Occitania had been our scientific and intellectual inferiors, rustic, unlettered, superstitious, essentially *medieval* with all the mud-spattered, gurning, Pythonesque barbarity the word implies.

For good or bad, I was about to have those misconceptions shattered.

As the sun settled behind the Throne of the Gods, a golden spume of cloud boiled up out of the west, moving so fast it was as if we were watching real-time animation. In fact, this being the nineties and UFOs being all the rage, we half expected the mother ship from *Close Encounters* to show up at any moment. We stared at the whirling mass of cloud, slack-jawed, taking a beat to realize it wasn't a bunch of benevolent aliens. It was a sudden, violent, late-summer storm and it was coming right at us. Forked lightning flickered within the thunderhead and seeing as we were perched on the very highest point in the land, we decided to make ourselves scarce.

As we started hastily down the timeworn steps we realized we were no longer alone in the castle. A stranger was standing silently in the courtyard below, seemingly unperturbed by the gathering tempest. He wore a black, hooded cloak or jellaba fashioned from coarse homespun—and judging by his long hair and beard, I took him to be one of the locals, some kind of far-out hermit or survivor of the hippie wars grown so used to the mountain's ways that the prospect of all that incoming voltage didn't seem to faze him one bit. Something about the man's pale face and the stillness of his gaze unsettled us and we made no attempt to address him.

We tried to take shelter at the base of the castle's eastern wall as the storm closed upon us. The cloud swirled about the peak as bolts began to strike into the keep as if its stones were somehow drawing the lightning. Cat clung to me in panic, four or five streamers of writhing white-hot plasma intertwining at a time, reaching down from the vortex like a vast inhuman hand.

"What's happening!?"

I saw a blinding incandescence streaming from the curiously angled embrasures in the castle walls and the east-facing gateway, known as the *Porte des Dieux*, or Gate of the Gods—a light so bright I thought I might never see anything again.

Incandescent plasma licked horizontally across the flanks of the mountain below, close enough to make our hair stand on end. Warm rain squalled over us as night descended in a rush and we huddled closer to each other, whimpering like trapped animals, trying to make ourselves as small as possible.

"Just make it go away. Whatever it is make it go away . . ."

Let's face it, we know very little about lightning, and if the supernatural is merely the natural to the power of ten, then this was the genuine article. A bolt of lightning can kill you without even touching you. The electromagnetic pulse given off by the strike alone is enough to stop the human heart, even at a distance, and there were literally hundreds of thousands of volts earthing themselves only a few feet away from us. The sheer existential terror of it came upon us as suddenly as if we had been caught in a riptide, the belittling sensation of being trapped in the jaws of something far bigger and more powerful than oneself.

I sniffed the air, catching a strange, half-familiar smell that I took at first to be the scent of the wet mountainside, a sweet smell vaguely reminiscent of rosebay or the burned icing on the bottom of a wedding cake—a hint of almonds.

"God . . ."

Cat had been making frightened, panicked sounds, but when that sweet smell began to grow stronger, she curled more tightly against me and fell silent as if she was too scared to even breathe, let alone open her eyes. It was as if the storm were a living animal trying to sniff us out, feeling about the mountaintop with fiery tendrils. There were sounds that seemed to come from within the storm. Ridiculous as it may seem, there were sounds like voices, like the cries of human souls burning in hell. Later I tried to justify this absurdity by telling myself it must have been the bellowing of cattle in the fields far below, their lowing amplified and distorted by the weird Alpine acoustics, but at the time I was reduced to a state of cowering, medieval terror, which is what I deserved for having been fool enough to take the Holy Grail as a joke to begin with.

I remember recalling a sign we had seen on the fence at Stonehenge—WARNING: Ancient Monuments Can Be Dangerous! We had joked about it then.

"What did they do here? What did they do in this place?!" Cat whispered. Those were the last coherent words I can recall from her, repeated in my mind through the long years to come, but at the time I had no answer.

The only way out was the way we had come, crawling on hands and knees toward the swirling maw of the keep and the source of that strobing, flickering incandescence. For a moment I cowered on the threshold, trying in vain to make sense of what I saw.

The hooded man was standing in a vortex of light but there seemed to be other figures moving around him, shadowy outlines that were harder to get a fix on. I rubbed my eyes, realizing there were whole sections of the courtyard that I couldn't quite bring into focus, the details of the architecture obscured by an odd, shifting gloom that I rationalized as the shadows of dense, fast-moving clouds, projected by random flashes of lightning against the stonework.

Then Cat began to scream.

Later I would learn the walls of the castle form a Faraday cage and the voltage coursing through them that night would surely have altered the electromagnetic field within the keep. All I knew at the time was that as Cat stepped through the arch, she began to quiver and thrash, eyes rolling up in their sockets, wet hair fluttering and twitching in the static as her body shuddered with such violence that I truly believed she was being attacked by some unseen presence from out of the dark. My eyesight is normally 20:20, but the lightning was playing hell with my night vision and between bursts the gloom was impenetrable.

Grabbing her flailing figure, I tried to put myself between Cat and her invisible attacker. The other figures in the courtyard utterly ignored us, so caught up in their strange rapture they seemed unaware of our presence. I remember envying them their calm and wishing I could understand who they were or what they were doing. Some part of me wanted to stick around to see what would happen next, but instead I helped Cat as best I could across the rain-swept courtyard toward the west-facing gate, the *Porte des hommes*, or Gate of Man, and started back down the mountain.

At a lower altitude Cat's breathing stabilized as the pain that afflicted her, psychosomatic or otherwise, sharply diminished.

Strange motes of emerald light filled the night and when we reached the tree line, we realized the woods were alive with glow worms, presumably roused by the sudden late summer rain.

Cat's breathing grew tortured as we approached the base of the slope and she began to tremble again, unable to move any farther on her own. Then another fusillade of lightning struck into the mountain-top and she collapsed into what I would have taken to be a fully blown grand mal had she any previous history of epilepsy.

Legend has it that after the fall of the castle in 1244, the last of the faithful of Montségur had been burned in the first level place where the crusaders could build a stockade and gather the necessary brushwood. Cat didn't know about that terrible history and I had no intention of telling her or allowing her to remain where she was. Hauling her to her feet, I led us, inch by inch, down the winding road toward the village.

Whatever we had encountered on the mountaintop seemed to follow us as we struggled back to the tiny auberge where we had taken lodging. I knew we were in over our heads and my first instinct was to get the hell out of there. I remember banging frantically on the door of Mike's room in an attempt to regain custody of the car keys. Although I sensed movement within and knew he couldn't possibly be asleep Mike refused, for whatever reason, to acknowledge my presence.

"Rich . . . ard . . ."

I heard Cat utter my name and as I turned the clasps holding the window's steel shutters were abruptly torn free by the storm. Cat's voice tailed off in a moan as the shutters slammed against the quivering frame, lashing crazily backward and forward in the grip of the tempest, white light blazing in at us as if whatever we had encountered in the keep was right there outside the window or perhaps already in the room. Cat's flailing hand caught hold of my right arm, gripping me so tightly the bruise took more than a week to fade, her body shuddering as if something were being forced out of her. Or into her. . . .

"Cat . . ."

Her eyes bulged, veins rising to the surface of her purpling skin. Her grip was so strong that for a moment I was almost afraid of her.

"Nuhhhhh . . ."

"You've gotta"—in that strange, flickering, shifting light Cat's face seemed as livid as a week-old corpse—"fight it!"

Digging her nails from my flesh, I lunged toward the window. Narrowing my eyes I reached blindly into the roaring void, catching hold of the swinging shutters. Then, drawing them closed I wedged them sensibly in place with a steel bar. At that very moment Cat caught her breath and folded to the floor, losing consciousness as if the plug had been pulled on whatever force had been at work. Crouching beside her I checked her pulse, relieved to find normal color returning to her cheeks. Lifting her onto the bed and getting her into the recovery position, I drew up a threadbare armchair, holding vigil. I was too shaken to sleep and while the storm howled outside, I began to read everything I could find on the castle's history.

I had vaguely heard of the medieval Christian heretics commonly known as the Cathars, but up to that point my understanding of their strange faith and the genocidal war that mainstream Christianity had waged against them was limited.

Those of you who already know this story should feel free to skip ahead. For the rest of you, what I learned was this . . .

2
A History of the Cathars

Take my hand and we shall attain together that abode where fire has no heat, water no fluidity, matter no substance and where is enjoyed the blessedness of loving endlessly.

MAURICE MAGRE (1877–1944)

Once upon a time, more than seven centuries ago, there existed between France and Spain a land known as Occitania that occupied the same place on the map as the ancient Septimania of the Gauls and Visigoths. It was not a nation-state as we currently understand a democracy to be, but a patchwork of feudal demesnes and warrior dukedoms much like modern Afghanistan, with every river valley under the sway of its own warlord and the whole bound together by complex ties of blood, marriage, and a common tongue. It seems to have been an oddly enlightened culture for its time, perhaps too enlightened, and the high concentration of Jews and Muslims among the population bears testimony to its tolerance and the overlapping disciplines that gave rise to old Occitania's artistic and scientific achievements.

Jews and Muslims had the same rights as any other citizen to trade, settle, and worship freely. They could seek employment from gentiles,

Fig. 2.1. The Martyr's Memorial on Montségur's field of the stake. Photo by Richard Stanley.

teach in universities, and were entitled to protection from the local lord. The Trencavel family who ruled the mighty city-state of Carcassonne had Jewish ministers of finance. As the fame of the Occitanian universities spread, rabbis could be found teaching at Vauvert and Narbonne, the principal city for Jewish emigrees. By the dawn of the thirteenth century, the world was lit only by fire, yet there was a school of Jewish medicine in Toulouse and a school of magic in Salamanca. Several of the cornerstone works of the Kabbalah were written during that period in northern Spain and the area saw the first flowering of gothic art and architecture.

There had been a Jewish influx to the region a millennia before. Surviving examples of Hebrew and Aramaic text found on the altar of the church of Robichaud and elsewhere indicate Jewish merchants were operating in the Pyrenees from the earliest days of Roman colonization.

There can be little doubt proto-Christian baptismal cults, fanning out from the Holy Land along the Roman trade routes, established an early toehold in this far corner of the empire, possibly giving rise to the enduring myth that Mary Magdalene herself found sanctuary in Septimania after the crucifixion, landing at Sainte Marie de la Mer and living out her remaining days at Sainte Baume.

Surely if Mary of Magdala had set foot on Occitan soil she would have found fertile and receptive ground for her teachings, the way prepared by untold generations. The tradition of the feminine divine has deep roots in the Pyrenees for where proto-Christian priestesses practiced their mysterious baptismal rites, the doves of Aphrodite had once fed from vestal hands and on the mountaintops the Gauls had lit their bonfires to Belisama or Belisenna, the "bright" or "shining one."

While not actively matriarchal, as some have claimed, Occitania embraced equal rights. Children often took their mother's surnames and women were allowed to inherit land, officiate as priests, and even command armies. A democracy of sorts existed in the form of elected magistrates, or *capitouls*, who acted as a check on the power of the church and the aristocracy. The cities of Toulouse, Carcassonne, Bézier, and Nimes were governed as independent city-states, almost mini republics. Every city had a council of elected capitouls with its presidency taken by the local lord. Decision-making was by vote of the council and the main responsibility was to protect residents in times of strife. The system worked well, and agriculture flourished as did the production of wine and olive oil. Cities established commercial trading agreements with coastal towns and favorable conditions were made available to foreign merchants. Ships from all nations came to anchor at Occitan ports with notable traders including the Genoese, Pisans, Greeks, and Normans. Moorish fabrics and silk from the Orient could be found in markets alongside spices with names not heard before in western Europe.

Above all, the citizens of Occitania embraced the code of chivalry, which allowed for a certain amount of movement between the classes. A burgher or serf could become a knight if he was valiant and loyal or knew how to compose music or poetry. Elsewhere in Europe, knighthood was inconceivable without nobility, but the attributes of Occitan knighthood—accessible to anyone regardless of race, country, or class—were nothing less than the sword, the word, and the lyre.

A troubadour could swear fidelity to his lady as if she were a feudal lord and from then on she would receive him according to the statutes of chivalry determined by the Courts of Love. This tradition, allegedly founded by Eleanor of Aquitaine, called on the noble ladies of the land to assemble once a year, usually in the spring, to adjudicate the social ecology of their world. From what scant documentation survives, these courts would seem to have been akin to quasi-Masonic lodges presided over by an elected high priestess or chatelaine who conferred with her peers to determine whether or not a knight or vassal had acted honorably, a sort of weaponized kaffeeklatsch of the highest order. Montségur's sister castle Puivert (literally the "green well") was one of the principal locations where these extraordinary gatherings held session, an ancient white-walled fortress overlooking a lake and a natural limestone maze known to this day as the green labyrinth. These courts recorded their proceedings, issued statutes, and referred to past rulings to determine fair judgment was passed. There were degrees of chivalry, like any secret society or initiatory process, for there was in those days a service of love just as there was a service of vassalage. There were four trials, four stations in that journey, four phases to a knight's devotion to his lady—first that of humble aspirant or *fegnedor*, then supplicant or *precador*, before they could be openly acknowledged as *entendedor*, or raised at last to the exalted realm of *drut*, or accepted love.

While honor and loyalty were cherished, truth remained the essential quality of knighthood, for it was believed in those far-off times that a knight who was true in heart could never fail in single combat.

It was the tolerance of the south that proved its undoing. The old pagan ways still lingered and the mountainous cradle of the Pyrenees became a haven for freethinkers and the nurturing ground of a variant form of Christianity that admitted no intermediaries between humankind and God. The nameless faith that flourished in these hills and vales in the late twelfth century eschewed material wealth and entertained Eastern concepts such as reincarnation and vegetarianism, perceiving animals to have souls similar to our own. Fish were commonly deemed fair game for the pot, thanks to a poor premedieval grasp of biology. The soul was commonly believed to reside in the breath and fish were thought to appear naturally like fruit or flowers. Modern neo-Cathars would doubtless be aware fish spawn through eggs and hence possess a similar motive essence to every other living being. At the point the so-called Cathar faith was driven underground, initiates were still debating whether dolphins and whales were fish or mammals, an issue that would not be resolved until generations later.

Some believe the Cathar faith was a surviving proto-Christianity, similar to the belief system of John the Baptist and the Essenes, while others maintain it was a Manichaean mutation derived from the Gnostic doctrines of Valentinus, Marcus of Memphis, and Priscillian of Avila. Priscillian has the dubious distinction of being considered the first heretic, the first Christian recorded to have been killed by other Christians over a variant interpretation of the scriptures. Priscillian was put to death by the sword in 380 CE after being accused of practicing magic (maleficium), holding nocturnal meetings with women, and praying in the nude. Certainly Priscillian of Avila's emphasis on asceticism, the distinction between darkness and light and flesh and Spirit echoes the later Cathar credentes. His persistence in studying the forbidden gospels of the apocrypha coupled with a heartfelt conviction that all living souls must strive toward perfection, an initiatory process Priscillian codified into three degrees, marks this freethinking, fourth-century martyr as being cut from the same spiritual cloth as the later adepts of Albi.

The Cathars believed infinite goodness was incapable of creating evil, hence as the world was filled with suffering it could not be the creation of the one God espoused by the three principal monotheisms. They suggested the flawed material world is an illusory veil woven by a lesser god, sometimes referred to as the demiurge or *Rex Mundi*, the "king of the earth." This demiurge is not necessarily a force of evil but imperfect and quite possibly unaware of its own imperfections. The Cathar adepts identified all clerical and secular rulers, principally the Holy Roman Church, as the manifestation of this demiurge and believed that either through multiple involuntary reincarnations or a form of direct initiation known as the consolamentum one might escape the cycles of time and the deterministic prison of the material world.

The consolamentum was a form of extreme unction given at the approach of death that involved the laying on of hands in a rite said to date back to the time of the apostles. After receiving the consolamentum the Cathar credentes would enter a state of *endura*, fasting themselves to death or deliberately exposing themselves to the elements in the hope of abandoning their physical bodies and returning to the stars, the domain of the true good God.

While the essential elements, the core beliefs of Catharism may have already been present in the syncretic petrie dish of the south, the heretical faith of Occitania did not gain a cohesive identity until the arrival of the legendary Bogomil missionary Nicetas in the late twelfth century. Papa Nicetas, as he is described in period sources, belonged to the *ordo* of Drugunthia/Dragovitia—an ordo being the sequence of consolamenta that allegedly linked them to the Apostles. Nicetas received his consolamentum from bishop Simon of Dragovitia, a controversial figure in his own right who was later denounced and excommunicated from the Bogomil church, effectively invalidating his lineage. Nicetas is said to have walked all the way to Toulouse from Lombardy and the Caucasus, bearing with him a mythical grand grimoire known as the Book of Love or the Book of the Seven Seals—a book that would supposedly only be opened at judgment day. The true identity of this long-lost text, the foundation document of the formal Cathar Church, has never been established although it is widely assumed to have been some sort of gnostic gospel. Prewar occultists commonly identified this tome with the lost Gospel of Saint John, a text that has subsequently been located among the Dead Sea scrolls at Kumran and is now available online, whereas modern pseudohistorians suggest it may have been either the lost Gospel of Mary Magdalene or even the "real-life Necronomicon" (see Kathleen McGowan, Michel Lamy, et al.).

The Bogomil saint and former archbishop of Constantinople, "Papa" Nicetas, certainly existed, even if his movements carry the stuff of myth about them. He laid the foundations of the new church at Saint-Felix de Caraman and arranged its bishoprics and dioceses, entrusting his precious book to his followers before departing for Sicily where he founded a parallel order—the *Fedeli d'Amore*, or Brotherhood of the Faithful in Love.

This metaphysical enlightenment spread through the south like a psychoactive virus as the common people turned en masse from the outmoded and restrictive practices of the Holy Roman Church, refusing to pay tithe and seeking a new way that promised the Earth could indeed become a paradise. The perfecti held services in fields and forests rather than churches and espoused birth control, believing indiscriminate coupling served only the devil by trapping more souls into "tunics of flesh." In Carcassonne, rich merchants who heard the word gave away their goods and belongings. In Montauban a man named Querigut scandalized the community by giving his wife to another man who loved her more deeply. Abandoning his home, he took to living in the forest and subsisting on roots and berries. Worse still, others followed his example. The heresy spread with uncanny speed and virulence, but ultimately it was the growing power wielded by the daughters of Occitania that really shook the patriarchal church to its foundations and kept the Roman pope awake at night.

At that time, being the early thirteenth century, the greatest of the Cathar high priestesses was the noble Esclarmonde de Foix, whose name can be translated as the "light of the world," etymologically linked to the French *eclair*, or lightning strike, just as *foix* literally means "faith." It is as if fate decreed that Esclarmonde would come to embody the guardian spirit of her land, incarnated at a time when her land needed her most.

Fig. 2.2. The castle of Foix. Photo by Otto Rahn.
Courtesy of the Otto Rahn Memorial website.

There are few deeper mysteries than the mysteries of blood. Esclarmonde de Foix was the daughter of an ancient Ibero-Celtic aristocracy with deep roots in in the Comminges that through marriage and good fortune would eventually flow into the royal bloodline of France. Many fancifully believe the so-called Grail family to be carriers of dragon, faery, or elf blood. It is scarcely surprising that popular folklore would subsequently blur the otherwordly figure of the great Esclarmonde with both the Guardian of the Grail and the Dame Blanche, the so-called "white lady" or Queen of the Elves. The term *elf* derives from *albi*, literally "white" or "shining one." From this same root, *albi*, comes the name commonly given to the Cathars, Albigensian (Albi + Gens), potentially meaning "of the elven blood."

Marked by a childhood encounter with the Bogomil mystic Nicetas in her father's hall, na Esclarmonda (as she would have been correctly addressed in the day) only took the cloth after living a full life as a wife and mother and devoted much of her energy to founding schools for women and shelters akin to heretical convents. They say she resembled divine wisdom made flesh and in her the Holy Roman Church found its most formidable opponent.

By the end of the twelfth century, the rise and exponential growth of the Cathar faith represented a genuine challenge to the faltering hegemony of the Roman church and a weakened papacy struggling to maintain its hold over mainland Europe after the fiasco of the third crusade.

In 1204 Pope Innocent III formulated a new authority to address the problem of the heretics, headed by Arnaud de Citeaux, whose Cistercian monks were given the task of restoring Occitania to the bosom of the mother church. Joining forces with the Spanish mendicant Domingo de Guzman, Citeaux criss-crossed the south with little success, finding his sermons greeted with apathy and opposition. Catharism had grown too strong to be dislodged by words alone.

Fig. 2.3. The Light of the World, Esclarmonde de Foix (1155–?), defender of Montségur.
Courtesy of Hamilton White.

Fig. 2.4. These rare postcard images are all that remain of a statue of the high priestess that was supposed to stand guard over the town square in Foix, the administrative capital of the Ariège. While a maquette was commissioned and built, the town council subsequently got cold feet and consigned the image to oblivion, not wanting to draw undue attention to the region's troubling history. Thanks to the determined efforts of the Inquisition, not a single representation of the Cathar high priestess, her comrades, and credentes has survived into the present day. According to folkloric belief, she is thought to have been a redhead.
Courtesy of Hamilton White.

In 1206 Domingo de Guzman and his fellow monks saw a fireball fall from the sky over the hilltop town of Fanjeaux, a bastion of heresy where na Esclarmonda had been initiated. Believing the unidentified atmospheric phenomena to be a blazing sign from God, Domingo vowed to found a new order that would wipe Catharism from the face of the Earth. Planting a fig tree to symbolize his newfound resolve, Domingo set about his life work, the creation of the *Domini canes*, or dogs of God, the black-garbed Dominican order destined to oversee the bureaucracy of the Inquisition, the system of terror, interrogation, and persecution that would serve as a template for the modern police state. Thanks to the "miracle of Fanjeaux," Domingo would subsequently be canonized as St. Dominic, patron saint of astronomers.

In 1207 the Count of Toulouse was excommunicated for allowing heretics to live on his lands, marking the start of a new phase of attacks on the population of Occitania. Conversion would now be by force rather than persuasion. An order was issued that all bishops must preach a crusade against the heretics *"who are worse than the Saracens."*

Emboldened by a sense of manifest destiny, Domingo confronted the arch-heretic Esclarmonde de Foix at the conference of Pamiers—a last attempt at peaceful debate between the Cathars and the Holy Roman Church. Domingo arranged a public ordeal by fire, placing a page from the Bible and a Cathar text side-by-side on the coals. The parchment burned to ashes while the page from the Bible flew up to the rafters, which Domingo took as a sure sign of the Roman church's God-given supremacy. When na Esclarmonda attempted to address the assembly, she was ordered to return to her spinning by the patriarchal Roman prelates, "Go back to your distaff, woman." The words still echo across the centuries. The southerners were known for their skills in spinning fabrics of a quality hitherto unknown to the northerners, indeed the heretics were often refered to as the weavers, their craft deeply connected to the magical lore of their ancestors. In southern churches the blessed virgin was often depicted holding a distaff in one hand and na Esclarmonda may well have felt she held the destiny of her kingdom in her supple fingers.

Convinced a cataclysm was descending upon Occitania, the high priestess made pilgrimage to the place where she felt strongest communion with the realm of Spirit, to the sacred mountain of Montségur high in the Ariège. Even then there was an old ruin on top of the mountain, possibly a Celtic or Roman temple aligned to the seasonal positions of the sun, moon, and stars.

Guided by her presentiment of doom, na Esclarmonda charged the young lord of Montségur, seventeen-year-old Raimond de Pereilha, to refortify the mountaintop. Drawing on the treasury of Foix to endow the work, the aging priestess personally oversaw the construction of granaries and cisterns dug deep into the rock, preparing the citadel to

Fig. 2.5. Lothario Conti, Pope Innocent III, architect of the Albigensian genocide.

receive the refugees from the coming apocalypse. The work was supervised by Raymond de Mirepoix and Raymond Blasco, with the walls of the keep rising a good 400 feet above the surrounding territory and a barbican constructed on a lower plateau to the west.

In 1208 Pope Innocent III dispatched several apostolic legates to Toulouse in the hope of setting an example strong enough to scare the people of the south back into the arms of the mother church. They chose as their first victim the venerable capitoul, Pierre Maurand, who had been the host of Nicetas during the Bulgarian mystic's visit to the south. The legates summoned Maurand, interrogated him, convicted him of heresy, and condemned him to death. Shocked by the severity of their judgment the elderly Maurand immediately recanted. He was stripped naked and forced to walk barefoot from the prison to the church of Saint Sernin between the bishop of Toulouse and one of the legates who beat him unmercifully with rods in what has come to be known as the walk of shame. Maurand's property and possessions were confiscated, and the old man was made to scourge himself and wander the streets naked for forty days before being exiled to the Holy Land to effectively serve as slave labor. The public was outraged by these high-handed actions and the threatening words of the legates who warned the Toulousians that their city would be destroyed unless they complied with the pope's demands. On the way back to Rome one of the legates, Pierre de Castelnau, was dragged from his horse and murdered while crossing the river Garonne near Fourques. Castelnau was allegedly run through with a spear by a knight who had ridden after them to avenge the honor of his master, Raymond IV, lord of Toulouse. This unfortunate event would provide the pretext for a military campaign against Occitania.

In 1209, Pope Innocent III authorized a punitive military campaign against the so-called heretics that would become a war of extermination, a last crusade fought on the soil of mainland Europe. To persuade men to join, the pope offered incentives in the form of papal indulgencies, the same offer made to those joining the crusades to the Holy Land—"Any person, as great a sinner as any, can escape the torments of hell if he fights against the heretics." In simple terms this was an offer from God's earthly representative for the forgiveness of all sins committed before or during the crusade.

I suspect the dogs of war were motivated by greed more than anything else, by the desire to possess the fertile lands and the notoriously beautiful daughters of the south, and the Holy See needed to find a way of scaring folk back into believing in the infallibility of the mother church after the shock of losing Jerusalem to the Moors, just as the United States saw fit to wage war on Iraq to make up for the trauma of 9/11.

A huge force rallied to the cause, an army like none assembled before in France converged on Lyon. The prelates assured the war hounds that in no more than forty days all would return home enriched with captured wealth and the promise of salvation.

The brilliant strategist Simon de Montfort was placed in overall command of the punitive force, a figure who was very much the

Fig. 2.6. Simon de Montfort—the lion of combat and butcher of the south.

Dick Cheney of his day, having honed his talents during his time in the Holy Land where he showed an extraordinary aptitude for reorganizing the administration and methodically asset stripping conquered cities and nations.

Besides Simon de Montfort, other aristocrats who rode with the last crusade included the duc de Borgogne, the counts of Nevers and St. Pol, and the seneschal of Anjou. The host (numbering between 10,000 and 20,000—some accounts estimate over 100,000) marched south, along the river Rhone, toward Provence. They were joined by Arnaud-Amaury, a papal legate who was granted titular leadership as spiritual advisor to the "holy" campaign.

Realizing the crusaders were heading toward his lands, the young prince of Carcassonne, Raimond Roger de Trencavel, who had been conducting frantic shuttle diplomacy between Foix and Toulouse, met the host in Montpellier, demanding an audience with their religious leader in order to "surrender to the church." Arnaud-Amaury stubbornly refused to receive the young prince, closing the door on further negotiation and the possibility of a peaceful resolution to the crisis. Knowing his people were about to be brutally attacked, Trencavel quickly returned to Carcassonne to organize his defenses, taking with him most of the Jewish population of Béziers to whom he promised safe passage.

On July 21, 1209, the crusaders reached Béziers and demanded the Cathars in the population be handed over. This hideous request was refused even by the Roman Catholics of the town. The next morning, on the feast day of Mary Magdalene, the defenders launched an ill-advised sortie that, when forced back through the gate, was closely pursued by a band of crusaders. Once inside the walls, the crusaders seized Béziers within an hour, beginning a mass slaughter of Catholics and Cathars alike, a massacre whose consequences will continue to reverberate through the narrows of time until its causes are understood. When asked by one of his warriors how to tell the difference between a good Christian and a heretic, Arnaud-Amaury delivered the notorious verdict, "Kill them all! God will recognize His own!"

Terrified women and children sought refuge in the cathedral of Marie Madeleine where they were duly cut down and burned by the dogs of war who spared no one in the city. Between 10,000 and 20,000 civilians are believed to have perished in the sack of Béziers with just over 200 estimated to have been heretics.

The massacre terrified other towns into surrendering without resistance and on August 1 the crusaders arrived before the walls of Carcassonne, a fortified city of twenty-six towers overlooking the Aude River. The town's population was swollen with fleeing Jews and heretics who looked to their beleaguered prince, Raimond Roger de Trencavel, for protection.

The Trencavel family were vassals to King Pedro II of Aragón, who came in person to the besieged city in an attempt to mediate. Once again Arnaud-Amaury refused to give quarter, and the Aragonese regent departed in anger, leaving the young prince to stand alone against the crusader army. A fierce siege ensued with both sides employing trebuchet and mangonel rotating-beam artillery. The crusaders succeeded in cutting off the defenders' access to the river, with thirst and spreading disease doing the rest, forcing Trencavel to seek terms for surrender. After being promised safe conduct, the young prince rode alone into the crusader camp to negotiate with de Montfort and Amaury, only to be taken prisoner—an act pinpointed by some historians as the death of the age of chivalry. Spirit broken by the loss of their heroic leader, Carcassonne capitulated, opening their gates to the crusaders. Rather than conduct another massacre, Amaury and de Montfort forced the residents to depart the walled city naked, "wearing nothing but their sins," their property and personal effects confiscated as spoils of war. The betrayed prince Raimond Roger de Trencavel would perish two months later in the dungeons of occupied Carcassonne. He was twenty-five years old.

The towns of Castelnaudary, Fanjeaux, Montréal, Limoux, Castres, Albi, and Lombers all surrendered to the crusaders without resistance and de Montfort was granted suzerainty over the stricken nation. The dogs of war fell upon the south in an ecstasy of rage. In Bram they

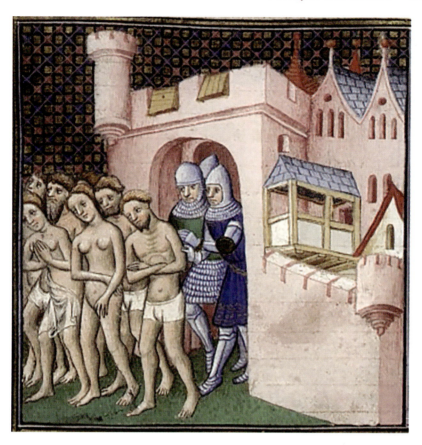

Fig. 2.7. Survivors of the siege of Carcassonne (August 1209) are unceremoniously herded out of the fallen city wearing "nothing but their sins."

cut off the faces and gouged out the eyes of everyone in the village, over a hundred citizens all told, leaving only one unfortunate with one eyeball to guide the walking wounded to the next settlement so that they could see what was coming and know to obey. Having dispensed with the codes of chivalry, the hounds of God opened the gates of hell, embracing nihilism and a new era of total war in the full knowledge their every crime would be forgiven.

When the crusaders seized Lavaur, the castle of Aimery de Montréal, de Montfort consigned the lord and his knights to the gallows. So many were hung the gibbet snapped, forcing the executioners to cut the throats of those remaining, which they did until the ground became wet and slippery with blood. De Montfort reserved special enmity for Lord Aimery's sister, Giralda de Laurac, who was a hugely respected figure in the community, a high priestess and chatelaine of the Courts of Love. They say her judgment was always fair and no one ever left her table with an empty stomach. Determined to set an example and send a message to the noblewomen of the land, Simon de Montfort turned dame Giralda over to his fighting men for their sexual amusement before ordering her still-living body to be flung into a well. This wasn't enough to kill Giralda so her followers were made to sit around the well and watch while stones were dropped on their chatelaine until she shut up. Then they butchered her followers.

In the English lands, the de Montfort family are celebrated as the founders of Britain's bicameral parliamentary system but in the mountains of Occitania their legacy is a bitter one with Simon's actions leaving wounds that have yet to heal. Despite being so shortsighted he was allegedly scarcely able to see the battlements of the castles he besieged or the despair in the eyes of those he condemned, Simon de Montfort was possessed by a genius for warfare, designing and building weapons unlike anything the world had seen. He frequently made use of "cats," armored platforms pushed up against castle walls to protect the sappers who tunneled beneath the buttresses. After a few days of digging, the wooden props in the "land mines" would be set afire and the walls would come tumbling down, allowing de Montfort's dogs of war to stream through. When the defenders learned to set the cats aflame with their arrows, de Montfort ordered horses and livestock to be slaughtered, fireproofing his siege engines by covering them in wet hides and offal. At Minerve he oversaw the creation of the largest and most powerful catapult in military history, a siege engine nicknamed *Malvoisine*, or bad neighbor, that swiftly pounded the castle into submission.

The first mass burning of Cathars took place after the fall of Minerve when the crusaders decided on the procedure of separating the heretics from other members of the community and consigning all who refused to recant to the flames, an infernal punishment that would soon become standard practice. Once sparked by de Montfort's crusaders, the Inquisitors and zealots who came after them would keep the witch fires burning for centuries.

As if guided by malign providence, the flames of this premiere auto-da-fé were kindled at Minerve on the feast day of Mary Magdalene, July 22, 1210, exactly one year after the massacre at Béziers. Approximately

Fig. 2.8. The fate of the Cathars.

150 heretics, men and women alike, faced an unspeakable death, burned offerings to a careless God, a deity seemingly blind and deaf to the suffering and perfidy of its creations.

Resentful of de Montfort's growing influence, the Catalan monarch, King Pedro II of Aragón, finally moved to oust the crusader army from the south. Having devoted himself to driving the Moors from Spain, the fiery Catalan leader considered himself to be the pope's champion and the strong right hand of God. After allegedly spending the evening before the decisive engagement, the night of September 11, 1213, in the arms of his concubine, the Spanish seeress, Maria Padhila, King Pedro laid siege to de Montfort at the castle of Muret. Despite commanding a vastly superior force, the monarch rapidly found himself outflanked and outmaneuvered by his crafty opponent and was slain in the rout, ending the dream of a greater Catalonia, breaking the power of the house of Aragon forever and sealing Occitania's fate as an independent nation.

The short supply lines and Occitania's lack of a unified political identity promised easy victory for the crusaders, but de Montfort did not live to see an end to the conflict. The military genius who would be remembered as the butcher of the south fell at the gates of Toulouse on midsummer's day, 1218, struck down by a rock fired from a mangonel, a rotating-beam weapon allegedly manned by a crew of women stationed on the roof of the chapterhouse where the capitouls once held session. The name of the woman responsible for the lucky shot has not come down to us but they say a flash of blonde hair was glimpsed on the rampart. Crusading was a family business and this proved a bad day for the de Montfort clan. Simon's younger brother, Guy, had just been struck in the groin by a crossbow bolt, a grievous wound he quipped would make him a hospitaller—a knight order renowned for their vows of chastity. When Simon came to his stricken brother's aid, the missile fired from the chapterhouse took off most of his head. Such was his ferocity, they say Simon de Montfort's body continued to chicken walk a few more steps toward the besieged city before pitching forward and bleeding out.

The loss of their military leader left the crusade in disarray, forcing the French king and the Holy Roman Church to redouble their efforts, sending fresh reinforcements to the south. Lacking the mechanization of the Nazis, it would take more than a century for the dogs of God, the black-garbed monks of the Inquisition, to achieve their aims. Not only were libraries and records burned and the written word outlawed, but the Occitan people were ultimately bred into extinction by laws making it illegal to marry anyone who did not eat meat or speak French. By the time the dust settled, the kingdom of Occitania had been wiped from the map and its language, a form of Anglo-Saxon not entirely dissimilar to English, known to later historians as Occitan, passed into oblivion.

As the cities fell to the crusaders, the mountainous heartland of Occitania, the forests and high pastures of the Ariège, held out against the invaders under the indomitable leadership of na Esclarmonda's impetuous brother, Roger Ramon, the redheaded Count of Foix. The count was a former troubadour who sang as he rode, having passed through all four stations in the trials of chivalry. Accordingly he was known to his people as Raimond Drut, or Raimond the beloved. Unlike his sister, Raimond Drut was no pacifist and proved a fierce defender of his lands, a veritable thorn in the side of Christendom who never suffered a captured crusader to go free without losing an eye, a hand, or a foot.

In February 1221, Raimond Drut burned Fanjeaux, the town where Domingo de Guzman founded his black order. It is recorded the vengeful redheaded count rode his horse into the burning church and tilted with his lance at the statue of Christ while yelling the immortal words, "Save yourself!"

After the murder of the prince of Carcassonne, Raimond Drut adopted his son, Roger de Trencavel II, spiriting the boy to Foix for safekeeping in the hope he might one day be capable of reuniting his shattered kingdom. In November 1215, Raimond Drut took his ten-year-old ward to Rome to petition Pope Innocent to return his lands and addressed the Fourth Lateran Council. When asked by the pope whether it was true he had killed priests, Raimond Drut coolly replied,

"My only regret, your holiness, is I have not killed more." It is perhaps unsurprising that Raimond Drut's requests for justice and redress fell on deaf ears. Eight years later, Prince Roger de Trencavel II, now in his teens, would lead a popular uprising to retake his father's lands by force, briefly recapturing Carcassonne.

Montségur's patron, protector, and spiritual light, na Esclarmonda managed to stay one step ahead of the Inquisition all her life, earning her the nickname the Fox of Foix. It is not known when death overtook her, but it is believed she ended her days in Montségur, the white-walled castle that became her sanctuary. It was the custom of the Inquisitors, who believed in physical resurrection at the end of time, to mutilate the corpses of those heretics they could not punish in life, sowing their ashes to the four winds. It is likely the Cathars hid the bodies of their leadership from their persecutors, and it did not take long for a myth to arise that na Esclarmonda still lived beyond the cycles of time and the reach of the papacy. High in the mists of the Ariège, her white-garbed figure was said to still reach her hands heavenward in the ancient sign of blessing, guiding her kingdom through the dark years that followed. To this day it is whispered na Esclarmonda never died but passed alive into the kingdom of heaven, like Christ or the prophet Elijah before her, her human form transfigured into Spirit, taking on the form of a dove, the living symbol of her nameless faith.

After her passing, a second na Esclarmonda arose, the niece of her saintly namesake, destined to become the castle's defender and heroine of the south. This second Esclarmonde was allegedly born out of wedlock along with her twin brother, Loup, after Raimond Drut's dalliance with a nun during a wolf hunt in the high Ariège. Conflicting data surrounding the birth of these troublesome twins suggests the story of their conception may have been distorted by Inquisition disinformation. It is possible Raimond Drut had his marriage to Countess Phillipa of Montcardo annulled after she took the cloth and was legally wed to the second Esclarmonde's mother, a figure named in some sources as Rixende (or Rixenda) of Teilho. The Holy Roman Church did not recognize divorce and doubtless found it prudent to disallow any claim this second Esclarmonde and her brother may have had to sovereignty.

Commonly believed to have been born to a raped abbess and raised at a distance from her father's court in Foix, the second Esclarmonde was rumored to be a sorceress who "consorted with certain dethroned pagan divinities whose language she spoke and whom she called down from the mountains to do her bidding" (Magre, *Le sang de Toulouse*, 1931. Author's translation.). When the crusaders finally ventured past the Forest of Toads and the Mountain of Fear to bring war to her woodland kin, "Esclarmonde the bastard" is said to have taken up a sword and donned armor to fight alongside her brother, Loup, so named after their father's exploit on the night of their conception.

According to a romantic tradition recorded by the thirteenth-century troubadour Guilhelm Montanhagol and popularized by Napoleon Peyrat's *Histoires des Albigeois* (1870), this second Esclarmonde organized shepherds to roll down rocks on the crusaders as they tried to pass through the gorges and lit the night beacons that were the only form of communication between the scattered bands of loyalists. She is said to have taken many lovers and like her venerable aunt, avoided capture, slipping effortlessly out of the pages of recorded history and into the warp and weave of legend. Maurice Magre, the foremost poet of the neo-Cathar revival memorably describes her as "the living incarnation of youth and freedom . . . her very name redolent of sin and damnation" (Magre, *Le sang de Toulouse*, 1931. Author's translation with James "JB" Bourne).

Raimond Drut succumbed to wounds received during the siege of Mirepoix on March 27, 1223. The redheaded count was sixty-three years old and had outwitted, outfought, and outlived most, if not all, of his earthly enemies. After his passing, his equally fiery daughter was forced to marry Bernard d'Alion, the lord of Usson who became her patron and protector. Bernard seems to have genuinely loved the young sorceress, building this second Esclarmonde her own castle in the Cathar stronghold of Montaillou. In return she bore him an heir and turned the castle of Usson into a vital staging post in the supply lines to Montségur, a safe haven for fleeing heretics setting out on the ratlines to Lombardy and beyond.

Under the stewardship of Esclarmonde de Foix, Montségur had become a new center for the Cathar faith and its final capital, a beacon of hope for the sundered nation. A document from the period, a letter drafted by Guilhabert de Castries, residing head of the Cathar Church and addressed to the lord of Montségur, Raimond de Pereilha, requests permission to take refuge in the fortress and for the "treasures of their faith" to be stored there *infra-castrum*, a term interpreted by historians to mean either literally "beneath the castle walls" or under the aegis of the castle. What these treasures may have been remains a matter of considerable speculation. Certainly they would have included books, quite possibly the foundation document of their order, the mythic Book of the Seven Seals, along with other titles unknown to us. Over the centuries a legend arose, suggesting the castle held among its treasures the most high Holy Grail—a concept that in all likelihood would have been alien to de Castries and his perfecti who didn't believe in the physical existence of Christ, let alone the cup of the last supper. Catharism was an initiatory tradition and at this distance in time it is not for us to know the secret lore and practices of its inner grades with any certitude. Some part of these treasures was surely monetary, for the Cathar hierarchy continued to pay their men-at-arms in gold ingots, known as *livres melgorien*, until the bitter end. A surviving deposition from the sergeant at arms Imbert de Salas refers to this fortune in heretic gold as *pecuniam infinitam*, literally "infinite money." The scale and composition of the treasure may have been exaggerated to encourage the dogs of war to scale the ramparts of na Esclarmonda's celestial fortress but there was certainly gold in the castle and where there is gold there is treachery, never more so than when kingdoms change hands.

Many of the great heroes of chivalry rallied to the defense of the heretics, men such as Lantar, Belissen, and Caraman (Magre, *Le Maitre Inconnu des Albigeois*, 1930). The dispossessed southern aristocrats-turned-outlaw were commonly known as *faidits*. Now these desperate men found themselves fighting a losing rear-guard action against the forces of the Holy Roman Church and the kings of France. Three times the holy mountain was besieged, yet the impenetrable citadel prevailed under the command of its military commander, Pierre Roger de Mirepoix, a faidit nicknamed the Peacock because of his jaunty good looks and ostentatious garb.

In those days the concept of divine monarchy was no joke, with many nobles believing they were literally the offspring of supernatural beings or minor divinities. In a similar manner to the Merovingian dynasty claiming a Lovecraftian sea monster or water elemental as its founder, so de Mirepoix believed, like many of the old families in the area, that he was directly descended from the pagan warrior goddess Belisenna, or Belisama, the lunar counterpart of the Celtic solar deity Belennos, whose name literally translates as "beautiful," "bright," or "shining one." De Mirepoix proudly bore the symbol of the crescent moon horns up on his blazon and is said to have perfected a form of phosphorescent paint used to decorate the skin and armor of the garrison so they would shine like ghosts to strike fear into the hearts of the superstitious Christians. In May 1242, de Mirepoix ordered the assassination of the chief Inquisitors of the south, Etienne de Saint-Thibery (Stephen of St. Thibery) and Guillaume-Arnaud (William Arnald), along with their assistants and notaries. The massacre was timed to coincide with the English invasion of southwestern France in the hope of sparking a mass uprising against their Christian oppressors. It is recorded that de Mirepoix ordered the decapitated head of Guillaume-Arnaud be brought back to Montségur so he could use it as a ceremonial cup.

This outrage, known as the Avignonet massacre, is one of the only times the pagan underground has succeeded in striking back against its oppressors with such determined ferocity. On the eve of the Feast of Ascension, the raiding party from Montségur, made up of the knights known as the sons and daughters of Belisama, or the children of Luna, slipped into the town of Avignonet under the cover of darkness and launched a surprise attack on the Inquisitors and their entourage. A number of friars tried to take refuge in the chapel and fell to their knees in front of the altar, where they were duly cut down. After the massacre was complete, their clothes, funds, and belongings were looted. More importantly, the Inquisition registers were confiscated and destroyed. When the children of the moon returned to rendezvous with their leader in a nearby forest known as Antioch Wood, de Mirepoix is said to have asked, "Where is my cup?"

"It is broken," replied Jean Acermat, one of the assassins.

"Oh, why did you not bring it?" chided the Peacock. "I would have bound it together with a circlet of gold and drunk from it all my days!"

This violent action provoked an equally swift and ruthless reprisal. An army of up to 10,000 crusaders under the command of Hugues des Arcis, seneschal of Carcassonne, and Pierre Amiel, the archbishop of Narbonne, was dispatched to Montségur to take the castle at all costs, cut off the serpent's head, and put an end to the clear and present danger it posed to Christendom.

The final siege lasted ten months, through the very worst of the Pyrenean winter as the castle's 500 inhabitants, including the garrison of 150 men-at-arms and fifteen knights under de Mirepoix stood alone against the pope, against the Inquisition, and the king of France, effectively against the world. It is clear these apocalyptic circumstances pushed the defenders beyond their limits, forcing them to renegotiate their relationship with God on a daily basis. As the perfecti sought to abandon the flawed and delusory material world that had rejected them, so others clung desperately to life. In January 1244, a brilliant young inventor, Bertrand de la Vacalarie, succeeded in breaching the lines and taught the defenders how to build their own ballistas from available materials, effectively prolonging the siege by another two months. On another occasion the son of the mad troubadour Pierre Vidal broke into the besieged castle to bring the defenders good news. He claimed to have encountered a faery knight on the road, an emissary of Elfland wearing a purple cloak and sapphire gloves, a sure sign victory would be theirs. Moments after making this bizarre proclamation, Vidal was killed by incoming ballista fire, an event that cast a further shadow over the defenders' spirits. As the desperate weeks wore on, no word came from the vacillating lord of Toulouse that relief was on the way, nor did any sign come from the forest that the sapphire knight and the hosts of Elfland and faery were rallying to their succor.

The castle fell to treachery just before the vernal equinox in the second year of the siege, when shepherds from the neighboring village of Camon guided a party of Basque mercenaries and Teutonic knights accustomed to the icy Alpine conditions, up a secret path on the sheer side of the mountain. The attack brought the keep and the small village on the east flank of the pog within range of crusader ballistas, forcing de Mirepoix to lead a desperate sortie to dislodge their oppressors from the mountain. The final battle raged all night and by dawn the bodies of most of the sons and daughters of the moon lay broken on the rocks below the cliffs, forcing the defenders to sound the great horn and call a ceasefire.

Negotiations for Montségur's surrender began on Wednesday, March 2, 1244, with de Mirepoix's brother-in-law, Raimond d'Aniort, lord of the Aude acting as intermediary between the head of the garrison and the seneschal of Carcassonne, Hugues des Arcis. I have already touched on the terms of the agreement. The men-at-arms were granted an unconditional amnesty and the knights who took part in the Avignonet massacre allowed to go free. Those who refused to recant, even in the face of certain death, were given fifteen days to consider their options and prepare themselves for the stake. It is hard to imagine what those fifteen days must have been like as the last of the faithful gave away their remaining earthly assets and bade their loved ones farewell.

During this period of grace, it is generally believed the castle's remaining treasures were smuggled to safety. Much of the gold had probably been carried out piecemeal over the course of the winter by a certain brother Matheus and his companions Amiel Aicart and Peter Bonnet, who came and went from the besieged fortress with surprising ease and frequency. The sergeant of the garrison, Imbert de Salas, later confessed under Inquisition interrogation that the perfecti had a secret understanding with the soldiers guarding the last road accessible from the pog and by this means much of the treasure was allegedly spirited away and buried in a nearby cave for later retrieval. Rather than the expected *pecuniam infinitam*, when the dogs of God finally took possession of the castle they found its coffers empty and storerooms bare.

On the day before the castle's capitulation, the priestess Rixende Donat and Bishop Bertrand Marty presided over a final ritual to mark the spring equinox, a date corresponding to the Manichaean feast day of Bema. It is not recorded what took place at this ceremony, but it is clear it had a profound effect on those who witnessed it. At least two of the surviving knights and several men-at-arms who had fought alongside the heretics for more than a year, converted to Catharism at the last moment and took the consolamentum, choosing to lay down their lives rather than walk away. To die in such a manner, on an obscure point of gnostic principle, is almost inconceivable but whatever they saw, whatever they experienced on top of the mountain that day made it impossible to choose otherwise.

Among those who made the leap of faith was the castle's chatelaine, Corba de Pereilha, who took the consolamentum on the evening of March 13, choosing to leave behind her husband, son, and two daughters. Her younger daughter, Esclarmonde, named after the castle's saintly guardian, was granted the consolomentum that same day. Esclarmonde de Pereilha was little more than a child and said to have been sickly, quite possibly already dying from malnutrition and hypothermia at that late stage of the siege. It is impossible to know whether she was even conscious at the time. They were joined by the noble lady Ermengarde d'Ussat and three younger women, Arssendis, Bruna, and Guilelme, all three married to men-at-arms who had become last-minute converts and who now chose to die beside their husbands.

On the morning of March 16, 1244, the seneschal and his knights presented themselves at the castle gates along with the bishop of Albi and two Inquisitors, brothers Ferrier and Duranti. The lord of Montségur, Raimond de Pereilha, knew full well that in giving up his castle he was also giving up his wife and daughter. History belongs to the victors and over the years it became convenient to suggest the Cathars went willingly to the flames, but closer examination of surviving documents suggests they were firmly chained by their necks and wrists. "They were brutally dragged forth from the fortress of Montségur," testified Arpaïs de Ravat, Corba's older daughter. The wounded and those too sick to walk were likewise dragged or carried to their doom.

It is generally agreed Bishop Bertrand Marty led this last procession down the holy mountain to a field "at the base of the rock" according to William de Puylaurens where their oppressors had "built a palisade of stakes and pales" filled with dry brushwood. The captives were herded into the palisade, allowing family members to die together. The brushwood was kindled at the four corners and the onlookers, God's representatives, retreated to a safe distance, chanting prayers and singing the Veni Creator Spiritus. In this way, some 225 men, women, and children perished on the Camp de Cremat, the field of the stake or place of the Burnt Ones.

Despite the terms of the surrender, not all the "pure ones" died that day.

According to Alzeu de Massabrac's later evidence to the Inquisition:

> When the *haeretici* came forth from the fortress of Montségur, which was perforce rendered up to the Church and the French Crown, Pierre Roger de Mirepoix held back within the said fortress Amiel Aicart and his friend Hugo, they being *haeretici*; and the night on which the other *haeretici* were burnt, he concealed the said heretics, and did cause them to escape; and this was done that the Church of the heretics might not lose its treasure, which was hidden in the forest; and the fugitives knew the place where it lay. (*Le Dossier de Montségur: Interrogatoires d'inquisition 1242–1247*, compiled and edited by Jean Duvernoy)

De Mirepoix risked his own freedom by concealing these surviving heretics in a safe place within the rock until the night of March 16 when they descended the sheer side of the mountain on ropes, escaping from the pages of recorded history. According to Bérenger de Lavalanet, a third man, Poitevin—sometimes referred to as Poitevin the Mason—went with them, vanishing into the night.

Under the terms of the agreement, Pierre Roger de Mirepoix was allowed to go free and is said to have ended his days in Spain. The fate of the second Esclarmonde (Esclarmonde the bastard) has not come down to us, although it is not thought she lived long after the castle's fall. Some accounts have it that this fierce opponent of Christendom escaped to the Aude while others insist na Esclarmonda and her earthly lover fled across the Tabor to take refuge in the caverns of Ussat where she was reunited with her brother, Loup. A legend of the high mountains recorded by Napoleon Peyrat in *Histoires des Albigeois: les Albigeois et l'Inquisition* (1870) suggests Esclarmonde d'Alion and her companions were hunted down by troops under the command of the seneschal of Toulouse. Unwilling to follow their quarry into the labyrinthine cave system in which they had taken refuge, their pursuers brought down the mountainside instead, entombing the last of the faithful alive within the rock.

Whatever Esclarmonde d'Alion's true fate may have been, it is easy to see how three women sharing the same name, three real-life historic personages from three successive generations, came to literally embody the three aspects of the pagan divinity, wise woman, warrior, and the innocent child, Esclarmonde de Pereilha, who perished in the flames of 1244, their identities blurred over the passage of centuries into a single figure, the guardian of the magic mountain, the mythical White Lady of the Pyrenees—Esclarmonde de Montségur. According to tradition, when the forces of darkness laid siege to the castle, na Esclarmonda was transformed into a dove that split the mountain with its beak. The holy treasure was cast into the rock, which closed around it. And so the Grail was saved.

For his part in the defense of Montségur and the dispersal of its treasures, Bernard d'Alion was arrested, tried, and convicted of aiding and abetting the heretics. He was publicly burned in the town square in Perpignan in 1258, and as his flesh blackened and sloughed from his bones, he might have had pause to regret marrying the living incarnation of youth and freedom. Perhaps it was her face he saw before him at the last.

After the fall, the castle was given to the de Levis family, who stationed a garrison of troops on the mountain to round up all those who still felt compelled to gather on the pog when the moon was full. While the Cathar faith staggered on for another century or so, surviving in exile in Lombardy and Spain, the spirit of the resistance was broken, leaving the forces of the Catholic Church, the agents of the one God, to preside over the long dark age that followed.

Today very little of the original fortress, the celestial citadel of Esclarmonde de Foix, remains—the castle has been rebuilt at least twice over the course of the centuries—nor has the site of the mass burning ever been established with certitude. Only two intact skeletons have ever been recovered from the pog, the remains of an unidentified elderly woman and a somewhat younger male interred in a shaft dug twenty-four meters (about seventy-nine feet) into the granite mountaintop. Whoever the occupants of this grave may have been, it is clear from the lengths taken by the defenders to hide their remains that they must have been extremely important figures.

The skeletons retrieved from the mountaintop both date to the time of the siege, at which point na Esclarmonda, had she still been alive, would have been eighty-nine years old. The sutures in the skull and signs of arthritis in the hands, feet, and joints of the female skeleton indicate the occupant of the grave perished at a similar age, a finding independently confirmed by forensic pathologists. The tip of a spear was found embedded in the skeleton's hip, indicating she probably died after being stabbed in the stomach or groin. Beside her was the body of a younger man slain by a crossbow bolt found still lodged in his back, their identity just one of the many mysteries that still haunt the mountain.

54   A History of the Cathars

Fig. 2.9. The light of the world? Could this be the skull of the Cathar high priestess Esclarmonde de Foix? Photograph by Richard Stanley.

If it was the practice of these persecuted heretics to conceal the remains of their dead, then we must concede they did so extraordinarily well. Many are known to have died at Montségur and from long before the final siege we find records of credentes and Cathar sympathizers choosing to spend their last days on the pog where they believed themselves to be closer to heaven and the stars from whence they had come. To date, the Cathar necropolis that must surely exist somewhere on the mountain has yet to be found, nor have archaeological investigations confirmed the presence of the subterranean galleries referred to in the texts. Geological examination has revealed the presence of a hidden river beneath the mountain feeding a lightless reservoir, an underground lake deep within the womb of the rock. No known access to this reservoir has been found, nor has any trace emerged of the missing

Cathar treasure. If the Holy Grail and the Book of the Seven Seals were spirited away before the fall of the castle, then they have vanished from history, leaving few clues to their true nature. If the lost book of the Cathars truly survived the final conflict, then why has it never subsequently come to light? The only explanation is that these mythic relics either never existed or never left the mountain.

Among the findings of the GRAME (Groupe de Recherches Archéologique de Montségur et Environs) currently in the collection of the museum of Montségur is a tiny strip of metal bearing lettering in an unknown alphabet. This cryptic relic strongly resembles decorative motifs and protective prayers found on the covers of twelfth-century Bibles such as the Stowe Missal. Esoteric historian Peter Levenda suggests the characters resemble Glagolithic, the forerunner of Old Church Slavonic, hinting at the Bogomil origins of the long lost book. Could this insignificant scrap of metal be all that remains of the mythic Book of the Seven Seals or Book of Love?

One of the most provocative relics associated with the Cathars is the stone dove of Montségur. The artifact was allegedly unearthed in the late 1920s by a wealthy antiquarian named Arthur Caussou who lived in the region and had taken a passionate interest in the history of the castle. Caussou claimed to have discovered two small sandstone pots hidden in a cavity on the mountain. One held the stone dove, allegedly the symbol of the Cathar faith while the other contained 200 gold coins

Fig. 2.10. Message in an unknown alphabet—a motif from the cover of a twelfth-century holy book found on the pog of Montségur.

Fig. 2.11. The stone dove of Montségur.

dating to the thirteenth century. The find was confirmed by a local archaeologist, Andre Glory, and the village priest Abbé Durand.

Otto Rahn claimed to have personally examined the relic during his visit to the area in 1929, claiming it was among the objects held in a private collection in Lavelanet. The current whereabouts of the artifact are unknown, nor has its true provenance ever been formally established. Only the photograph reproduced in figure 2.11 remains as proof this elusive relic ever existed. Nonetheless, the mysterious carving has become central to the myth complex associating the symbol of the dove with the dualist faith. No primary documents from the twelfth or thirteenth centuries exist that make any mention of the symbol and, in the absence of further evidence, the true relevance of the dove, the bearer of the laurel, to the Cathar faith remains, at best, circumstantial. This has not discouraged modern gurus and tour operators alike from using the stylized dove as a symbol for Pays Cathar and the vanished faith of Amor.

According to local gossip, the relic did not bring Caussou himself any luck. It is said that from the day of the discovery, he was afflicted by ill fortune, losing his wealth and property to eventually die in penury. The only things he was able to leave his heirs were the old coins and the small white stone dove.

After the fall of Montségur, the light of the true faith was slowly and painfully extinguished. The Inquisitors fought Catharism as if it were a biological contamination, a psychoactive virus to be contained and cauterized by fire. Knowing the consolomentum was a direct transmission spread by the touch of the hand from one adept to another, the Inquisition sought to isolate, denounce, and destroy all those who carried the seed of heresy within them in a merciless act of cold-blooded social surgery. They hoped in time all memory of their victims would be erased, but in this they were less successful.

A small group of the faithful, led by charismatic pastor Pierre Paraire, struggled on for ten more years under the protection of the lord of Quéribus, Chabert de Barbaira, until they too were delivered to the flames in May 1255. Other congregations are believed to have survived in secret in the Aude and the Corbières thanks in part to the influence of the Templar order and the collusion of the local aristocracy.

The last fully initiated Cathar *perfect* Guilhelm Bélibaste was born into a wealthy family at Cubières but was forced to flee the area after killing a shepherd. On the run from the law, he made common cause with the fleeing heretics Pierre and Jacques Authié. After receiving the consolomentum, Bélibaste became a preacher himself, finding safe haven in Morella, Spain, where he attempted to lead an inconspicuous secular life weaving baskets and making carding combs. The Inquisition had not forgotten this unfortunate man and efforts were made by Father Jacques Fournier (later to become Pope Benedict XII) to have Bélibaste returned to Pamiers for trial. By elaborate trickery, the last *bonhomme* was convinced to cross the border into the Ariège where a trap was laid by the bounty hunter, Arnaud Sicré who had entered into a profitable arrangement with the chief Inquisitor. Guilhelm Bélibaste was seized, interrogated, and executed for the crime of murder committed in his youth.

Fig. 2.12. The Morenci Cross—the face of Belennos gazes across the centuries. The face was carved on a great rock on the summit of the mountain facing Montségur, a neolithic necropolis that has yielded a number of curious archaeological findings. The site was christianized in the seventeenth century when the rock was carved into the cross that exists today.
Photo by Martin Chaput.

When Bélibaste burned at the stake in the town of Villerouge-Termenes in 1321, the chain of direct initiation was broken forever. Before perishing, the last adept allegedly uttered a cryptic prophecy whose exact wording has been debated ever since. Realizing he had no hope of escape, Bélibaste is said to have cursed his earthly oppressors, predicting that after seven centuries, the power of the Roman church would crumble. "People will rise against people and kingdom against kingdom; a descendant of the house of Aragon will graze their horse upon the altar in Rome."

After the passage of seven hundred years, Bélibaste claimed, the old ways would return. "The laurel will turn green again . . ."

3
Who Was Otto Rahn?

When the ploughman returns from plowing
Quand lo boièr ven de laurar
He plants his cattle prod
Planta son agulhada
AEIOU
He finds his wife at the foot of the fire
Tròba sa femna al pè del fuòc
Totally inconsolable
Tota desconsolada . . .

Lo Boier/le Bouvier,
Anonymous, ca. twelfth century

Seven hundred and forty-six years after the fall of Montségur, I found myself sitting in a threadbare armchair in one of the oldest houses in the village, waiting for an oddly violent summer storm to abate, trying to make sense of the facts as they'd been handed down to me. My girlfriend, Cat Knightly, lay unconscious on the bed beside me, lost in a deep and dreamless sleep. Dawn was clear and cloudless, as if the night before had never happened. My writer friend, Mike Dee, was sullen and withdrawn at breakfast, refusing to discuss the events

Fig. 3.1. The pog of Montségur.
Photo by Richard Stanley.

of the previous evening other than to complain about us disturbing his sleep. When pushed on the subject, he suggested we must have either been on drugs or had been suffering some form of shared hallucination as a result of the endorphins released into our bloodstream by the panic induced by the storm.

Lightning is perfectly capable of scrambling one's brainwaves and Mike went on to politely suggest the electromagnetic field inside the castle might have dramatically affected our perception of what we thought we had seen. It was not the last time I would hear such an explanation in the course of my inquiries, but for now it was the only rationale available.

"And the voices? What about them? The screams? I've never heard anything like that in my life. It sounded like . . ." I struggled to find words. "Like souls in pain."

"Farm animals," Mike grunted, clearly uncomfortable with this subject. "Pigs can sound a lot like human beings, especially when they're all squealing at once."

"But I don't think there are any pigs in this valley. At least I haven't seen any. It's all dairy."

"Cows, then. Bellowing in fear." Mike toyed with his croissant, pushing it from one side of the plate to another.

"It didn't sound like cows. It sounded like screams."

"You'd be surprised." Deciding his croissant was too stale to eat, Mike pushed back his chair. "When they're scared enough,cows can cover a few octaves."

I'd barely slept a wink, but my mind was racing. The only person who seemed to lend my story any credence was our hostess, the auberge's landlady, Aimeé Couquet.

We were lodging in what turned out to be the oldest house in the village and Madame Couquet had lived there all her life, and her father and grandfather before her. She had seen enough to know Cat and I weren't hallucinating and when I politely inquired about what we had seen on the mountaintop she simply smiled and nodded, putting it down to *les anciens*—the old ones—a phrase that only put the hook in me further. I tried to explain our story and Madame seemed to listen without judgment, adding at length that it came as no surprise we'd had a somewhat restless night. After all, she told us, we had been sleeping in Otto's room.

And who the hell was Otto?

Not Otto Skorzeny, as it turned out. The yarn told by Colonel Howard Buechner in his batty book was, as I had guessed, largely fantastical, a fiction that nonetheless contained a tiny grain of truth. The Nazis had been here after all, but not Skorzeny.

Rahn. Otto Rahn.

Fig. 3.2. Maison Couquet. Aimeé Couquet at the window of Otto Rahn's former room in Montségur, summer 1998. Photo by James "JB" Bourne.

Fig. 3.3. Aimeé Couquet. Photo by Richard Stanley.

64   Who Was Otto Rahn?

Fig. 3.4. Otto Wilhelm Rahn.
Drawing by W. Goetz, circa 1932.

Aimeé had been a little girl at the time, but she remembered the tall, silent German and had kept his room much as it had been in the day. Rahn had experienced something on that mountain, something that failed to gel with his rational German intellect, something he couldn't adequately explain that drew him back to the castle again and again and ultimately turned him against the corrupt regime he served. If it was impossible to believe in the physical existence of the Ark of the Covenant and the Holy Grail, then it was almost as difficult to imagine Otto Rahn himself existed.

It took Cat a while to surface after the travails of the night before, and while she rested I asked around the village to see if I could find anyone else who had been there since the war, in the hope of uncovering more witnesses who might remember the elusive SS officer. My initial inquiries were encouraging and I was assured by the village's former mayor, Marius Mounié, that Rahn himself was still alive, having apparently escaped the death assigned to him in Buechner's colorful account. Otto Rahn was apparently an old man by now but, according to Marius, he still visited the area often. If Otto had really found the mysterious treasure of the Cathars, as some suggested, then he was evidently worth talking to and I resolved to try to track him down in the hope of interviewing him for British television.

The deeper I dug into the backstory behind Buechner's book, the more bizarre the discrepancies between the text and the facts on the ground seemed to become. It was clear some sort of massacre had taken place in the village during the dying days of the war but the details stubbornly refused to come into focus. It came as a shock to learn that the ruins gradually blending back into the undergrowth behind the village had once housed prisoners of war, Indo-Chinese captives known locally as *anamites* who had been effectively used as slave labor by the Montséguriens. From what I was able to gather, a private enterprise known as the French Wood Gas Company had patented a process for turning wood into gasoline, an enterprise encouraged by the Vichy regime who believed it was essential to the war effort. Accordingly a detachment of prisoners was assigned to log the valley.

Working without proper training or safety considerations, under conditions of appalling hardship, many of the anamites died or were seriously injured. Others were "repurposed" for menial work in the village, something that could not have been easy given the traditional racism and hostility of the hardy Ariègeois.

The Nazi tanks came in the spring of 1944, just in time for the 700th anniversary of the fall of the castle, an event around which a considerable mythology has accrued. It is hard to imagine why anyone bothered to send heavy armor to such a remote region so late in the war. Buechner implies the tanks were dispatched to help Skorzeny secure the "treasure of the ages" but the true nature of the Third Panzer Division's mission may have been of a more prosaic nature. Surviving Vichy-era documents unearthed from an archive in Paris suggest they were chasing partizans who were conducting raids across the border into Franco's Spain. Three of these alleged partisans were apparently executed on the spot and the barracks of the anamites burned to the ground. What became of the unfortunate slave laborers has not been recorded.

According to Buechner, the pog was subsequently overflown by a Luftwaffe plane that used a smoke trail to inscribe a huge Celtic cross over the castle, a sign that Skorzeny had succeeded in his mission. The sign in the sky was supposedly left on the morning of March 16, 1944, and was witnessed by a group of neo-Cathars who assembled on the mountaintop to mark the anniversary and celebrate the greening of the laurel. Buechner implies Heinrich Himmler, the reichsführer SS, was aboard the plane and that the following day, an official delegation composed of Reichsminister Alfred Rosenburg and Colonel Wolfram Sievers of the Ahnenerbe SS (literally the "folk memory" or "folk legacy" department) arrived to congratulate Skorzeny. Records, however, clearly indicate Skorzeny was in Hungary that day, trying in vain to defend the crumbling Reich, and Himmler, Rosenburg, and Sievers were themselves otherwise engaged hundred of miles from the French Pyrenees, leaving us none the wiser as to what really happened in these remote backwoods. The only thing I could be sure of is men died here and buildings were destroyed. But who were they fighting and why?

On my first inspection of the ruins, it was clear someone somewhere knew what had happened here in the spring of 1944 and felt the need to commemorate this long-forgotten skirmish. The remains of the buildings had been recently tagged with graffiti allegedly painted by a neo-Nazi formation operating out of Provence who were clearly aware of the Panzer Division's historic presence in the valley, yet I was loathe to reach out to them.

One of Madame Couquet's friends, a bearlike old farmer named Antoine Laffont dropped by the auberge just after lunch to fix the clock in the dining room. Word had started to spread via the tiny community's bush telegraph that there were three researchers in town, working

Fig. 3.5. Crocuses bloom on an ancient battlefield hidden deep in an area of the Montségur woods known as *la Reboule*, literally the "round" or "circle." A *wolfsangel*—the blazon of the Third Panzer Division (Das Reich) is daubed on the walls of a ruined barracks, former quarters of Indo-Chinese prisoners of war.

for an unspecified television show and a number of Montséguriens who still remembered the war were keen to talk.

Antoine had been in his early teens on March 16, 1944, but still remembered the day vividly. It had been a bright, early spring morning and Antoine had been working in the fields when he heard the sound of gunfire coming from the village. Antoine told me in broken English that he turned at once and began to run toward the settlement but then Madame put her hand on his shoulder and hushed him, telling him softly in French that there was no need to talk about it now, that some things were best forgotten. I made a mental note to get the rest of his story when Madame Couquet wasn't eavesdropping, but the opportunity never arose, not that day. Mike was keen to get moving, assuming the Rahn affair to be another wild goose chase.

It took me more than ten years to finally gain access to the documents on file in Paris that named Madame Couquet's uncle, the former

Fig. 3.6. Antoine Laffont repairs the clock in the dining room of Mme. Couquet's auberge, setting its dusty hands in motion once more. Photo by James "JB" Bourne.

mayor, as having identified the partisans to the Nazis, effectively signing their death warrants. The mayor had risen to power in the community after ridding himself of any potential opposition, shouldering the responsibility of cutting the D9, the first tar road linking Montségur to the outside world. Of course, Madame knew all this and didn't want her buddy running his mouth off on camera, but by the time I understood the context Antoine Laffont was already dead.

It was early afternoon by the time Cat managed to get back on her feet. She insisted she felt stronger and cleaner, as if somehow purged by her ordeal in the castle. She had only a fragmentary memory of what had happened and no recollection of how we had gotten back to the auberge. Mike was eager to get moving and put the whole affair behind us. Piling into our rental car we decided to check out the deep, glacier cut valley of the Ariège on the far side of the massif known as the

Throne of the Gods. There were stories Rahn and the Nazis had been there too, apparently searching for the treasure smuggled out of the castle at the time of the siege.

The long dry summer was drawing to a close in a suitably biblical manner and by late afternoon another storm was brewing, great thunderheads banking up along the mountainous horizon. Reassuring Cat I had no desire to spend another night in the open, let alone on top of a mountain, we resolved to pitch camp in one of the caves that honeycombed the valley. We were spoiled for choice as the Ariège is the largest limestone district in Europe and the labyrinthine recesses below its mountains have been continuously inhabited since Cro-Magnon times. Cave paintings such as the therianthropic sorcerer of Trois Frères hint of ancient ritual usage and archaeological finds in the region include some of the very first representations of the human form, fertility goddesses, white ladies carved from horse's teeth, and mammoth's tusks that date back to the last ice age and the mists of unrecorded time.

Fig. 3.7. The *Dame de Brassempouy* or *Dame à la Capuche*—Lady in the Hood—a fragmentary ivory figurine discovered in a cave at Brassempouy, France. Approximately 25,000 years old, it is one of the earliest known representations of the human face.

Manhandling the hollow trunk of a fallen tree into the mouth of one of the grottoes, we kindled a comforting blaze that burned through the night, keeping us surprisingly warm and dry.

The cave, known locally as the *eglise* had served as a church in ancient times, its vaulted, limestone walls pockmarked by sconces that served as admirable candleholders, filling the natural cavity with a comforting, flickering glow. We were just laying out our sleeping bags and settling down when we were surprised by the appearance of a stranger who stepped silently out of the rain-lashed darkness, a bearded man swathed in a damp, homespun jellaba very similar to the ones I had seen those shadowy figures wearing in the castle the previous evening. This newcomer was unable to converse in either English or French but from what little we could work out his name was apparently Uriel. Judging from his wild beard, mane of unkempt hair, quasi-medieval clothing, and zoned-out eyes we assumed he was some sort of hermit who must have been living rough on the hillside and had presumably been drawn to the light of our fire in the hope of finding sanctuary from the downpour. He seemed friendly enough and exuded such an aura of calm that we did not hesitate to admit him to our circle. The lack of any common tongue put further conversation out of the question but as we made ourselves comfortable Uriel slipped a wooden flute from the folds of his robe and began to play.

It was the first time I had heard the folk music of old Occitania and to my untrained ear its coiling, mesmeric cadences had a distinctly Middle Eastern flavor, redolent of distant lands and vanished kingdoms. As the storm howled outside and the candles flickered in the sconces cut into the cavern walls, I curled deeper into my sleeping bag, allowing my thoughts to drift, realizing I had come to the edge of something I could scarcely comprehend.

It was no surprise to find the next morning that Uriel had disappeared, quietly taking his leave while we slept as if he had never existed. The sun was already high in the firmament. The storms had passed, at least for now, and the sky was a rich, deep, cloudless blue.

Fig. 3.8. The grotto of Ornolac—known to the European Rosicrucian movement as the *eglise*, or church. When I first spent the night in the grotto in the summer of 1990, I had no idea the cave marked the first station on an initiatory journey, the point at which the candidate has to be prepared to leave their old life behind and step into the unknown. Photo by Chrzu Lindstrom, March 2017.

Mike Dee and myself were divided over the final report submitted to Channel Four. At length, I bowed to pressure and omitted all mention of Rahn and the chateau from the treatment, yet the affair continued to haunt me. I confided in a professional Reich historian affiliated with the BBC's contemporary history department, who showed no small interest in the matter, telling me it indicated "just how irrational the Nazis really were." Yet these words proved troubling ones as I had started to give credence to Rahn's thesis.

Returning to the Pyrenees on my own coin, I spent months camped out on the holy mountain, accompanied by my friend, the German cameraman Immo Horn, who had worked with me in Afghanistan. Covering every conceivable angle of the mountain with locked off cameras, we hoped to capture the "hand of God" and those fiery fingers of living plasma on film for all to see, but we waited in vain. Moreover, our search for the missing Grail historian proved just as fruitless.

I tried telling myself that what I witnessed in the castle of Montségur had simply been a freak storm and the voltage coursing through the walls of the keep had somehow affected Cat's brainwaves, triggering the violent seizure. Despite all I had seen, my conscious mind refused to give in to the thought that she really had been possessed, or that the citadel truly was the castle of the Holy Grail.

4
Otto's Quest for the Grail
The Crown of Lucifer

I am that dark, that thrice dishonored prince of Aquitaine. The star upon my scutcheon long hath faded. The black sun upon my lute doth yet remain.

GERARD DE NERVAL

Otto Rahn's gaunt figure, swathed in characteristic black coat and fedora, casts a long shadow out of the years between the wars, a great silhouette around which the most extravagant myths have accrued. He is variously said to have been a Rosicrucian, a Luciferian, an agent of the Thule Gesellschaft, an initiated Cathar adept, and even the leader of an international secret society known as the Polaires. As American author Philip Kerr put it, Rahn's contemporaries might not have been surprised to see "the Scarlet Woman and the Great beast come flying out of the front door" of his apartment on Tiergarten Strasse. The former mayor of Montségur, Marius Mounié, claimed Rahn was still alive while others believed he turned against his Nazi superiors and died in the war.

Colonel Howard Buechner suggested Rahn was imprisoned in

Fig. 4.1. Otto Rahn (1904–1939), the original "man in black."

Dachau while others insisted he escaped with the Holy Grail to a secret Arctic base and the entrance of the Hollow Earth. The French investigative journalist and former head of TF1, Christian Bernadac, was convinced Otto survived the war, swapping identities with his dead brother, Rudolph, to rise to power as the head of Coca-Cola Europe.

One of the only things I could be sure of when I first started on his trail was that Otto Wilhelm Rahn had been born. It is recorded he came into this world in Michelstadt on February 18, 1904, and spent his formative years in a region of Germany rich in history and folklore. At an early age he was captivated by the trips he took with his father to the Odentwalt (Odin's Forest) and the ruins of Schloss Wildenburg where Wolfram von Eschenbach had penned his celebrated thirteenth-century Grail epic.

"When I was very young, Otto's father, my grandfather Karl, who was by then a very old man and almost blind, took me up into the hills," recalled Ingeborgh Roemer-Rahn, gazing out the window at the leafless trees, focused on the past. "He told me if I closed my eyes and took his hand I'd be able to see heaven."

"And did you?"

Otto Rahn's niece smiled thinly, briefly meeting my gaze. Ingeborgh had her uncle's profile, cheekbones, and icy green eyes, cool and distant as snowmelt. "I took his hand and it was like a lightning flash. I don't know what I felt." She shook her head, then smiled again, more openly this time, trusting me with her truth. "He said, do you feel that? That feeling, that is heaven. The angels, those seraphim, they exist! It was a form of inheritance. A gift. Ever since then I've been able to see those angels myself and sometimes I hear their voices . . ."

I nodded, stirring my chai, envying her certitude, her faith in things unknown, in the emissaries of the invisible world.

"Otto must have inherited that gift from his father too. I think the seventh sight must run in our blood."

I felt like asking what happened to the "sixth sense" but that would have been cheeky. It was good of her to invite me into her home, a beautiful wooden house overlooking the forest near Amorbach. Ingeborgh was recently divorced and lived alone with her ailing mother, earning a pittance as a psychiatrist and naturopath.

"Otto's father, Karl, was a man of few words. I think he was looking for a kind of religion and perhaps he found it in nature." Ingeborgh returned her attention to the lusterless, wintery sky and the wind moving in the trees outside the rambling wooden house. "When he saw a tree, he would say that is God. His partner Clara, however, was a very materialistic woman and could never understand this spiritual side of him. She had difficulties expressing affection, especially toward her son. After Otto died she became introspective. When the war ended she burned his books and papers and never spoke of him again."

Fig. 4.2. Otto Rahn and his brother.

Fig. 4.3. The Rahn brothers with their father, Karl, on the balcony of the family home in Michelstadt.

Fig. 4.4. Rahn family album—Karl, Clara, and the brothers.

78   Otto's Quest for the Grail

Ingeborgh told me Otto's father, Karl, had been a magistrate who was often transferred from town to town, which made it hard for the two boys to form lasting friendships. Otto had been a lonely, introverted child who was frequently bullied at school. "A farmer's victim," Ingeborgh called him. There is no doubt the untimely death of Otto Rahn's older brother and his inability to form a loving relationship with his mother, Clara, affected him deeply. Retreating into his imagination, the young Rahn became a precocious scholar, assimilating the bare bones of German Romanticism through his childhood reading of Greek, Roman, and Nordic mythology.

"I think he felt a genuine calling. It was his destiny. He was always searching, looking for the faraway, for the outside." Ingeborgh pulled down a family album containing the vanished Grail seeker's school photographs. When she spoke of Otto she spoke of him tenderly as if she was proud of his actions. "I know this feeling, but it's like a disease. Always searching. Never finding."

Fig. 4.5. Otto Rahn's school days.

Fig. 4.6. The Rahn brothers go to school.

Ingeborgh had worn her uncle's hand-me-down clothes as a child and still had Otto's threadbare teddy bear on a shelf in the bedroom. She proudly displayed an incense burner the Grail hunter had brought back from a journey to Iceland with the Ahnenerbe SS, some crystal glasses, a handful of old photographs, curling postcards, and a lump of amber the size of a hen's egg—Otto Rahn's surviving personal effects. I was half hoping he might have left an old cup lying about somewhere but no such luck. She had managed to hold on to a number of her uncle's unpublished manuscripts, but sadly I was unable to find any trace of the missing final third of his Grail thesis.

In the closing pages of *The Court of Lucifer* (1937), Rahn describes that very same lump of amber serving as a paperweight, resting atop a pile of densely written notes that would form the substance of his third and final opus, a vanished text entitled "Orpheus: A Journey to Hell and Beyond." Like the proverbial *verbum dismissum* of the alchemists, it seems somehow unsurprising that the third book of Rahn should be lost to mortal ken, the mystery left naggingly incomplete. There were plenty of typescripts among the works in Ingeborgh's safekeeping but most were handwritten in Otto Rahn's customary wilting scrawl. To transcribe and translate the material was beyond my resources but the titles alone charted the wilder shores of Rahn's interests, ranging from "Count Sainte Germaine: Magician or Charlatan" to "Lauren," a ninety-page manuscript concerning the legendary king of the Little People, the ruler of the German faery folk (see appendix 1).

In the end all Ingeborgh could do was give me a hug and make me promise to keep her posted on anything we could find out about her mysterious uncle. Still mulling over what we had learned and indeed whether we had learned anything at all, Mr. Horn and I opted to spend the night camped in the nearby ruins of the Schloss Wildenburg where Wolfram von Eschenbach had penned *Parzival*.

It seemed appropriate, necessary even, to visit the place where Otto Rahn's trail had begun, to return to the source.

Fig. 4.7. Otto Rahn playing with the family dog.

The ruins of Wildenburg are far more extensive than Montségur and the Cathar remains of the south, provoking thoughts of an almost unimaginable vanished grandeur. On the wall of one chamber overlooking the misty valley far below, an inscription is carved in High German, mirroring a line from Wolfram's masterpiece and possibly predating it. The words read: Ach Mutter, Was Ist Gott? (Oh Mother, what is God?). In that same roofless chamber, its mottled stonework crawling with Masonic glyphs, is a massive hearth and the remains of a chimney, possibly the same prodigious fireplace, large enough to spit an ox, that gives rise to another line in *Parzival* when Wolfram remarks, "In the castle of the Holy Grail there are fireplaces even larger than Wildenburg."

Mr. Horn and I foraged for brushwood, salvaging a few dryish logs left from the autumn deadfall, enough to build an impressive pyre, and as if on cue a troupe of teenagers appeared like ghosts from the gloom, members of the Wandervogel in matching hats and animal-hide backpacks, axes dangling from their belts. They had been hiking in the woods and stopped to warm themselves. They were well aware of the castle's history and producing a guitar, played troubadour songs late into the night.

Firelight spilled across the snow and the sere frost glistened on the timeworn flags. An owl hooted in the distance as I huddled closer to the hearth, the same hearth those who came before me had stared into in past centuries. The story really started here. A tale told in the Odenwald. A legend whispered as a charm against the dark. A cure for the world's pain. A medicine for melancholy. A tale of a lost love, a knight, a quest, and a cup.

From an early age, Otto Rahn developed an interest in the stories of Parzival, Lohengrin, the Nibelungenlied, and the legends of Jacob and Benjamin Grimm, fellow denizens of the Black Forest, whom he saw as role models in his chosen career as philologist and folklorist. While attending the University of Giessen, he was encouraged by his professor, Freiherr von Gall, to focus his studies on the history of witchcraft and heresy, finishing his higher education in 1924 with a baccalaureate in literary history and the languages of medieval France. Fascinated and compelled by the history of persecution suffered by the pagans and heretics of his homeland, the high Hesse, Rahn wrote at length about the abominable career of the Inquisitor and witch hunter Konrad von Marburg (1180–1233) whose reign of terror all but depopulated the countryside, wiping entire villages from the map. "My ancestors were witches and I am a heretic," Rahn proclaimed, clearly identifying with the oppressed outsiders.

Otto Rahn completed his schooling in Giessen and would certainly have been familiar with the Wandervogel, or wandering birds, established in 1901 as a stridently anti-industrial, back-to-nature youth organization emphasizing freedom, self-responsibility, and the spirit of adventure. Like modern hippies, the Wandervogel's membership was largely drawn from the middle classes and promoted the concept of *Jugendkultur*, a culture of youth led by youth in which individuality was prized. Giessen was one of the Wandervogel's principal centers and a surviving photograph shows the young Rahn posing with guitar-wielding members of the group.

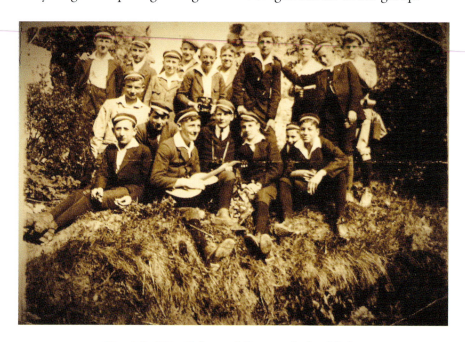

Fig. 4.8. Otto Rahn and the wandering birds.
Courtesy of Hamilton White.

The Wandervogel drew inspiration from the troubadours, reviving interest in all but forgotten folk songs and idealized Teutonic values. The movement initially refused to admit girls and nurtured distinctly homoerotic characteristics that must have appealed to Rahn's nascent sexuality, including the promotion of naturism and neo-paganism. The wandering birds were richly imbued in the folklore of their homeland and were directly responsible for introducing the celebration of the main pagan holidays or Sabbats (Beltane, Lammas, Samhain, Yuletide, and Imbolc) into the scouting movement and hence into the modern New Age neo-pagan community.

In 1928 Rahn embarked on a lifelong correspondence and subsequent friendship with the author Albert Rausch, who wrote under the pseudonym Henry Benrath. Rausch had close ties to the Wandervogel and was a frequent visitor to the home of one of the movement's prewar leaders Wilhelm Jansen, commonly known as Uncle Willie. In 1933 Rausch won the Georg Büchner prize for literature and wrote an introduction to a book entitled *Kreuz und Gral* (Cross and Grail). Rausch was twenty years older than Rahn and proudly, openly gay. Through their correspondence we are afforded some small view of Rahn's inner nature and the passions that drove him.

Rahn observed the culture of the medieval Cathars bore a strong resemblance to the ancient Druids whose wisdom he believed had been preserved in part by the troubadours or *minnesingers* (literally "remembrance singers"), the traveling poets and minstrels of medieval Europe. Rahn's 1924 dissertation concerned the true identity of Master Kyot, or Gyot de Provence, the Languedocian troubadour whose long-lost ballads allegedly inspired Wolfram's *Parzival*.

Interest in Wolfram's chivalric romance had been revived in the nineteenth century by Richard Wagner's opera and Rahn hoped to uncover the real-life underpinnings to the popular myth. Inspired by the adventures of amateur archaeologist Heinrich Schliemann whose theory that Homer's *Iliad* reflected actual historic events led to the discovery of the lost city of Troy, Rahn dreamed of achieving similarly sensational results by proving there was a factual basis to Wolfram's epic narrative.

Wolfram's poem, written in the early thirteenth century, concerns the Arthurian hero Parzival and his circuitous quest for the Holy Grail following his initial failure to attain it. It is hard not to see Rahn's own life journey as a reflection of the source material that drove him. Born and raised by the princess Herzeloyde (High German: "heart's sorrow") in the wilderness of Soltane, the young Parzival sets out to resolve the mystery of his own identity and win a seat at the Round Table. In doing so he breaks his mother's heart and leaves her to die.

After slaying the red knight, Sir Ither, Parzival is tutored by the black knight, Gurnemanz, who teaches him never to ask questions. Rescuing and subsequently marrying the besieged queen, Condwiramurs, the young champion finds himself welcomed into the Grail castle of Montsalvaesche. Mindful of Gurnemanz's advice, Parzival fails to ask his host, the fisher king Amfortas, about his mysterious wound or the magical objects paraded before him in the great hall. When Parzival awakens with the dawn, he finds the castle deserted, leading him to believe his experiences of the night before were an illusion conjured by malevolent spirits to ensnare him. As he rides away, a voice calls after the young knight, telling him he is a goose.

Returning to Arthur's court, Parzival seeks to take his place at the Round Table, only to be challenged by the wild woman, Cundrie, the messenger of the Grail. Cundrie curses Parzival in the name of the Grail, rudely interrupting the festivities to announce that the young knight has lost his honor. Parzival leaves the court in utter humiliation, incapable of comprehending the depths of his guilt.

After five years in self-imposed exile, wandering and fighting, Parzival wins a new horse, the former steed of a Grail knight. On Good Friday, the horse leads Parzival to the holy hermit, Trevrizent, who lives in the cave of the wild fountain and espouses a creed of pacifism and vegetarianism, choosing to eat neither flesh nor fowl. Over the course of a fourteen-day sojourn in the subterranean sanctuary, Trevrizent initiates Parzival into the true mysteries of the Grail, awakening his spirit. After battling his own brother, Fierefiz, to a standstill, Parzival lays down his broken sword, realizing "I was against my own self."

Cundrie now reappears, rejuvenated, to announce that Parzival's name has appeared upon the Grail, proclaiming him the new Grail King. Reunited with his bride, Condwiramurs, Parzival rides with his brother to the holy mountain of Montsalvaesche to claim his destiny as guardian of the Grail.

Parzival is one of the great masterpieces of the Middle Ages, recorded in sixteen books composed of thirty-line stanzas, dictated in the early years of the thirteenth century. The exact date of the composition is unknown and the details of Wolfram von Eschenbach's biography are equally sketchy. The likelihood is that Wolfram was a landless knight and itinerant singer who wended his way from court to court. The dates of his birth and death carved into his gravestone in the Church of Our Lady in Eschenbach had already been worn to the point of being unreadable by the fifteenth century.

Wolfram claimed to be illiterate, implying his source for the Grail myth was an oral one. "Reading is unknown to me. I do not know a single word, neither what is written in books, for that fact I am ignorant."

According to Wolfram, the saga of the Grail quest was related to him by a master storyteller named Kyot—a figure many literary historians assume to be a fictional creation, invented to legitimize the fanciful account. This wise master, Wolfram tells us, drew on Arabic and Angevin sources, including the occult legacy of an equally liminal figure, a Muslim storyteller and astronomer named Flegetanis the Moor, a descendant of Solomon who allegedly found the secrets of the Grail "written in the stars." While this attribution to Flegetanis suggests a possibly Persian origin for the quest narrative, Wolfram's account clearly owes its greatest debt to a pre-existing romance, *Perceval, the Story of the Grail*, left incomplete by French poet and trouvère Chrétien de Troyes. Wolfram is known to have spoken French, albeit clumsily, so would have been able to understand the bardic tales without any need for translation. It can be assumed that after listening to the troubadours he decided to create his own story based around their work.

In his thesis, Otto Rahn suggests Wolfram's master may have been a troubadour from Northern France, a certain Guyot of Provence, a real-life personage, a renowned poet and musician who frequented the courts of Occitania and Aquitania. Guyot is recorded to have attended an event in Germany, arranged by the emperor Frederick Barbarossa at Maguncia on Whitsunday 1184. It is not inconceivable von Eschenbach was present at this gathering. It is equally likely their paths may have crossed on the Wartburg in the court of the Landgrave Hermann of Thuringia where Wolfram sojourned in 1203.

Wolfram insists Kyot was the true source of the legend of the Grail and that Chrétien de Troyes "has done wrong by this story." Otto Rahn observed that Kyot/Gyot celebrated the lives and deeds of his wealthy patrons, suggesting the character of Parzival's mother, Herzeloyde, was none other than the Viscountess Adélaide de Carcassonne, high priestess of the Court of Love and domina of King Alfonso II of Aragon and Catalonia, a figure referred to as "Alfonso the chaste" or "Castis" in Wolfram's poem. Adélaide's son was the heroic prince of Carcassonne, Raimond Roger de Trencavel, a name that can be translated as "pierced through the heart"—the name of Parzival, the young quest knight who seeks the cure to the world's pain.

Wolfram's poem codifies the essential quest narrative, drawing on themes present for centuries in the oral tradition. In truth, nobody really knows what a grail is, let alone whom it is supposed to serve. The old French term *graal* as it appears in the earliest surviving accounts betokens a cup or bowl, cognate with the Old Occitan *grazal* or the Old Catalan *gresal*. Chrétien de Troyes, who first recorded the myth in his *Les Contes del Graal* describes the holy relic as a sort of dish or serving platter emblazoned with the Christian fish symbol, a real-life historic artifact currently in the collection of the Louvre in Paris.

While the symbol of the life-giving cup or font stems from earlier pagan archetypes such as Bran's cauldron or the horn of plenty, the fabled cornucopia, the Grail was rapidly repurposed for Catholic use. Robert de Boron was the first to suggest the chalice was really the cup of the Last Supper, used by Joseph of Arimathea to gather Christ's blood, a notion advanced in his romance *Joseph d'Arimathie*, composed between 1191 and 1202.

Walter Johannes Stein writing in *The Ninth Century and the Holy Grail* (1928) links the myth to the literal blood of Christ, brought back from the Holy Land by Dietrich of Alsace and gifted to the town of Bruges where the glass phial containing the sanguinary powder is venerated to this day. Stein sees Parsifal as a symbol of the sun, his quest embodying the yearly solar passage through the houses of the zodiac and the death and rebirth of the land.

By the time Wolfram retold the saga in his thirteenth-century epic, the Grail had been reconfigured into a "hard, dark stone" a mysterious symbol of Christ's suffering and humanity's redemption.

"It is well known to me," Wolfram recounts, "that many formidable fighting-men dwell at Munsalvaesche with the Gral. They are continually riding out on sorties in quest of adventure . . . I will tell you how they are nourished. They live from a Stone whose essence is most pure. If you have never heard of it I shall name it for you here. It is called '*Lapsit exillis*.' By virtue of this stone the Phoenix is burned to ashes, in which he is reborn—Thus does the Phoenix moult its feathers! Which done, it shines dazzling bright and lovely as before! Further: however ill a mortal may be, from the day on which he sees the Stone he cannot die for that week, nor does he lose his colour. For if anyone, maid or man, were to look at the Gral for two hundred years, you would have to admit that his colour was as fresh as in his early prime, except that his hair would be grey!—Such powers does the Stone confer on mortal men that their flesh and bones are soon made young again. This stone is also called 'The Gral' . . ." (Von Eschenbach, *Parzival*).

Other legends portrayed this mythic Grail as a book or graven tablet, possibly the lost Gospel of Saint John or the Book of Love, the vanished grimoire of the Cathars. Latter-day conspiracy theorists and pseudohistorians, inspired by Baigent, Lincoln, and Leigh's *The Holy Blood and the Holy Grail* (1982) insist the Sangraal or Sang Real is literally the bloodline of Christ and Mary Magdalene, his wife and high priestess, a proposition as far-fetched as the New Age notion of the Grail as a power object fashioned by extraterrestrials or Atlanteans or some blurry crypto-theosophical combination of both.

The path of the Grail is not an easy trail to tread in the so-called real world, nor does a spiritual vocation put bread on the table, least of all in the Weimar Republic when hyperinflation was dragging Germany to the edge of ruin. In an effort to please his father, Rahn attempted to study law at Freiburg and later at Heidelberg although it was clear he had little taste or talent for it.

Dropping out of higher education in 1928, Rahn relocated to Berlin where he took a job as cinema usher and tried his hand at screenwriting,

Fig. 4.9. Otto Rahn and friend, circa 1928.
Courtesy of Hamilton White.

finding temporary employment with the Lux-Europa Filmgesellschaft. Rahn was fascinated by the potential of the cinematic medium and deeply taken with the work of director Arnold Fanck (1889–1974) whose film *Der Heilge Berg* (1929) features a vision of the Grail experienced by a dying climber on the brink of succumbing to hypothermia. Leni Riefenstahl makes a striking debut in this production, essaying a dual role as a dancer and hallucinatory guardian of the Grail, embodying the tainted essence of a spiritual symbol destined to be hijacked for the bitter purposes of Nazi propaganda.

Several photographs taken during Rahn's subsequent exploration of the Pyrenees echo images from Arnold Fanck's work. Possibly the most striking of these surviving photographs depicts Rahn as a silhouetted figure stepping across a chasm, acting out the tarnished ideal promulgated by the prewar "mountain movies." For a while Rahn futzed around the edges of the film industry and was present on the set of George Wilhelm Pabst's debut feature *Westfront 1918*, appearing as an extra in various silent movie productions before seeking more stable employment as a translator in Geneva.

In November 1928, Otto Rahn met the love of his life, a young Swiss citizen named Raymond Perrier who took lodging with his parents in the hope of learning the German language. "Nineteen years old. Beautiful. Even very beautiful," Rahn wrote breathlessly to Rausch, "and from Geneva!" Raymond was five years younger than Rahn, a scion of the Swiss mineral water dynasty and nephew to Geneva's Honorary-Chancellor of the Republic, Brett Perrier. Rahn's unguarded comments to Rausch and others makes his attraction to Raymond clear; he shows no disinclination toward identifying as gay. These youthful romantic confessions would come back to haunt Otto Rahn in his later career.

"The time of my love with Otto was the happiest in my short life," Perrier would later write to Rausch, although in this same missive he pointedly describes his relationship with Rahn as a "friendship." The pair toured Switzerland and stayed at Perrier's family home in Nyon for two months while Rahn completed work on his thesis, "The Research of Master Kyot of Wolfram von Eschenbach." This epic work in progress, intended as a stepping-stone to Rahn's doctorate in philology, was submitted at the behest of a certain professor Friedrich Gundelfinger, a prominent Jewish writer and critic. While Rahn made no attempt to hide his affection for Raymond, and by inference his sexual orientation, it is hard to know to what extent he identified as a Jew. It would later emerge that Rahn's mother, Clara Margaret Hamburger, descended from a Semitic lineage through her father, Simeon, and mother, Lea Cucer, a detail of ancestry that placed her son on an inevitable collision course with the coming storm of Hitler's Reich.

For a while Rahn managed to hold down a job as a German language teacher at a Catholic school in Geneva where he lived on the Rue Croix d'Or under typically impecunious circumstances. For two reasonably happy years, Rahn continued to pursue his relationship with Raymond, writing and reading prodigiously, studying Rousseau, Voltaire, and the history of the witch hunts. The consistent lack of funds however clearly took its toll on the young man. After meeting Rahn for the first time, the southern French poet Jean-Baptiste Fauré-Lacaussade commented on how under-nourished and sickly the young German appeared, his skin the color of unglazed porcelain. Rahn was driven by what Fauré-Lacaussade described as a "great but disorderly intelligence," caught up in his research and obsessed with the agendas of past times.

In 1929, Albert Rausch relocated to Paris where he was engaged as press officer to the International Red Cross. Rahn managed to save enough money to follow his friend and mentor to the great city of Isis, briefly taking up lodging in the Rue de Lille, where he hoped to pursue his dream of becoming a writer.

Taking Rahn under his wing, Rausch introduced the young man to a circle of French associates who shared their interests in occultism, medievalism, and Grail lore. Among them was the author, Buddhist scholar, and ardent Occitan nationalist Maurice Magre.

Fig. 4.10. Maurice Magre (1874–1944) writer, poet, and neo-Cathar sympathizer. Courtesy of Hamilton White.

Magre could be considered the poet laureate of Catharism, a sort of southern French equivalent of J. R. R. Tolkien and Robert E. Howard rolled into one. Beyond that, he had a prodigious appetite for opium, a fondness for hashish, and a penchant for flamboyant neckties.

In 1924, a journalist from *Le Figaro* wrote: "Magre is an anarchist, an individualist, a sadist, an opium addict. He has all the faults. He is a very great writer. You must read his work."

Drawing heavily on romantic traditions promulgated by Baptist pastor Napoleon Peyrat, Magre's work may not always be historically accurate, yet through his words we sense the tastes, textures, and passions of his native Occitania. His pursuit of the hidden tradition led to a lifelong involvement with the occult demimonde, Freemasonry, Martinism, spiritism, and Madame Helena Petrovna Blavatsky's Theosophical Society. The publication of *The Book of Half-Open Lotuses* (1926), *The Light of China: The Romance of Confucius* (1927), and *Why I Am a Buddhist* (1928) would secure his reputation as a Buddhist scholar and in later life, after making pilgrimage to mother India and sojourning in an ashram at Pondicherry, he would declare himself a Hindu at heart.

At the time of his first meeting with Otto Rahn, Magre was researching his occult magnum opus, *Magiciens et illuminés* (Magicians and Illuminati)—subsequently translated into English as *Return of the Magi*. The book is a collection of essays outlining the transmission of esoteric knowledge from age to age with entries on Apollonius of Tyana, the Rosicrucians, the Templars, Count Saint Germaine, Cagliostro, Nicolas Flamel, and the philosopher's stone. The book stands as a concise and highly readable introduction to the arcanum and includes a lengthy essay on the heretical faith of the south entitled "The Unknown Master of the Albigenses."

Believing Catharism to have been a Western tranche of Buddhism, Magre would continue to chronicle the rise and fall of the Languedocian heresy in his masterpiece *Le sang de Toulouse* (The blood of Toulouse, 1931) and *The Treasure of the Albigenses* (1938). There is no doubt his prose struck a deep chord in Otto Rahn, enflaming the young German's imagination with tales of old Occitania and fanning his passion for the quest.

Taking Rahn into his confidence, Magre introduced him to the charismatic figure of the Countess Miryanne de Pujol Murat, an initiate of Jules Doinel's Église Gnostique de France. The countess claimed descendency from both Esclarmonde de Foix and Hugues de Payens, founder of the Templar order and was by all accounts an impressive figure, believed by some to be if not the reincarnation of the Cathar high priestess, then an expression of the same guardian spirit. In the years between the wars, Miryanne de Pujol Murat served as midwife, den mother, and de facto patron to the neo-Cathar revival and was the guiding light of a Franco-Italian secret society known as the Polaires.

The countess and the spiritual dilettantes drawn to her circle nursed the earnest hope that the time of prophecy was at hand, the time foretold by Guilhelm Bélibaste when the hegemony of the Roman church would falter and the old ways return. Counting seven long centuries from the fall of Montségur and the mass burning of March 16, 1244, gave the hopeful the due date of March 16, 1944, encouraging the belief a better world was not only possible but within reach, a world without war, poverty, or oppression, united in Spirit under the dove and the

Grail. It seemed after the horrors of the First World War the big lie was breaking down and the long, dark age, the Kali Yuga was finally drawing to an end. Theosophists, Anthroposophists, occultists, and neo-Cathars alike dreamed of a new aeon, the dawning of a Satya Yuga or Aquarian age, a global evolution in consciousness when the underground stream might flow into the light and the human race realize their true nature as spiritual beings.

In 1890, Jules Doinel announced the "beginning of the era of Gnosis restored," founding the Église Gnostique de France and declaring himself Gnostic patriarch of Paris. The sect's central rite, a eucharistic ceremony known as the Gnostic mass had allegedly been channeled directly from disembodied Cathar adepts during a dramatic séance conducted in the salon of the medium Lady Marie Caithness. These channeling sessions were a conscious attempt to reach across the centuries and repair the web of time where it had been broken, restoring an initiatory tradition that had been lost when the last known recipient of the consolomentum, Guilhelm Bélibaste, went to the stake in 1321. As a priestess of Doinel's church the Countess Miryanne de Pujol Murat would have been familiar with this ceremony. Moreover she believed herself to be guided by the spirit of her own ancestor, the great na Esclarmonda.

Doinel's Gnostic mass was adopted as one of the central practices in Aleister Crowley's initiatory organization the Ordo Templi Orientis, nor is the O.T.O. the only secret society to consider Montségur their Mount Sinai. Both the Masons and the European Rosicrucian movement hold the magic mountain in high regard, along with countless other latter-day sects such as the Raellians, Ramtha, and the Ordre du Temple Solaire (O.T.S.).

Caught up in this escalating esoteric delirium, Otto Rahn pursued his research in the Bibliothèque Nationale, becoming acquainted with the work of Joséphin Péladan whose text *Le secret des troubadours* speculated on the possible Cathar and Templar origins of the Grail myth, linking the castle of Munsalvaesche in Wolfram's *Parzival* to the heretic stronghold of Montségur, the last known repository of the sacred treasure.

Montségur had been cursed by the Vatican and anathematized by successive papacies, with the rite repeated annually to ensure the serpent's head would never rise again. Every year for seven centuries on the anniversary of the castle's fall, the unfortunate villagers were made to drag a cross through the streets and process to the field of the stake where they would have to repeat the words of the Veni Creator Spiritus sung at the original auto-da-fé. This practice was abandoned in 1925, when it was deemed irrelevant to the modern world, just four years before the first secret societies arrived in the village and the neo-Cathar conferences began in earnest. After the passage of seven centuries, the magic mountain seemed to be reawakening as if a force that had lain dormant since the crusade was stirring and gathering its cohorts.

It is clear Montségur held a particular significance to the Countess de Pujol Murat who served as Rahn's initiator. When she invited him to the south to attend a wedding in the remote village and pursue his research in situ, he could barely contain his excitement. She opened her home to the young German, a lavish ancestral castle on the Black Mountain and even placed her car and private chauffeur at his disposal.

The village of Montségur was not so different in those days, at the fag end of the 1920s when Otto Rahn found himself on the doorstep of the Maison Couquet, the only hostelry in the area. If anything, the settlement was more vibrant, more filled with life, both human and animal, before the coming of the tar road drained the community's youth and vitality. Children still played in the narrow streets and shepherds and *païsan* rubbed shoulders with occultists and treasure hunters.

The auberge where Rahn took lodging played an incubatory role in the neo-Cathar revival that gathered like an esoteric storm around the long table in the downstairs parlor. Few outsiders could imagine the colorful characters who met behind the facade of this obscure mountain hostelry. Spiritualists, poets, artists, and initiates from any number of

Fig. 4.11. Postcards from Montségur.
Courtesy of Hamilton White.

exotic orders gathered about the bright yellow tablecloth to rekindle the spark of the all but forgotten heresy.

"Otto Rahn arrived in Montségur around the time of the first neo-Cathar conferences organized by Déodat Roché," confirmed Suzanne Nelli, the director of the Centre d'Études Cathares in one of several recordings I made with her.

> He was introduced to our circle by the writer Maurice Magre and the Countess Miryanne de Pujol Murat, whom he met in Paris. It is certain Rahn felt at home in this milieu because he recognized the people of the Ariège as having common Aryan roots. It is possible he was sent to France on a mission supported by the politics of the time. . . . Many people came here who were interested in the revival of the faith, the old tradition, the way of the Cathars. There would maybe be twenty or thirty of us seated around this table and it was truly enthralling because each person would share their thoughts and impressions sincerely. Obviously there were mistakes. Myths still existed and we had not yet defined and purified the atmosphere of Catharism but there was a truly human exchange, a human warmth that I haven't found since. Often, at the very beginning, my husband came here with the countess Fanita de Pierrfeu and Lancon del Vasto, the troubadour, who would sit by the fire with his guitar and play the old Occitan songs—and superbly well at that! That was the beginning of the movement, if you will. . . . There were many different types of people. The countess was as likely to entertain the Prince of Saxe or a philosopher like Gabriel Marcel as she would a hippy. The hippies didn't come here because they weren't interested in Catharism in the '60s and '70s, although it is certain some key figures in the situationist movement, particularly Guy de Bord, drew inspiration from the Cathar resistance.

Otto Rahn was introduced to Maurice Magre's inner circle, a loose affiliation of poets, occultists, and folklorists known as *les Amis de*

Fig. 4.12. Suzanne Nelli née Martine Suzette Madeleine Ramon (1918–2007).

Montségur et du Graal. Among them was a former schoolteacher from the Ariège who would exert an enormous influence over the young Grail hunter—Antonin Gadal. Gadal was a minister of tourism for the region and claimed to have been the recipient of an oral tradition passed down to him from the time of the Cathars. In later years he would declare himself to be the Cathar patriarch of the Sabarthès.

Fig. 4.13. Antonin Gadal (1877–1962), self-proclaimed Cathar patriarch of the Sabarthés. Courtesy of Rozekruis Pers.

Magre's well intentioned Grail fellowship was destined to implode when members failed to agree on even the most basic principles of Cathar dogma. Suzanne Nelli's husband, the writer and poet René Nelli, viewed the bygone faith as a form of gnostic dualism, a concept codified in his book *The Doctrine of the Two Principles* whereas Magre considered Catharism to be a Western stream of Buddhism and Déodat Roché saw the so-called heretics as descendants of Mithraism, reflecting the ancient light of Zoroaster.

Figs. 4.14a and 4.14b. René Nelli (1906–1982), founder of the Centre d'Études Cathares, the Centre of Cathar Studies in Carcassonne whose archives played a key role in preserving documents from the time of the crusade.

Fig. 4.15. Déodat Roché, the "pope of neo-Catharism" (1877–1978).

Fig. 4.16. The pope of neo-Catharism in the Gate of the Gods (Porte des Dieux). Déodat Roché in the east-facing gate of the fortress of Montségur.

Fig. 4.17. Déodat Roché's apron—Roché was initiated into the Grand Orient de France through the lodge Les Vrais Amis Réunis in Carcassonne.

Déodat Roché was a vastly respected figure in the neo-Cathar community, a disciple of Steiner, and a prominent Freemason. A lawyer and magistrate with a seat in the high court of Carcassonne, Roché was initiated into Freemasonry in the Grand Orient de France through the lodge Les Vrais Amis Réunis. He would become master of the lodge, a position held until death.

Like the countess, Roché was initiated into Doinel's Église Gnostique de France and ordained in 1903 as Gnostic bishop of Carcassonne—"His Greatness Tau Theodotos." In 1929, he was granted audience with Rudolph Steiner at Dornach and remained a lifelong adherent. Roché's spiritual views would lead to his expulsion from the judiciary by the Vichy government in 1941, although he subsequently served as general councillor of Couiza after the Liberation and mayor of Arques.

In April 1950, Roché founded the Société du Souvenir et des Études Cathares (the Society of the Memory), responsible for erecting and

Fig. 4.18. The founders of the Sociéte du Souvenir et des Études Cathares—Lucienne Julien, Déodat Roché, and René Nelli, whose widow, Suzanne, would later become one of my principal informants.

maintaining the stele, or Martyr's Memorial on Montségur's field of the stake, the only official monument to Catharism. The memorial was inaugurated on May 21, 1961, and would become a focus for Occitan nationalists and neo-Cathar sympathizers in generations to come.

Every year from 1956 onward, Roché and the Société's general secretary, resistance heroine Lucienne Julien, organized summer camps in the Rialsès valley in the Hautes-Corbières. A day at one of these neo-Cathar camps typically began before sunrise with group meditation followed by a full program of polyphonic singing, paneurhythmy, and painting lessons.

Roché would live to be over 100 years old, becoming known as the pope of neo-Catharism. At the time of his death in 1978, Roché left a formidable body of written work, none of which has ever been translated from the original French. A sampling of principle titles includes "Ancient gnosis and modern thought" (1906), "Catharism and spiritual science" (1955), "Survival and Immortality of the Soul—Ghosts of the living and the dead—Successive lives and luminous bodies of resurrection" (1955).

Fig. 4.19. As above, so below: The stele, or Martyr's Memorial, in Montségur's field of the stake erected by Roché's Society of the Memory. Photos by Richard Stanley.

Otto's Quest for the Grail   103

It is impossible to know what transpired between Rahn and Roché. The young German is said to have borrowed money from Roché to prolong his stay, possibly with the intent of buying property in the village. Inspired and deeply moved by the potent spiritual energies of the pog, Rahn spent as much time as he could on the magic mountain, finding himself in the presence of a mystery whose solution would become his lifework. Weather allowing, he held vigil on the battlement, taking hundreds of photographs and noting the curious orientation of the castle, convinced the place names and geofeatures in the area held vital clues. Rahn clearly held a romantic view of the past, yet nothing he found in Montségur disappointed or disillusioned him. Instead the silence and mystery of the mountaintop citadel only served to fan the flames of his already chimeric imagination.

Marius Mounié claimed Rahn attempted to purchase a plot of land from his father with a view of the castle, but his plans were thwarted

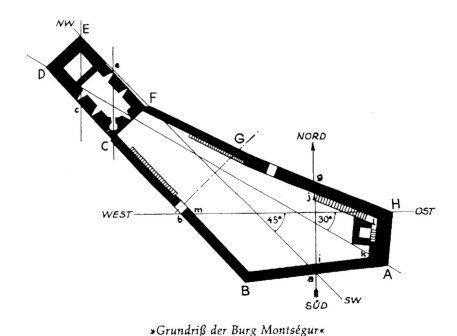

»Grundriß der Burg Montségur«

Fig. 4.20. Orientation of the castle of Montségur, diagram by Otto Rahn.

Fig. 4.21. Archaeologist Fabrice Chambon in the ruins of the thirteenth-century Cathar village on the east face of the pog, the only surviving structures that can be readily dated to the time of the siege. The rest of the fortress has been rebuilt so many times that dating the individual layers of stone would require more sophisticated technology than was available to the GRAME (Groupe de Recherches Archéologiques de Montségur et Environs) when they conducted the official survey in the years between 1969 and 1976. Since then, no further archaeological investigation of the pog has been authorized.
Photo by Richard Stanley.

when the locals closed ranks against him. Rahn's command of French was imperfect and memory of the First World War too fresh for the Montséguriens to admit a German into their insular community. There was, perhaps, something a little otherwordly about Rahn's manner that failed to inspire their confidence.

After prevailing on Roché's generosity, Rahn apparently failed to repay the loan and was allegedly expelled from Montségur by locals who drove him out with pitchforks and horsewhips. If Suzanne Nelli was right about Rahn serving as an occult envoy, then something must have gone very wrong with his mission.

While the rift with Roché and the neo-Cathars of Montségur discouraged Rahn, it did not deter him from his increasingly quixotic quest. Relocating to the neighboring valley of the Ariège, he continued to explore the area by foot. The data he compiled during this period would provide the substance of his first book *Crusade against the Grail* (1933), one of the earliest accounts of the Albigensian genocide to appear outside of France.

Rahn's writing makes it clear his quest was a spiritual journey in search of a lost link between humanity and the divine, a reconciliation symbolized by the Grail. In Rahn's private cosmology, the war of the Holy Roman Church against the Albigenses was simply another manifestation of an ongoing apocalyptic struggle between the forces of light and darkness on whose constantly shifting balance everything in our illusory material universe is supposedly predicated. If the physical universe is merely the three-dimensional shadow of a spiritual reality, the material manifestation of an etheric truth, then Rahn's search for a physical relic hidden within the mountains was no contradiction in terms. The outer journey traditionally mirrors and informs the seeker's progress through the inner labyrinth.

In his published writings, Rahn identifies the Grail with the crown of Lucifer, citing a folktale he allegedly heard in the Ariège. While walking in the heights of the Tabor, Rahn claims to have taken shelter from a violent summer storm in an ancient shepherd's hut near the Lac du Diable, the so-called Devil's Lake. Here he claims to have encountered an elderly païsan, a descendant of the Cathars. While lightning crashed and flickered outside, the old man told the young German a curious tale—the story of Lucifer's diadem. Of course, we have no proof this garrulous sage of the high pastures ever really existed any more than Wolfram's Master Kyot. The whole episode carries the smell of myth, if not a subtle hint of brimstone.

"In the days before the fall," said the shepherd, "Lucifer was the fairest of God's angels and wore on his brow an emerald diadem. The crown fell from the peacock angel's brow when he fell from grace with

Fig. 4.22. The Gate of the Gods (Porte des Dieux).
Photo by Richard Stanley.

God and was cast out of heaven with his minions. The diadem was lost and the light bearer cast down into the abyss of manifestation. According to tradition, the crown of Lucifer fell to Earth in the Hindu Kush, where it was fashioned by master Afghan craftsmen into a cup used by Salem to consecrate the temple Abraham built in Ur of the Chaldees. The cup became part of the sacred treasure of the temple of Solomon and was said in time to have been borne back to Europe.

"Before the fall of Montségur, the castle preserved within its walls the most high Holy Grail. But the legions of Hell laid siege to the castle, seeking to regain their master's lost diadem. Na Esclarmonda, the guardian of the Grail, transformed herself into a dove that split the mountain with its beak. The sacred treasure was concealed within the rock, which closed around it. And so the Grail was saved. When the devils entered the castle the treasure was nowhere to be found. In their rage, they seized the pure ones, burning them alive on the Camp de Cremat—the field of the stake" (Otto Rahn, *Crusade against the Grail*, 1934, Inner Traditions).

According to Rahn's mysterious shepherd, the servants of Lucifer still search for their master's fallen crown so he might one day regain his rightful place in the kingdom of heaven. Searching from one lifetime to the next, down through the ages . . .

5
A Visit to the Devil's Lake

Summer 1998

Don't elves play in the moonlight around the crystal clear springs in their native Pyrenees? Don't the oak trees on the Tabor speak to the shepherds, who are so far from God's world, by rustling their leaves? The guaranteed authentic story that the ninety-year-old peasant of Ornolac told me shows that the grandchildren of the Druids and bards, of the Cathars and troubadours, are todays mystics and poets. He asserted he saw a snake on the trail that bit its tail and shook itself as it formed a circle at the abyss of the Sabarthès towards the snow-covered summit of Montcalm. Three times the Tabor was cursed and three times it burned in flames. Six hundred years later, a day worker from the town of Ornolac claims to have seen the symbol of eternity: a snake that bites its tail. Esclarmonde did not die, a shepherd told me on the Pathway of the Cathars. She continues to live . . .

OTTO RAHN, CRUSADE AGAINST THE GRAIL

I inched forward, lying motionless as a lizard in the sun at close to 3,300 feet, staring down into the abyss. The waters of the Lac du Diable were as clear as glass, rocky bed shelving away into depths beyond knowing, blue as lapis lazuli, shot through with bands of rippling green. I had never seen water so clear, so pure, like a piece of the sky fallen to earth. This was where the river rose all right, welling from the heart of the Tabor and lapping over the lake's outermost rim to snake downward through the impenetrable ravines of the Pic de Saint-Barthélemy, forming the icy stream whose emerald torrents had, over the course of millenia, cut the valley of Montségur and still feed the unseen waters beneath the castle—but was it also the source of the mountain's mysterious power?

A light moved in the depths, golden, watery beams coruscating up from the aqueous gloom. Dancing. Turning. Beckoning. A wheel of silent, liquid fire.

The lakes of the Tabor lie serene, so high above the clouds they touch a different air, like vast scrying mirrors that reflect only the flawless blue of the firmament. The surrounding cliffs that soar upward to the dim spires of the vast natural amphitheater commonly known as the Throne of the Gods, topped by the beetling summits of Soularac and Saint-Barthélemy, so far above the human world that snow still lingers in their clefts even in late summer. On the plateau below the Devil's Lake lies a second tarn, the Lac des Truit, alternatively described as the Lake of the Trout or the Lake of the Druids, depending on one's interpretation of old Occitan. I'd tried fishing it and there were no trout to be had, although trout can fool you. Otto Rahn, with typically mythopoeic zeal, dubbed it the *Druidenzee* and tacitly accepted the silent tarn's magical properties, believing it to be an ancient ceremonial site, which wasn't hard to believe, given it looked like a '70s gatefold album cover—specifically one of Roger Dean's artworks for the British prog rock band YES wrought in three-dimensional life.

In ancient times this Olympian peak was consecrated to the solar deity Abelio and as early as the fourth century, the massif became known as the Tabor, or mountain of transfiguration. The highest summit of the natural amphitheater was dedicated to Saint Bartholomew, the apostle of India and Persia. It is surely tantalizing to see this as another clue to the origins of the Grail myth in distant Khorazin, a legend of paradise lost transmitted to southern Europe by the Moorish philosopher Flegetanis and united with the Western stream. There is no doubt this initiatory mountain held a special significance to the vanished Cathars and the Gauls and Celts before them who scaled its heights to bring themselves closer to God. Otto Rahn suggests the pog of Montségur and the peaks of Soularac and Saint-Barthélemy symbolize the holy trinity—the Paraclete, the Demiurge, and the unknown.

Mr. Horn and our buddy James "JB" Bourne, a British ex-pat who had recently purchased a farm in the area, were slowly but steadily working their way around the perimeter of the lake, scrambling over the

Fig. 5.1. The Devil's Lake (Lac du Diable).
Photo by Martin Chaput.

Fig. 5.2. Gateway to Shambhala—reflections in the Devil's Lake.
Photo by Richard Stanley.

scree. I could distantly hear JB's voice echoing off the rubble, singing as he went. "Yippie yi yi yippie yi. She'll be coming round the mountain when she comes, when she comes . . ."

It was here, on this barren shore, Otto Rahn claimed to have encountered the anonymous shepherd who first told him the saga of na Esclarmonda and the crown of Lucifer. Na Esclarmonda—the undying guardian of the Grail, whose iconic figure straddled two worlds—at once a Christian priestess and the living avatar of the Mountain Mother, the heathen Goddess that was the true sovereignty of this land—a historic personage transmuted into myth, transfigured into the symbol of her faith. Rahn claims he shared bread and wine with this unnamed sage after summiting Soularac in the summer of 1931, although there is no

Fig. 5.3. The Route of the Bonhomme—the author on the summit of the Tabor. Photo by Momo Milla Gross.

Fig. 5.4. The forests of the Tabor. Photo by Richard Stanley.

way of testing the fable's provenance. The shepherd described how the Cathar holy men made pilgrimage to the place where the earth meets the sky, the first stop on the journey to the stars. It is easy enough to imagine the perfecti in their ragged mantles, seated in the shade of a cromlech, repeating the stories of the days of old to their disciples, just as the Druids before them had scaled these heights to celebrate their mysteries.

The Devil's Lake lies halfway between the Cathar fortress of Montségur and the castle of Lordat on an almost impassable pilgrimage route known as the path of the bonhomme. Esclarmonde the bastard, the illegitimate niece of the fabled high priestess, and her companions, Amiel Aicart, Poitevin the Mason, and Brother Matheus, were said to have passed this way when they fled Montségur the night after the burning. Some maintain the fleeing heretics cast their treasure into the bottomless lake as they passed. Others believe its waters hide the cursed treasure of Delphi that had been dragged through the streets of Toulouse by the Visigoths before being flung into the lake in order to lift a plague from the land. Supposedly that plague will return if treasure hunters ever attempt to penetrate its azure depths or disturb the sunken hoard below.

According to a tradition, first recorded in the fifteenth century, the lake is the mouth of hell and if you throw a stone into its waters a storm will be sure to come. During the drought of 1840 a local baker was said to have thrown a cat into its waters. The cat began to thrash and struggle in the middle of the lake, scratching at the water so hard the devil was enraged and caused it to rain for seven weeks. As in myths the world over, the source of the river is connected to the all-powerful rain-making magic and the life of the land. Ever since the far-off days when pagan gods held sway over these mountains, the inhabitants of the surrounding villages made a yearly torch-lit pilgrimage to the Devil's Lake on the eve of August 23, the feast day of Saint Barthélemy, building bonfires and keeping vigil until dawn. This practice apparently had its origins in the bacchanalia and fertility rites of their pre-Christian ancestors and the outraged local clergy complained that like crabs drawn to their spawning ground by the new moon, so the young Ariègeois would be drawn to the shores of the Devil's Lake to sing ribald songs, make love, and participate in naked sun worship. Of course, we only have the period clergy's typically prurient word for it, as the practice was discontinued in the late nineteenth century, but it seems nocturnal gatherings on lonely mountaintops and other places of power have always been a bone of contention to the mother church. The powers that be have never liked folk having free access to the otherworld and attempts to deliberately suppress the old religion and bar access to their holy places continue to the present, unconsciously or otherwise.

Alone on the shore of that all but unreachable tarn, I had to admit it was one of the most otherworldly landscapes I had ever set foot in. Shortly after we got there, JB found a pair of pale, sinewy white tentacles, presumably the mutilated remains of a squid or freshwater hydra caught in the reeds at the mouth of the lake. Squid, to the best of my knowledge, only thrive in salt water and have no place in an isolated freshwater source such as the Lac du Diable. The best available explanations, that the squid was either carried up the mountain and cut up for bait by a passing fisherman or was somehow borne all the way from the Mediterranean by a stray seagull, failed to entirely convince, yet I was unwilling to submit to the beguilingly freaky notion that these calm waters hid the existence of a tendriled Lovecraftian beast, hitherto unknown to science. For a moment I found myself recalling those nameless dethroned pagan divinities na Esclarmonda, immortal white lady of Montségur, was supposed to have called down from the mountains to do her bidding but then I tried to put the thought from my mind. The only borderline cryptozoological critter known to exist in these parts other than the Pyrenean giant toads were a unique species of golden salamander, appropriately a symbol of eternal life, of humanity and nature made whole.

Gazing out from a precipitous crag that jutted like a pulpit over the silent waters, I watched as vaporous masses started to form up over the center of the lake, clouds briefly taking on the shape of wings, hands, or shrouded figures before melting back into thin air, presumably the result of some sort of temperature inversion between the tarn's upper layers, warmed by the afternoon sun and the freezing lower depths fed by the snows of the Saint-Barthélemy. Otto Rahn might well have sat on that very ledge, seventy years gone by. A shoal of fish, too small to be rainbow trout or brownies, glided below, their shadows crossing several objects that from where I rested resembled broken tablets lying strewn across the lake's stony bed. Even at a distance, I imagined I could almost read the glyphs that might be scrawled on their fractured surfaces, almost scry their secrets, like speaking a language I'd never learned. There were old bones down there too. The head of what looked like a femur and what might have been part of an animal skull rotting into the mulch. Then the wind blew and the view was lost, breaking up into dancing shadows, shards of light flickering across the wavelets like blazing butterflies.

 Easing my aching body from the rocks, I stood on the edge of the abyss, breathing in through my nose and out through my mouth, filling my lungs with cold, clean mountain air. Then, going with the flow, I put my head down, straightened my arms and pushed myself off into space. A moment in midair, a moment of falling—then the snowmelt burst in a shower of green sparks around me and I found myself kicking my way downward into the crystal depths. It was not as cold as I had expected, at least not at first. The stones that had looked like broken tablets lay before me, still beyond reach. I forced myself deeper, my fingertips brushing the silt of the lakebed. For a moment I could have been almost anywhere or anywhen, drifting through a huge room lit in various shades of blue, beautifully graduated from light to dark. I went toward the palest color even though it seemed to be to one side of me rather than above—and an instant before I broke surface I saw the ghostly disc of the sun through the meniscus of the water, liquid and transformed. Then the disc exploded in my face and I drew myself gasping and shivering from the tarn.

 I was at the very edge of the cursed lake, where it flowed out over

Fig. 5.5. The author on the edge of the Devil's Lake, summer 1998. Photo by James "JB" Bourne.

the lip of the plateau to trickle away down the mountainside toward the lake of the Druids, the treeline, and the undulating carpet of cloud beyond. I caught my breath, feeling as if I had been baptized anew in the name of some unknown god, looking down on the scarcely created world that unfurled itself like a mirage before me. There was something in my hand, and opening my trembling fingers I found I was clutching a single ringlet from what looked like a piece of rusted chain mail. It was probably nothing, but I turned the bit of metal in my palm and, closing my eyes, made a wish. I tried to imagine her face hanging before me and for a moment found myself wondering whether the immortal high priestess of the Albigensians really had red hair like her brother.

Raimond Drut, Raimond the Beloved, the redheaded Count of Foix had been this land's fiercest and most stubborn defender, yet no image of him or his saintly sister survives. The crusaders and the Inquisitors who followed tried to ensure that all record of those far-off days was eradicated along with any paintings or sculptures that might have existed of the heretical faith's greatest heroes and leaders. A statue of the great Esclarmonde was commissioned in the early years of the twentieth century by the city of Foix but once the maquette was completed the town council got cold feet, removing the effigy from public display and consigning it to oblivion. It seems poor reward for a lifetime of selfless service as guardian of the faith that na Esclarmonda should be effectively canceled from history, nor have I ever been able to locate a single photograph of the mysterious Countess Miryanne de Pujol Murat who claimed descendency from her line.

Otto Rahn describes his mentor, after a pleasant afternoon at the Mediterranean seaside, seated in an armchair beside the baronial hearth of her castle on the Black Mountain, knitting fiercely as she continued to expound on the injustices suffered by her family. Both of them, the countess and her young neophyte are gone now, part of an older Europe long since washed away on a tide of blood and ash, yet it is my fancy that they still exist, just as all things exist somewhere in the abyss of time, nor is it impossible to conjure them back into being, like reflected light still caught in the fathomless waters of the Devil's Lake.

If I listen carefully enough, I can almost hear their voices.

"Lucifer is not the devil," the countess hissed, needles glinting in the firelight as she completed another row. "Because *Lucifer* means 'Bearer of Light'! The Cathars recognized him by another name." She glanced up at the young German as if to make sure he was still paying attention, eyes like black holes in the masklike parchment of her face. "Lucibel. He was not the devil! The Jews and the papists wished to debase him by confounding him in this way."

A log split on the hearth, sending their shadows dancing out across the musty walls of the great hall, a plume of sparks rising past the blackened blazon beside the flue, twin opposing salamanders, the symbol of life eternal.

"As far as the Grail is concerned," she continued, voice falling to a whisper, "it must surely be, as your shepherd says, a stone fallen from Lucifer's crown."

Reaching for a poker, Otto Rahn delicately tidied back the embers. He knew not to interrupt la comtesse, but instead listened carefully, or at least gave the impression of listening. Despite his poor French, his inability to grasp the nuances of what she was trying to tell him, his aristocratic hostess couldn't help but wonder if this strange young man was really the only one who still believed in her, the last of the faithful. One of her cats stirred, turning in a semicircle before settling itself once more beside the hearth.

"This is why the church revindicated the Grail, to christianize this Luciferian symbol," she insisted. "The pog of Montségur was the mountain of the Grail, of which Esclarmonde was mistress." She finished another row, almost ready to cast off, the pullover she was working on steadily taking shape. Turning toward the table, Otto glanced at the books he had fetched from her private library, among them a monograph on the funerary rites of her all but vanished faith and the Albigensian tombs recently unearthed not far from the countess's ancestral seat. In one communal pit, twelve skeletons had been found, heads placed together, bodies radiating outward like the spokes of a wheel, a practice, the monograph suggested, possibly linked to a bygone sun-worshipping cult.

"The church, after leading a war of the Cross against the Grail, appropriated this non-Christian religious symbol for its own and milked it for all it was worth." Leaning forward, the countess stared up at Otto with unwavering eyes. "It wasn't enough to pretend the Grail was simply the chalice Jesus shared with his disciples at the Last Supper and later was supposedly used to gather his blood at Golgotha. No, they had to make believe the Benedictine monastery of Montserrat, in the

A Visit to the Devil's Lake   119

Fig. 5.6. The view from the Tabor, summer 1998. Immo Horn uses a clockwork Bolex to record a time-lapse image on the cloudscape. Photo by Richard Stanley.

south of these mountains, was the true temple of the Grail." Shaking her head at this perfidy, she subsided back into her chair with a hiss. "After the Cathars—dismissed as Luciferians by the Inquisitors—had guarded the Grail stone in the north of the Pyrenees, it was now the Catholic monks who claimed to hold it in the south, having transformed it into a run-of-the-mill relic, conferred by Jesus, the conqueror of the Prince of Darkness, to his faithful. I don't have to remind you that Montserrat, the bastion of the Dark Mother, was where Loyola conceived his infernal spiritual exercises." Setting aside her knitting, the Countess Miryanne de Pujol Murat gazed into the surging embers before offering her young disciple a final piece of advice. "If I were you, I would look into these points, very carefully."

6

Into the Labyrinth of the Pyrenees

In the silent darkness, the bishops no doubt uttered the words which promised divine pardon as a result of the imminence of death and the liberation of the spirit. No doubt they stretched forth their hands over bowed heads in the invisible gesture of the consolamentum. The mountains above the Ariège have kept the secret of the mass without candles, the death without grave or winding sheet. The book of Nicetas which was kept among the treasure, the lovers' kiss, the bishops' gesture of blessing, must have turned to stone from the absence of air. The last of the Albigenses, motionless, clothed in stone, still celebrate their final ritual amidst dead vegetation and lustureless crystals in a basilica of darkness. . . .

MAURICE MAGRE

According to tradition, after the fall of Montségur, the surviving heretics fled across the Tabor and down into the valley of Ussat where they took refuge in the labyrinthine caverns that became the treasure's final resting place. This enduring myth first found expression in the work of Napoleon Peyrat, a baptist pastor from Saint Germaine-en-Laye who described how the last of the faithful were entombed alive by the Crusaders who didn't dare to follow them into the lightless tunnels. Neither Magre nor Peyrat give any indication of a historic source for this unhappy legend, a local variant on the myth of the eternal return, not far removed from stories commonly told in England and Wales about

Fig. 6.1. The fortified grotto of Bouan.
Photo by Otto Rahn.

Arthur, Merlin, and the knights of the Round Table still sleeping beneath one hill or another, waiting for the day they might rise again. Otto Rahn seemed to give these stories credence. After his unseemly departure from Montségur, Rahn settled in Ussat-les-Bains in the Ariège and began to explore the many caves honeycombing the region in the hope of finding the key to the treasure hidden within the coils of the largest limestone region in Europe. Whether that treasure was a physical or spiritual one remained to be seen but to fully appraise the merits of Rahn's case it was clear I would have to follow in his steps.

My companion and guide on my first visit to the caves of Ussat was Christian Bernadac, the former head of TF1, France's national television channel. Christian had been born and bred in the Ariège and the Rahn enigma had become an obsession to him. He was an avid vintage car collector and arrived at our rendezvous in a World War II era jeep, which seemed entirely appropriate.

Turning in a slow pirouette on the patio outside the hotel bar in Tarascon, a gauloise clenched in one hand and a cocktail glass in

Fig. 6.2. The Grotto of Ornolac or the "eglise."
Photo by Richard Stanley.

the other, Christian indicated the surrounding cradle of mountains, unpacking an unlikely sounding story that each peak represented a different animal in the Egyptian creation myth.

"And that one?" He gestured at another crag, this time a shorter, humpier formation overlooking the turbulent waters of the Ariège. "What kind of animal do you think that is?"

I shrugged, finding it difficult to follow his train of thought.

"C'est un marmot! It's a marmot!" sighed Christian as if this were somehow self-evident. And at that moment, I recall the young French lady who was translating for me that day, leaning closer and whispering in my ear, "Richard, do you think maybe Christian did too much acid back in the hippie days?"

I didn't care to reflect too deeply on Christian's brain chemistry or how many cocktails he downed before leaving the bar. Strapping myself into the jeep's passenger seat I tried not to look too nervous as we set out on what I knew would be a journey like none other.

"My grandfather owned the only car in this region back in the '30s," Christian informed me, stepping on the gas. "All the archaeologists

Fig. 6.3. Christian Bernadac and his jeep, summer 1998.
Photo by James "JB" Bourne.

Fig. 6.4. Touring the Ariège, summer 1932.
Courtesy of Hamilton White.

back then were either schoolteachers, lecturers, or priests. They always wanted to go to the caves and my grandfather would take them there. Then in '31 a young German arrived in Ussat who wanted to carry out research concerning the Grail, Montségur, and the Cathars. Obviously, since Rahn wanted to move about and he had become acquainted with a certain Antonin Gadal, who had been interested in Grail research for many years, they came to see my grandfather about the car, which was a Renault, a B-14."

I nodded, listening to Christian's take on the story as the rickety wooden jeep hurtled up a precipitous road high above the valley, propelling me ever deeper into his paranoid worldview.

Paul Bernadac, Christian's grandfather, had been an ardent amateur spelunker with an extensive knowledge of the local cave systems. In the spring of 1932, Paul was recruited to become Otto Rahn's guide and driver, accompanying him on his daily expeditions to the caves, just as his grandson would later accompany me. In this manner they charted all the major caverns marked on the hand-drawn map Rahn prepared for publication in his first book.

Into the Labyrinth of the Pyrenees

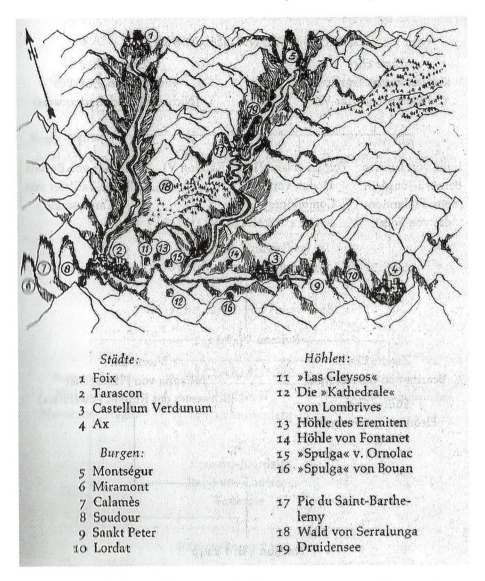

Städte:
1. Foix
2. Tarascon
3. Castellum Verdunum
4. Ax

Burgen:
5. Montségur
6. Miramont
7. Calamès
8. Soudour
9. Sankt Peter
10. Lordat

Höhlen:
11. »Las Gleysos«
12. Die »Kathedrale« von Lombrives
13. Höhle des Eremiten
14. Höhle von Fontanet
15. »Spulga« v. Ornolac
16. »Spulga« von Bouan

17. Pic du Saint-Barthelemy
18. Wald von Serralunga
19. Druidensee

Fig. 6.5. The key to the treasure is the treasure—a map of the quest drawn by Grail hunter Otto Wilhelm Rahn.

According to Christian, Rahn visited the Lombrives, the Cave of the Hermit, Fontanet, Bédeilhac, Niaux, Ornolac, the fortified grotto of Bouan, and the subterranean river of la Bouiche where his father, Paul Bernadac, served as boatman, paddling the dugout canoe that bore the young Grail seeker into the heart of the mountain. Christian told me it was his grandfather's tradition to always carry a flask of absinthe, known locally as *la Fée Verte* (the "green faery"), a concoction Rahn would imbibe with a lump of sugar and a sip of cold water so it would melt on his tongue.

On other occasions, Rahn is known to have borrowed the countess's car along with her chauffeur, Joseph Widigger, who can be seen holding one of the carbide lanterns in a surviving photograph. The locals in Ussat-les-Bains mistrusted Widigger instinctively, believing him to be just as unsavory as the other members of Rahn's growing entourage and possibly capable of violence. Rahn's nickname for Widigger was Lazybones.

On his subterranean outings, Otto Rahn frequently traveled in the company of Antonin Gadal (1877–1962), who served as minister of tourism for the region. Gadal was by all accounts a complex and controversial figure. Born in Ussat, Gadal claimed to have been the recipient of an oral tradition bequeathed to him by an old blind man he had nursed in his youth, a local historian and folklorist named Adolphe Garigou (1802–1897) who served as his initiator into the mysteries of the Cathar faith. Gadal believed the caves surrounding his hometown had played an important role in those mysteries, providing shelter and places of worship for the so-called heretics. Gadal referred to his initiator as Papa Garigou and would become known as the self-proclaimed patriarch of the Sabarthès, frequently boasting his surname was an anagram for Galaad or Galahad, the quest knight.

As head of the Syndicat d'Initiative of Ussat-Ornolac, Gadal effectively claimed ownership of the caves. Otto Rahn needed unfettered access to these sites to pursue his quest and was forced to knock on Gadal's door. In time, Gadal opened that door for him and became his friend and quite possibly his patron. Otto Rahn would write that he "owed everything" to Gadal and it is possible Gadal saw in him a potential heir and acolyte. Together they set out in quest of a treasure they believed had been lost to humanity for seven centuries.

Into the Labyrinth of the Pyrenees   127

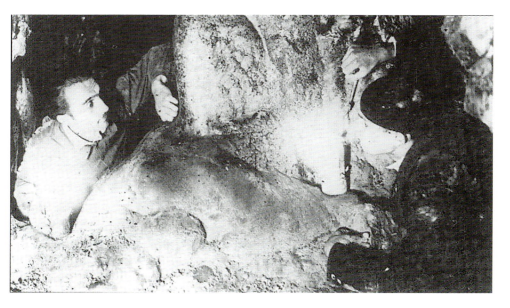

Fig. 6.6. Otto Rahn explores the Cave of the Hermit, a pristine limestone system protected by three long crawls, accompanied by Joseph "Lazybones" Widigger, seen on the left holding a carbide lantern.

Fig. 6.7. Antonin Gadal (*far right*) with spelunkers at the Lombrives, circa 1932. Courtesy of Hamilton White.

Fig. 6.8. Postcards home—a card addressed to Otto Rahn's father, Karl, showing Ussat-les-Bains and the highway to Andora. The location of the Hotel des Marronniers has been labeled in Otto's handwriting.

Into the Labyrinth of the Pyrenees 129

In order to pursue his research, Otto Rahn took over the lease of a guesthouse on the main highway to Andorra—the Hotel des Marronniers. It is difficult, if not impossible, to trace the source of the funding for this largesse. Rahn was no businessman and had little or no financial reserves of his own. The young German was dogged throughout his life by bad debts and unrecovered loans. With Germany in the grip of an apocalyptic recession, Rahn's family was in no position to bankroll such an ill-starred venture, nor does the surviving correspondence with his father indicate that he was soliciting financial support from his parents. Rahn's postcards paint a rosy picture of his circumstances in the Ariège, offering no clue to the source of the necessary income to underwrite his ongoing quest.

Some suggest it was Antonin Gadal who advanced the deposit to secure the Hotel des Marronier's lease, but Christian Bernadac was convinced the cash flow could only have come from the coffers of a major European secret society, suggesting the Thule Gesellschaft were underwriting the young Grail seeker's research.

Christian cornered sharply, taking the trail toward the caves. This was the first time I had heard anyone mention the Thule Society in connection to the Rahn affair and there was nothing in the surviving documentation to substantiate Christian's claims. In their prime the Thule sponsored the creation of the Deutsche Arbeiterpartei (German Worker's Party or DAP), which Adolph Hitler subsequently reorganized into the National Socialist German Workers' Party or Nazi party, but by the summer of 1931, the lodge had already been dissolved. I looked at Christian askance, refusing to believe the Thule could have had anything to do with securing Rahn's lease. The clue to the identity of Otto's paymasters, Christian insisted, could be found in the jumper he frequently wore at the time, emblazoned with a prominent *sieg* rune, known to be one of the symbols of the Thule.

"It is not difficult to suppose Otto Rahn was sent here on a mission," Christian continued. "A secret mission to turn the neo-Cathar movement toward the Nazi cause. It is certainly strange that he was already

Fig. 6.9. Postcards home—cards addressed to Otto Rahn's father, Karl, circa 1931.

Fig. 6.10. The Hotel des Marronniers depicted on a postcard Otto Rahn sent to his father in early 1932, boasting of his achievements. The Grail hunter's handwriting appears on the bottom left, labeling the room he used as his study.

marked by a lightning bolt, his garments emblazoned with the symbol of the SS long years before the Black Order even came into existence."

I nodded, admitting that it seemed beyond coincidence, but then so were a lot of things pertaining to this affair.

Christian Bernadac suggested the sweater had been knitted by Otto's mother who is pictured beside him in a photograph showing her son proudly displaying the garment. I later learned from Rahn's niece, Ingeborgh Roemer-Rahn, that she had turned this hand-me-down knitted garment, inherited from her uncle, into a pair of play trousers for her son.

"This is where the mystery really begins," Christian insisted—and who was I to doubt him?

Otto Rahn seems to have undertaken his exploration of the Pyrenean caves and mountaintops at his own behest, driven by personal

Fig. 6.11. Otto Rahn, his proud mother, Clara, and the notorious sieg rune sweater.

obsession. There is no evidence to suggest his work was carried out under the aegis of either the Thule Society or the nascent Schutzstaffel, so what was the true significance of that incriminating lightning bolt on the Grail seeker's sweater?

While it remains pure supposition, subsequent research suggested a possibility Christian Bernadac hadn't considered.

The Wandervogel commonly use occult symbols such as the Wolf's Engel among their insignia and the badge of the Nerother Bund's *Donnerkeile* formation features a jagged sieg rune strikingly similar to the one depicted on Rahn's jumper. His close friend Albert Rausch was familiar with the movement's leadership and Rahn seems to have maintained a relationship with the Wandervogel that began during his school days in Giessen and extended beyond his death.

In 1964, members of the Nerother Bund, under the direction of a certain Pater Martin Kuhn, constructed a curious memorial at their order castle in the forest of Hunsruck, the only monument to Rahn's memory. At the base of a circular pedestal of stones, carried one by one from the heretic citadel of Montségur, appears a simple, sobering phrase drawn from Wolfram's *Parzival*, "Caution, these ways lead astray!" Clearly someone in the Bund's hierarchy shared Rahn's passion for the Grail myth.

The Nerother Bund was a breakaway formation led by the charismatic Robert Oelbermann, who established his new order on March 27, 1921, an act perceived by many as a sort of coup d'état within the Wandervogel. Robert Oelbermann wanted to preserve the conservative core of the movement from reform, separating the Bund from any and all formations that had the temerity to admit girls to their ranks. He hoped to expand the Bund's influence into the Rhineland by purchasing and restoring the ruined fortress at Waldeck to serve as the formation's headquarters. Three subsidiary orders were formed and pledged their allegiance to Oelbermann's covenant, the Orders of the Raven's Claw, the Goat Riders, and the Werewolves. The names of these orders might have sprung directly from J. K. Rowling's Harry Potter franchise, an impression further enforced by the gothic circumstances of the castle and the magical curriculum. If Oelbermann sought to establish a real-life Hogwarts, then it was an exclusively male one. The silver swan became their blazon and the red and blue of the Neroth Wandering Bird were adopted as the formation's official colors.

The Bund was formally dissolved when the Nazis seized power in 1933 and Waldeck was occupied by the Hitler Youth, the SA, and the SS. Former members continued to gather in secret and in 1934 Robert Oelbermann set up the Burg Waldeck Working Group to try to regain control of the castle. Oelbermann was promptly accused of pedophilia and arrested for alleged violations of Section 175, the notorious Nazi-era addition to the German penal code that criminalized homosexuality. Approximately 150 members of the Bund between the ages of thirteen and forty were arrested and severely tortured in the Ulmer Höhe prison in Düsseldorf to extract false statements and further accusations against

Fig. 6.12. Robert and Karl Oelbermann.

Oelbermann and his brother Karl who was in South Africa at the time. Robert Oelbermann was subsequently transferred from civilian prison to the concentration camps of Oranienburg and Sachsenhausen before perishing in Dachau in 1941.

In 1950, Karl Oelbermann returned from exile, having spent the war in a South African internment camp. Assuming leadership of the revived Bund, he set about restoring the order castle, inaugurating the practice of erecting memorial stones on the property. "King Oelb," as he came to be known, had a particular fondness for the French Pyrenees and in later years spent a good deal of time in Montségur where he lodged at the Maison Couquet, counting Rahn's former landlady Aimeé Couquet as a friend. After King Oelb's passing, the Bund continued to use Maison Couquet as a base of operations in Cathar country, sketching their colorful blazons in the pages of Aimeé's guestbook, a relationship that extended to the present day. A further 46 kg of stones were removed from the castle of Montségur in 1995 and carried back to Waldeck by members of the

Bund who continue to hold the summer solstice as their major festival.

But why had the Bund chosen to erect a memorial to Rahn, especially one bearing such a numinous inscription? Did Rahn perform some secret duty to the Bund, putting his life in danger as a consequence? I was starting to wonder if the answer didn't lie beyond the gates of KZ Dachau. Certainly the paths of all too many of the players in this strange drama seemed to end there.

Whatever the import of that enigmatic lightning bolt, I sensed I was no closer to tracing the true source of Rahn's funding. Without visible means of support, the young Grail hunter made use of pickaxes, shovels, carbide lanterns, and cameras during his systematic exploration of the caves. In the course of his research, he took hundreds of photographs, converting the hotel attic into a darkroom.

Under Rahn's management the Hotel des Marronniers would become the focus for a convoluted web of local legend. Its patrons are said to have included emissaries of obscure occult formations, fancy women from Toulouse, British clairvoyants, Basque, Occitan, and Catalan nationalists, Italian fascists, German fifth columnists, and flamboyant local personalities such as historian Isabelle Sandy and the mysterious Mr. Baby. Rahn would write to Gadal that his time in Ussat was all but ruined by the behavior of one of his guests—the seemingly inevitable *lupus in fabula*—the wolf in the story. In this case, the source of Rahn's troubles turned out to be a rotund, bullet-headed gay American from Rochester, New York, named Nat Wolff. Wolff claimed to have formerly lived in Marrakesh and to be on a photographic mission on behalf of the American consulate in Paris but Christian Bernadac and the other locals in Ussat clearly believed him to be a Nazi fifth columnist.

Wolff lodged at Chez Cousture at the far end of the park but would usually spend his evenings with Rahn at des Marronniers, often in the company of two seedy looking companions, a penurious traveling salesman named Salvador Barcos Escude and a mediocre artist named Alain Albert Haustrate. According to Paul Arques, the former chef at des Marronniers, Wolff and Otto Rahn seemed to know each other intimately and did not meet by chance. Most evenings they would spend in the tiny photographic studio above the bar and in the winter of 1931 they traveled together to Carcassonne, Portes-Vendres, Cerbère, Marseilles, and Puigcerdà on undisclosed business related to Rahn's research. Another aging resident of Ussat-les-Bains, Edmond Abatout described how he had gone with Rahn, Wolff, Widigger, and the others to visit the aluminium factory of Sabart, but instead of photographing the caves, the group seemed more interested in documenting the industrial installation from every angle. Abatout believed Wolff had been sent by his German superiors to "keep an eye on Otto." He said they frequently quarreled and that after Wolff's visits Otto would appear livid with clenched teeth. Another time, Wolff came back to the hotel with his face covered in blood, claiming to have been set upon by the locals.

Wolff did not get along well with Gadal, pestering him with far-fetched money-making schemes, going so far as to suggest converting the Bethlehem Grotto, one of the most important initiatory caverns, into a bar-restaurant. The British occultist Walter Birks, who met Wolff during this period, described him as "positively repulsive and evil" and tried to warn Gadal against him, believing him to stand in antithesis to everything the Grail represented. Christian Bernadac claimed Wolff often went by the name "Karl," arguing this was the same Karl Wolff who would later emerge as Heinrich Himmler's personal adjutant, his beloved "Wolffchen" or "Wolffie," but this theory can be easily disproved. The whereabouts of the real Karl Wolff, whose path would cross Otto Rahn's several years later to tragic effect, are well known, but the true identity of the Nat Wolff who plagued the young Grail hunter in the Pyrenees remains a mystery. Surviving records indicate a certain Nathaniel Wolff of Rochester, New York, filed a deposition in 1933, identifying himself as a Jew who had been physically assaulted by Nazis in Berlin. He is further identified as the proprietor of the Lyceum Theatre in Rochester that filed for bankruptcy in 1934. In 1938, the French authorities learned this same Nathaniel Wolff had been traveling on two passports bearing conflicting birth dates issued under the names Kurt Hermann and Hermann Kußt, leading to an expulsion order from the minister of the interior on suspicion of being a German agent. I can find no further record of his existence beyond that date.

If Rahn's relations with Wolff were less than cordial, he did find one friend at des Marronniers, striking up an unlikely acquaintance with the seven-foot-tall Senegalese barman, Habdu. This friendly giant would become his traveling companion and de facto bodyguard, saving the young Grail seeker's life when he was nearly swept away by rising floodwaters in the grotto of Fontanet.

"Habdu was his name," confirms Otto Rahn, speaking of his companion in the past tense in a 1934 interview on the Berliner Illustrirte Zeitung and Southwest German broadcasting. "A strange name and an equally strange fellow. He was a tree-sized negro from Senegal, almost two meters tall. Even though the floodwaters (in the cavern of Fontanet) were up to his chin, Habdu lifted me onto his shoulders and waded through the waters, guided by the lamp I had retrieved from my backpack. He carried me in this fashion and such dreadful conditions for three hours, after which the waters began to recede. This item of good news was outweighed however by the fact that our carbide lamp burned out and we had no candles. All that remained to light our way were two boxes of matches! I'll never forget that awful journey, stumbling every step of the way, our bodies soaked, cold and shivering. As the last match burned down we finally reached the main cavern just one kilometre from the outside world. We walked the last stretch in darkness."

Some believe Rahn and Habdu became lovers. Typically, Rahn makes no mention of Habdu in his published works, nor does he make any reference to Nat Wolff, Antonin Gadal, Joseph Widigger, Paul Ladame, or Paul Bernadac, stating in *The Court of Lucifer* that his sole companion during the exploration of the caves was his cat.

But what in heaven or Earth did he hope to find beneath the Tabor?

"For Rahn the Grail was a stone, fallen from the sky. It's not a vase, a cut emerald or a grasale, which is what we, in the Pyrenees, call a dish

Fig. 6.13. Otto Rahn in the "cathedral" of the Lombrives. Rahn believed the graffiti preserved on the cave walls held clues to the whereabouts of the sacred treasure.

. . . the dish in which Joseph of Arimathea was said to have gathered the blood of Christ." Christian Bernadac pulled the jeep to a halt outside a sagging stone building he indicated had been his grandfather's house, his words hinting once again at the existence of a physical relic, rather than a symbol or a spiritual ideal. The aging Dien Bien Phu vet had recently retired from TF1 to run as a candidate in a coming election and clearly took the whole Grail business very seriously. Motioning for me to follow, Christian led me up a winding trail behind the house to a cave known as the Bethlehem Grotto, the same cavity Nat Wolff had once hoped to turn into a bar.

Reputedly a ray of light falls on a natural stone altar in the center of this cavern on December 25 every year, giving rise to the appropriately biblical name.

Into the Labyrinth of the Pyrenees 139

Fig. 6.14. The Bethlehem Grotto.
Photo by Richard Stanley.

Fig. 6.15. Landscape as Rorschach—the stone pentagram in the Bethlehem Grotto. Photo by Richard Stanley.

The Bethlehem Grotto, commanding a magisterial view of the valley of Ussat, has allegedly been a place of worship since ancient times although candle wax on the rocks pointed at more recent ritual usage.

Above the altar, Christian drew my attention to a pentagonal depression on the limestone wall, a feature that held particular importance for Gadal and the neo-Cathars of Rahn's day. Judging by the recent scuff marks on the wall it was still important to someone now.

In his landmark book, *Les Catharisme*, Déodat Roché claims the figure of Mithras, complete with Phrygian cap and surrounded by the sacred animals of Mithraism (the bull, the serpent, the dog, and the horse) can clearly be seen on the surface on the pentagon. Firsthand examination of the site however made it impossible to believe Roché was seeing anything other than natural markings in the limestone onto which the pope of neo-Catharism had projected his own quixotic interpretation. If nothing else, it was a splendid example of landscape as Rorschach. While Christian Bernadac viewed Gadal and Roché's claims with marked hostility, he was equally prone to pareidolia, the natural human tendency to perceive meaningful images in random chaotic patterns, more often than not faces or the shapes of animals, a talent he had ably demonstrated in the hotel bar.

Gesturing earnestly at the depression on the wall, Christian told me that back in the summer of 1930, Otto Rahn had drawn a woman's face in the center of the pentagon. According to Christian, Rahn had been caught red-handed by a certain Joseph Mandement, a member of the local tourist board, who allegedly threw the young German from the cave and "hurled his crayons after him." Later, Christian claimed, the face had been scrubbed from the wall by René Nelli, Suzanne Nelli's husband, Rahn's translator.

"But who was she?" I asked, bewildered.

"Who was who?"

"The woman whose face he drew? The woman on the wall? I mean, it seems like a pretty weird thing to do." I stared at the pentagon, trying to puzzle it out.

"I don't know. An unrequited love. Beatrice perhaps, who accompanied Dante on his journey to hell." Christian shook his head. "Who knows what drove Rahn to come here?"

Like so many elements in the Rahn mystery, the tale of the enigmatic face in the pentagram only provoked further questions.

Joseph Mandement, the man who allegedly threw Otto Rahn out of the Bethlehem Grotto, was president of the Syndicat d'initiative of Tarascon and an ardent spelunker. To some extent, he was Rahn and Gadal's direct competitor.

In the summer of 1932, while exploring the ruins of the castle of Montréal-de-Sos, Mandement discovered a mysterious painting in a cave below the fortress that would come to be known as the Graal blazon.

The shield-like square surmounted by twelve crosses and containing six tongues of fire or drops of blood is believed to represent the ark or tabernacle of the Grail. Déodat Roché suggested the sword and sun

Fig. 6.16. The AEIOU express—Joseph Mandement explores the subterranean river of la Bouiche. Published in the newspaper *L'Illustration* on February 21, 1925, Toulouse municipal archives, REV301.

disc were proof of the lost link between Catharism and the Mithraic mystery traditions. Roché proposed that the castle of Montréal-de-Sos had been home to a secret knight order closely related to the Cathars and implied the treasure of Montségur had been hidden there after the siege of 1244.

In true anthroposophical fashion, Roché perceived the Grail not to be a physical object but a spiritual current that flowed through every manifestation of the Western mystery tradition from the Druids and priests of Mithras to the Cathars and Templars and on to the present day. Others believe the mural is a modern-day forgery painted by Mandement himself to draw tourists to the site.

Otto Rahn makes no mention of the blazon and by the time I photographed the mural, less than a hundred years after its "discovery," it had faded badly. In 2014 the so-called Graal blazon was vandalized, its outline painted over in a "monkey Christ" restoration, making it impossible for future researchers to date its true provenance.

If Mandement had been moved to manufacture occult graffiti to drum up tourism revenues, then it was only natural he might have been tempted to shift the blame onto the taciturn young German who had explored the region only a year before this alleged discovery.

Neither Rahn nor Antonin Gadal were qualified archaeologists, moreover both were amateur mystics and natural fantasists making it impossible to take their sensational claims at face value. Had they really uncovered vital clues to the true nature of the most sacred relic in Christendom or were they simply spiraling into self-induced delirium?

Certainly the silence and darkness of the caves was conducive to the opening of the heart and spirit; there is no doubt that sensory deprivation weaves its subtle, psychogenic spell over all who venture into those stygian depths. It is tempting to see Rahn's obsession with the caves as

Fig. 6.17. The Graal blazon—anatomy of a fraud.
Photo by Richard Stanley.

a sort of return to the source, to the protective womb of the earth, but had he really found something more than just a spiritual link to the past? Did the diadem of Lucifer exist in physical form and, if so, had it been removed to the dark sanctuary of the SS order castle and later spirited to Antarctica as Buechner suggested or did it remain, even now, within the confines of the valley of Ussat?

Fig. 6.18. The Grotte de Lombrives—explored by
Otto Rahn and Antonin Gadal in the summer of 1931.
Joseph Mandement can be seen on the far right of the group.
Courtesy of Hamilton White.

Into the Labyrinth of the Pyrenees   **145**

Fig. 6.19. The Grotte de Lombrives, explored by the author in the summer of 1998. Photo by James "JB" Bourne.

Wet limestone, on its way to becoming crystal, shimmered in our flashlight beams as Christian Bernadac guided Mr. Horn and myself deeper into the coils of the Lombrives, the largest cave system in Western Europe. The descent seemed endless as if we had literally been swallowed by the earth. The rock faces crawled with ancient graffiti and Christian pointed out the signature of his grandfather at the base of one of the stalactites. Beside it I recognized the name of the former mayor of Montségur, Marius Mounié.

Otto Rahn apparently attached a great deal of importance to the graffiti on these walls, taking dozens of photographs, each one neatly labeled in the vanished Grail seeker's wilting hand. He seemed to believe the Cathars and Knights Templar shared hiding places and these scrawled sigils proved an obscure linkage between them, a connection apparently vital to the lineage of the modern-day Masons. Some, Christian included, believed it was really Rahn and Gadal, the wily minister of tourism, who had covertly tagged the limestone with crudely rendered designer esoterica.

Everywhere I looked pentagrams, pyramids, and stylized spiders danced and wriggled across the dank stone, hinting at a unified conspiracy theory that was still beyond my comprehension. In one inscription a young man asked God why he took his wife and the mother of his children.

Another, dated 1850, echoes the words graven on the wall at Wildenberg, a question that still awaits a reply, "What is God?"

The immense chamber at the heart of the labyrinth, known as the cathedral, with its 260-foot-high ceiling had once been used as a temple by the Druids and Visigoths. Otto Rahn believed the Cathars had sojourned there along with their mythic treasure. While Christian spoke scathingly of Otto it was equally clear he believed the young German had found something here, a secret that had been lost to mankind for seven centuries.

"Deeply stirred," wrote Otto Rahn, "I wandered through the crystal halls and marble crypts. My hands set aside the blackened bones of fallen knights. Evidence of a war in the darkness . . ."

But where was the Grail hunter now? If the relic he sought was really capable of prolonging life, then was it possible Rahn still walked among us?

According to Wolfram von Eschenbach's *Parzival*, anyone who comes in contact with the Grail "will have eternal life and will be healed." Christian Bernadac, like Marius and several others, believed Rahn had survived the holocaust, assumed a false identity, and risen to a position of considerable wealth and power in postwar Europe.

"I don't know if he's alive or dead. I don't know if there was a body. I don't think there was a body," hissed Christian, staring moodily out from the hotel balcony as shadows deepened across the Ariège. "No death certificate was ever issued, so technically he's still alive. What is extraordinary is that Rahn's death was announced in an SS journal by Karl Wolff, Himmler's personal adjutant who had helped act as a conduit for the funds during his excavations in Ussat. With Otto Rahn it would have been easy to create a second or third identity who could relocate to Holland, to Finland, or even to the Middle East. It's the ABC, the most well-known ploy of the secret services. I don't believe in spontaneous statements made twenty, thirty, or forty years later. They're not true. I don't know who found Otto Rahn's body.

Fig. 6.20. Otto Rahn inspects the graffiti in the cathedral of the Lombrives.

Fig. 6.21. Detail of grafitti.

Fig. 6.22. In Rahn's footsteps.

Fig. 6.23. Grail hunter. Photo by Otto Rahn.

I don't know if he was buried. I don't know if the parents were there. It would be necessary, little by little, to dig, to reconstruct, and why not, exhume the corpse, the skeleton of Otto Rahn and see if it corresponds with his dental pattern, his height, his bones, maybe even his hair."

Christian puffed furiously on his gauloise as he spoke, pausing only to emit the occasional hacking cough for emphasis.

"I can supply further proof that Rahn's secretary, Tita Laubert, whom he needed for all his typing, left Himmler's cabinet at the time of his alleged demise in 1939 and curiously turned up in the Vatican with a second person who went by the name of Rudolf Rahn. This Rudolf Rahn, during his youth had a brother who died named Otto and would often himself go by the name of Otto. Rahn made a deal with the head of the CIA, which had been created around '42 or '43. Rahn ended up becoming the director of the Coca-Cola Company in Munich. It's hard to imagine a Nazi could become the director of Coca-Cola Europe without the collusion of the CIA. Of course, the SS had completely monopolized the European bottling industry before the war began. By using forced labor at their bottling plant in Dachau they were able to dramatically reduce the cost of production. That's how Rahn's lover, Raymond Perrier, the heir to the Perrier bottling dynasty, got his foot onto the ladder."

Otto's sexual orientation was rapidly becoming an issue. Indeed it is hard to imagine how anyone could have been openly gay at the time of the Hitler dictatorship when such an attitude might consign one to the camps. Rahn was certainly close to Raymond Perrier and on the balance of their surviving correspondence it would seem Christian Bernadac was right about them being lovers. Raymond's name was redacted from some of the initial documents sourced from the Bundesarchiv and this only served to further put the hook in me. A letter from Raymond Perrier, addressed to Heinrich Himmler, thanks the reichsführer SS for the tour of his "marvelous facility"—namely the bottling plant at KZ Dachau—adding that the visit will "benefit him immeasurably" in his work.

Christian claimed Otto Rahn had taken the identity of his dead brother, Rudolph, and with the cooperation of the CIA, had survived

Into the Labyrinth of the Pyrenees 151

the war to become the head of Coca-Cola Europe. It was an attractive, if paranoid, proposition but the facts fell wide of the mark. Otto Rahn did have a dead brother named Rudolph and there was a very real Rudolph Rahn who had taken charge of the eponymous soft drink company after the war, but subsequent research indicated they were not the same man. By the outbreak of hostilities in 1939, the SS had cornered 100 percent of the European bottling interests and there is no doubt Coca-Cola, and later Fanta, were bottled by slave labor. But Rudolph wasn't Otto. It wasn't that simple.

The light was almost gone now. Taking my leave of Christian I went looking for a drink.

When Otto Rahn took over the lease of des Marronniers, his sudden solvency led Christian Bernadac to suspect he was a fifth columnist, ostensibly in the pay of the Thule Society, but it seemed just as likely his funds came from the deep pockets of the ailing countess. At one point, in his fragmentary account of the period, Rahn refers to des Marronniers as "her inn" as if it were the countess's property all along, although perhaps there is some nuance here that has been lost in translation. His time in Ussat would appear to have been the happiest period in Otto Rahn's short, weird life—or would have been had it not been for the irritation he experienced as a result of Wolff's overbearing presence. It was certainly the closest Rahn came to finding a home or creating a semi-functional family unit about himself. Rejected by his birth mother, Clara, he seems to have found a surrogate mother in the aging countess while Gadal served as a second father. During this period his research took on concrete form and he spent each day exploring the caves with pick and flashlight. The countess was too frail to accompany Rahn on these arduous daily explorations but would wait for her young acolyte at the inn. At times she placed her personal chauffeur, Joseph "Lazybones" Widigger, at his disposal. On Rahn's return, she would help him develop his photographs in the improvised darkroom in the hostelry's attic while Habdu prepared their evening meal. After dinner it was Rahn's habit to settle himself at the piano (installed on

Fig. 6.24. The grotto of Ornolac.
Photo by Richard Stanley.

the countess's instructions) and interpret the day in music, always finding a fresh tune to fit the circumstance. In his journal, Rahn describes playing an improvisation on Handel's *The Gods Go a'Begging* and then hearing, as he closed the lid of the piano, the valley literally come to life with the cries of a thousand owls, their plaintive voices echoing off the cliffs with almost supernatural clarity.

"Do you hear, mon ami," murmured the countess, dragging at Otto's sleeve. "How the souls of my ancestors complain? They accuse Rome and its paradise! The first who massacred them was a Caesar, a Roman. Then came the Franks who invaded and tried to exterminate them. Then the crusaders and Inquisitors who tortured and burned all those who had another faith to their own, because they too were in Rome's service. Finally, the Huguenots were persecuted and martyred, because Rome could not tolerate them. Now we are all supposedly 'Roman Catholics' and make up a part of France that boasts of being the 'eldest daughter of the Church.' My ancestors are complaining, and they accuse. Can you not hear them?"

Otto Rahn nodded, gazing into the dark, imagining the phantom flights of the night birds as they gathered around the hotel.

"I am an old lady and my days are numbered," the countess sighed. "I have done all I could to vindicate my ancestors. Would you promise me to continue this work when I am no longer?" Otto nodded again, more slowly this time. "I promise." And the screeching of the owls came from out of the night as if in answer. "And what I cannot achieve will be completed by the hands of the ones that come after me."

7

Infiltrating the Order of the Polaires

The living are deaf...
WILLIAM PETER BLATTY

On March 6, 1932, an article appeared in the Ariège's daily newspaper, *la Depeche*, under the headline "Is this a new gold rush?" claiming an international secret society known as the Polaires, under the direction of a shadowy German named Rams were excavating the ruins of the castle of Lordat and the caves above Ussat-les-Bains, allegedly in the hope of uncovering the treasure of the Cathars or possibly the legendary Book of the Seven Seals.

A follow-up article ran under the caption, "Who are the Polaires? And what is Mr Rams doing in Ussat?" On March 10 the newspaper printed a letter that began with the words: "My dear sirs . . . you are entirely mistaken. My name is Rahn, not Rams . . ."

In the subsequent missive, Otto Rahn not only corrects the journalist's spelling, but rebuts the accusations, claiming to have nothing to do with the aforementioned secret society, insisting the whole affair is a simple case of mistaken identity. It does seem odd the journalist not only assumed Rahn to be a member of this obscure occult fraternity, but their de facto leader. Closer examination of the few facts given in the article reveals the ruins of Lordat were the private property of Rahn's astrally inspired mentor, the Countess Miryanne de Pujol Murat.

To all intents and purposes, the French Polaires were disbanded at the onset of the war in 1939. Their records were deposited at the Theosophical Society's Paris headquarters and subsequently looted and destroyed during the Occupation, meeting the same fate as the internal memoranda of a great many other secret societies of the period. I heard rumors during my time in France, notably from investigative journalist Christian Bernadac, that a sister movement continued to thrive in the United Kingdom in the form of a spiritualist church known as the White Eagle Lodge who had carried over the vanished prewar society's core teachings and practices. The only way to know for sure whether Otto Rahn had been a card-carrying member of the Polaires, or indeed their leader, was to infiltrate the order and access their records. Knowing the White Eagle Lodge maintained close ties with the Spiritualist Association of Great Britain and recruited from their membership, I began attending platform medium sessions at the SAGB's moldering headquarters in London's Belgrave Square.

Founded in 1872, the SAGB's stated goal is "to offer evidence to the bereaved that man survives the change called death and, because he is a spiritual being, retains the faculties of individuality, personality and intelligence, and can willingly return to those left on earth."

Despite their claims to strive toward a kind of scientific mediumship, I confess I was underwhelmed by the sessions I sat in on, the mediums carrying more than a whiff of carny about them. Given the circumstances, it was relatively easy to pass myself off as a fellow "clairvoyant," a routine abetted by my friend, television crystal-ball gazer Andre Phillipe. Andre is perhaps best known for his serial appearances on UK quiz shows, notably on *Blind Date* where he successfully predicted his own victory in front of bemused hostess Cilla Black. Andre proved an able tutor, pressing my limited skills as a close-up magician into service to help sell the overall effect. If you want to convince folk you have supernatural powers, it helps to look like a mystic. Accordingly I dressed in formal attire, trimmed my whiskers in suitably Mephistophelean manner and practiced my patent Aleister Crowley gaze.

Grief is a powerful emotion, and it is all too easy for the unscrupulous to exploit those touched by Mater Lachrymarum, for she touches everyone sooner or later. Given the unfathomable depths of human misery and the ceaseless calling of the bereaved for vanished faces, it is only natural a whole cadre of charlatans has sprung up over the centuries to service this inexhaustible market. Much of what takes place in the séance room is no different from any sideshow mentalist routine, generally opening with a one-size-fits-all statement such as "There's an old woman with me who's recently passed over to Spirit. She has a message for someone here. I see a hospital room . . ."—a gambit guaranteed to connect with at least one or more members of the public present at the sitting. The punters attracted to this sort of thing are usually of a certain age, so you can count on most having lost one, if not both, parents and all too often a hospital room would have been the scene of the unhappy event. Once a "client" is hooked, it's relatively easy to reel them in, playing on the million and one unconscious tells in their body language, in the natural human propensity to lean closer when they hear what they want and draw back when something doesn't connect. If you really strike out, you can always take the "shopping bag" approach, telling sitters who are confused or upset by insensitive or contradictory advice to "take it with them" as if the true meaning of your cryptic words will dawn on them later when they are safely in the parking lot. Folks seldom kick up a fuss. Most feel humbled and threatened by the presence of the so-called supernatural and are prepared to go through all kinds of mental contortions to avoid facing their own mortality and the irrevocable truth that they will in all likelihood never see or hear from their loved ones again.

Sir Arthur Conan Doyle (1859–1930) is best remembered as the creator of Sherlock Holmes, but he was also a long-standing Freemason and the SAGB's most prominent spokesperson. Doyle had long been intrigued by paranormal phenomena, but after the death of his son in the war, his interest in these matters took a more serious turn. In 1920, Doyle debated the claims of Spiritualism with arch-skeptic Joseph McCabe in a notorious verbal showdown at Queen's Hall, London. McCabe published his rebuttal to Doyle's arguments in a booklet entitled "Is Spiritualism Based on Fraud?" suggesting Sir Arthur had been gulled into believing in the existence of life after death by elementary carny trickery. Doyle's celebrated friendship with the American illusionist and escapologist Harry Houdini foundered on these same issues of faith. While Houdini insisted that Spiritualist mediums owed their paranormal powers to trickery and consistently exposed them as frauds, Doyle became convinced Houdini himself possessed psychic abilities he refused to admit to. Despite penning two turgid manifestos on what he perceived to be an emergent religion, *The New Revelation* (1918) and *The Vital Message* (1919), Conan Doyle was clearly not above a little trickery of his own. In 1922 he endorsed the notorious Cottingley fairy hoax in his book *The Coming of the Fairies* and in the same year showed footage of Willis O'Brien's stop-motion monsters, created for the first film adaptation of Doyle's novel *The Lost World*, to the Society of American Magicians, claiming them to be real dinosaurs—an act that may have been intended as a way of getting revenge on Houdini, who was present at the screening. Several notable Fortean researchers, including science historian Richard Milner, have theorized that Doyle may have been the perpetrator of the Piltdown Man hoax of 1912, creating a counterfeit hominid fossil that fooled academia for over forty years. Milner suggests Doyle was motived by the desire to avenge himself on the scientific community for debunking the Spiritualist movement. The events that followed Sir Arthur's death on July 7, 1930, proved even more bizarre, further conflating fact and fiction, openhearted belief and transparent deception.

After being struck down by a heart attack at the age of seventy-one, Sir Arthur Conan Doyle was "channeled" from beyond the grave by

Fig. 7.1. Grace Cooke and the spirit of Sir Arthur Conan Doyle.

one of the SAGB's rising stars, Welsh platform medium Grace Cooke, herself a fully initiated member of the Polaires, the very same occult fraternity Otto Rahn was accused of leading.

Grace Cooke embarked on her mediumistic career with the foundation of a small Spiritualist church in Middlesex, only to distance herself from its activities when its leadership became increasingly focused on finding quantifiable proof of life after death. Grace, operating under the pseudonym Minesta, shifted her emphasis to psychic healing and channeling the "teachings" of her spirit guide, a benevolent Native American shaman named White Eagle, a service she deemed more important, not to mention more lucrative, than the continuing quest for concrete evidence of the posthumous survival of consciousness.

After Sir Arthur's death, Grace Cooke seems to have made an inspired bid for leadership of the Spiritualist movement by channeling their figurehead in a series of private sittings with the Doyle family. In the summer of 1931, Grace showed up in the Ariège as a guest of the Countess Miryanne de Pujol Murat and was photographed picnicking with the Polaires at the site of their excavations in the ruins of the château of Lordat. At that time, the young Welsh medium believed herself to be in astral contact with the Albigensian high priestess Esclarmonde de Foix and the ascended Cathar perfecti who reached out to her in waking dreams, ultimately directing her to found the White Eagle Lodge.

It took little more than forty-eight hours and a couple of dodgy handshakes to insinuate myself into a gathering of the lodge's West London chapter at a lavishly converted chapel a block or two from Harrods. My curiosity whetted, I sat in on a healing session in the lodge's inner sanctum. Initiates in white labcoats went through the motions of psychically drawing negative energy out of a row of elderly patients seated on cushions before the altar. There was no cross in this church. Instead the watery British sunlight fell on a massive plaster eagle resembling the Luftwaffe symbol and the high priest and priestess wore the same turquoise gowns that had once adorned the French Polaires in the days before the war. Those vivid blue robes, the unisex labcoats, and the manner in which the healers scrubbed down before and after the ceremony only added to the oddly clinical impression as if I had stumbled into something that had been dreamed up by Canadian director David Cronenberg and his resident production designer Carole Spier. I was just an observer at the ceremony, seated toward the back of the assembly with my buddy Andre who had come along to act as a reliable witness to my increasingly paranoid claims. We were the only ones in the congregation wearing black.

"May the Great White Spirit bless you," intoned the priestess, a formidable raven-haired woman named Jenny Dent who exerted an effortless authority over the lodge. Her stewardship of the movement was clearly a dynastic role as she was directly descended from the lodge's founder, being the granddaughter of Grace Cooke herself. "The age of Aquarius is at hand, the age of Spirit," she continued. "You in this lodge have the power to lead by your thoughts, your speech, and your actions." As she spoke my attention was caught by the pendant she wore about her neck, a tiny six-pointed star that was all too familiar. "The early Christian brethren of the Piscean Age served faithfully. You are Brethren of the Aquarian Age, and you too must serve . . ."

In truth I was no longer paying attention to her words, which were pretty much the same sort of neo-Christian New Age sophistry I had come to expect from the Spiritualist community. Instead I found my thoughts led by the sight of that tiny, glinting hexagram, drawn back on a Möbius strip into the past as I tried to wrap my head around where this story really began and how it fit with the murky facts of the Rahn affair.

Another man had worn an identical hexagram back then, an enigmatic, turbaned swami known as Zam Bhotiva who had attended the sittings with the Doyle family. The swami led the credulous membership of the SAGB to believe he was one of the illustrious "masters of the East" and none dared question him, such was the intensity of his gaze, although they noted his exotic regalia, the outer signs of an unknown initiatory order that had allegedly risen up from the dust of the centuries. Beneath the greasepaint, however, the fraudulent guru was just a man like any other, a Franco-Italian confidence trickster named Cesar Accomani, the co-founder of the Polaires. It comes as no surprise that on closer inspection, Sir Arthur's posthumous message, as "channeled" by Grace and Zam from beyond the grave, turns out to be little more than blatant propaganda for the ambitious European secret society who were clearly seeking to expand their operations into the British Isles.

"Behold! A new star rises in the east," proclaimed Grace to the recently bereaved Lady Doyle. "It is a six-pointed star—the star of the Polaires."

Accomani relished the opportunity to impersonate a theosophical master, having dress rehearsed his Zam Bhotiva persona in 1929, when he used the pseudonym to co-author the baffling tome *Asia Mysteriosa*, an all but incomprehensible text purporting to be a direct transmission from the hidden rulers of the world.

The meandering manuscript of *Asia Mysteriosa* was cowritten by Accomani and Mario Fille, a former vaudevillian and dance hall composer commonly acknowledged as the fraternity's cofounder. This curious book, which serves as the manifesto of the Polaires, lays out the history and goals of the movement and comes complete with an introduction cowritten by Fernand Divoire and Jean Marqués-Riviére along with prominent Buddhist scholar, Freemason, and foremost poet of neo-Catharism Maurice Magre—all three seemingly passionate adherents of the nascent occult order—but from where had this shadowy secret society sprung? From whence its true roots? The account given in the order's foundation document is certainly hard to accept at face value.

According to the convoluted text, the fraternity trace their origins to 1908, when the fourteen-year-old Mario Fille was holidaying in Bagnaia, a small town near Viterbo, about sixty miles north of Rome. During his long walks on the densely forested slopes of Monte Cimino, he came across a mysterious hermit, a sunburnt old man with deep-set eyes and curling whiskers who affected a coarse, monkish habit. The villagers shunned the old man whom they regarded with fear, believing him to be a sorcerer. He lived like a wild man in the woods, fed on herbs and fruits, and was scorned by the Christian community who never saw him cross the threshold of the local church. In spite of dire rumors of spells and ancient sorceries, the young Fille swiftly befriended the hermit after coming across his isolated retreat. Eerily, the old man, whom Fille refers to as Padre Giuliano, seemed to have been expecting his young visitor. Fille offered him money and food but the hermit refused help, telling his guest he already had all he needed. Slowly a bond formed between them as Fille's visits became more frequent and their conversations more lengthy. The hermit spoke meaningfully of brotherhood, pain, sacrifice, and the path of the sorcerer—a way that can only be walked alone.

One day on going up the trail to the hermit's dwelling, Fille came across Padre Giuliano lying unconscious in the road, badly wounded in the knee. Fille dressed the wound and helped the old man back to his shelter. The next morning, he was astounded to find the hermit already up and about and noticed that within three days the wound had completely healed. Fille did not dare ask how such a thing could be possible and Padre Giuliano, for his part, when questioned on such matters would choose to hold his silence as if lost in a dream.

At the end of his holiday, Fille paid the old man a final visit. For the first time the mysterious adept called Fille his "son" and when the moment came to make their farewells, he pressed into his hands a sheath of parchments, yellowed by time.

These were, Padre Giuliano explained, "some pages taken from the Book of the Science of Life and Death. These pages contain a method of mathematical divination—a numerical oracle. Should you at any time require counsel you have only to follow the instructions contained herein—and you will receive a reply. If you seek the answer to an important question, then write that question down, add your first and last name as well as your mother's name. Then convert the letters into numbers and carry out the necessary calculations. The calculations are lengthy and difficult—but do not let this put you off, because when you finally convert the results back into letters, you will always have the correct answer to any question you ask. But know, you are the only one who has the key and are commanded not to pass this knowledge on without the authorization of the Unknown Superiors" (Ivan Cooke, *Thy Kingdom Come*, 1930).

Padre Giuliano warned Fille the oracle should only be used in times of dire need, telling the boy if he ever divulged the secret to anyone, insanity and death would surely follow. Fille took the old man's words to heart and did not attempt to apply the occult calculi until twelve years later during a time of deep personal crisis. In the spring of 1920, Mario Fille painstakingly followed the hermit's directions and after several hours of work, a final series of numbers emerged that, when translated into letters, gave a cogent answer to his question. With mounting trepidation, Fille realized the hermit had bequeathed him a magical system of almost unimaginable potential that was destined to transform the course of his life.

Later that year, Fille made his first visit to Egypt and, while waiting out a sandstorm in Cairo, fell into the company of a flamboyant fellow traveler, the budding occultist and all-round esoteric opportunist Cesar Accomani. After telling Accomani about his encounter with Padre Giuliano, the two began to experiment with the oracle. The two seekers were amazed to find that while they phrased their questions in Italian, the answers sometimes came back in English, French, or German. During one of these early sessions, the mysterious mathematical system revealed its name: *l'Oracle de Force Astrale*, or the Oracle of Astral Force. Fille and Accomani rapidly concluded the oracle was a direct channel of communication with what they termed the Rosicrucian Initiatic Center of Mysterious Asia. This secret center, known as Agharta or Agharti, was apparently a hidden monastery located somewhere in the heartland of the Himalayas, the Hindu Kush, or the Karakorums that served as the headquarters of the *secret rulers of the world*, a mysterious cabal of enlightened adepts called the Supreme Sages or the Great White Brotherhood, a term popularized in the late nineteenth century by the Theosophical Society under Annie Besant and Madame Helena Petrovna Blavatsky.

The myth of the White Lodge or Great White Brotherhood is an enduring one, dating back to the mid-eighteenth century and Baron von Hund's Freemasonry of the Strict Observance with its *Unknown Superiors*—a term referenced by Mario Fille in his account of the meeting with the mysterious hermit Padre Giuliano. Von Hund was referring to the hidden Rosicrucian masters of the early seventeenth century who, according to French metaphysicist René Guénon, fled Europe during the Thirty Years War, taking refuge in the mountains of Asia. Guénon's pseudohistorical speculations united the Western tradition with popular notions of the unknown "masters of the East" and the initiatory centers of the Hindu and Buddhist faiths, notably the legend of Shambhala. The lost city is described in the Kalacakra Tantra and the ancient Tibetan Zhangzhun texts as the domain of the Maitreya, or future Buddha, a notion akin to the Sufi concept of the hidden imam or the mythical kingdom where the Kalki avatar of the Hindu faith, the final incarnation of Vishnu will be born in order to usher in the long awaited Golden Age or Satya Yuga. The first concrete reports to reach the West concerning this enlightened realm came from the Portuguese Catholic missionary Estêvão Cacella, who believed Shambhala (which he transcribed as "Xembala"), was merely another name for Cathay or China. Over the course of the centuries, numerous expeditions have set out to locate this lost world, notably Nicholas and Helena Roerich's 1924–28 excursion. Writing in 1833, the Hungarian esoteric scholar Sándor Kőrösi Csoma went so far as to give us the lost city's precise coordinates, claiming it was situated between latitude 45° and 50° north, which would situate it in the hills of modern-day Kazakhstan, whereas my own questing in the late eighties took me to the mountain-locked valleys of Kafiristan. I had gone looking for a Bactrian sun temple known as Shams-i-Balkh (from the Persian *Sham-i-Bala*, the "high light" or "elevated candle") but found little more than abandoned rock dwellings and a few curiously carved marker stones. It was enough to keep the door in my mind open, at least a crack.

Despite the lack of physical evidence, the myth prevailed, a legend popularized by the theosophists of an antediluvian spiritual center that once existed at the Pole only to be subsequently relocated to the Gobi Desert, the Himalayas, or even the Hollow Earth. Along the way this secret center had been polarized, split into twin (equally mythic) city-states, one light, one dark, Agharta and Shambhala, perennially locked in mysterious rivalry. This dualist spin on the myth can be sourced to the work of nineteenth-century esotericist and "synarchist" Alexandre Saint-Yves d'Alveydre who claimed the lost city was an actual geographic location in Tibet that will only be "accessible for all mankind . . . when the anarchy that exists in our world is replaced by the Synarchy"—in other words, the direct rule of humanity by a secret elite, themselves the servitors of an unknown god. Given that Saint-Yves d'Alveydre attained this insight through channeling—or what he referred to as "psychic attunement"—it follows we should take his claims with a suitable dose of salt. With the advent of ground penetrating radar and satellite mapping, even the most ardent believers in these elusive initiatory centers are now compelled to accept they may not be on Earth at all, but possibly in another galaxy, vibrational frequency, or quantum world—always somewhere conveniently beyond the reach of uninitiated eyes.

The cofounders of the Brotherhood of the Polaires, Mario Fille and Cesar Accomani, were clearly influenced by Saint-Yves d'Alveydre's ideals as much as the teachings of the theosophists and the peculiar brand of mystical Rosicrucianism espoused by René Guénon, believing that in the Oracle de Force Astrale they had found a synthesis of these streams—literally a hotline to the secret rulers of the Earth. Accomani saw tremendous potential in this miraculous method of mathematical mediumship, imagining himself to be one of the elite of the world to come. It was Fille alone who held the key to the oracle's operation however, a secret he resolutely refused to divulge.

Returning to Europe, Fille decided it was time to pay another visit to his occult mentor, Padre Giuliano, only to find the old man had disappeared. The hermitage on Monte Cimino lay abandoned, home only to swallows and lizards, nor did the locals have any clue what had become of its occupant. Turning to the oracle, Fille learned to his amazement the unassuming old hermit had secretly been one of the most powerful adepts on the planet. Since their meeting, Padre Giuliano had been recalled to Agharta from whence he was now telepathically preparing humanity for the transition from the Piscean to the Aquarian age.

The oracle directed Fille and Accomani to depart at once for Paris where, fired by a growing sense of mission, they recruited the first members of the secret society they believed was destined to bring about the "coming of the Spirit under the sign of the Rose and Cross." Lodging in Montmartre, the two Italians proceeded to demonstrate the oracle's preternatural powers to an invited audience of Gallic writers and occult VIPs including René Guénon, Fernand Divoire, Jean Dorsenne, Jean Marquès-Rivière, and Maurice Magre.

The excitement and momentum of these Parisian sessions was such that in 1929 the group known as la Fraternité des Polaires was formally inaugurated, taking its name from the mythical initiatory mountain believed to have existed at the pole in Hyperborean times. The oracle chose their insignia, the emblem of the Pole Star, a hexagram composed of two interlacing triangles, a symbol allegedly descended from Hyperborean times that still resonated with a powerful elder magic.

The Brotherhood's rules and rituals were all dictated by the oracle. The fraternity's first formal meetings took place at the offices of a daily newspaper on the rue Richelieu, whose editor allowed the secret society to use the premises during the evenings. On August 27, 1930, the group moved into more spacious quarters paid for by private donations at 38 avenue Junot in the 18th arrondissement. Fille and Accomani seem to have taken the address as a sign their headquarters were under the protection of the ascended masters—36 and 18 being multiples of 3 and 9, numbers that recur throughout the Brotherhood's internal organization. This is, of course, exactly the kind of mathematical malarky one might expect from a secret society designed and administered by a numerical oracle. Membership fees were fixed at nine Francs, the order's official publication *Le Bulletin des Polaires* appeared on the ninth day of every month and the group was administered by a central committee known as "the Nine" (*Les Neuf*), doubtless in emulation of the nine secret rulers of the world.

Fig. 7.2. *Le Bulletin des Polaires.*

The lodge on avenue Junot was furnished in grand style, complete with a round table and throne-like chairs. There was initially a statue of the Chinese goddess of compassion, Kuan Yin, positioned on a plinth beside the lodge's entrance, but this effigy was later removed after ongoing doctrinal disputes among the membership.

Fille and Accomani boldly insisted the order was a resurfacing of the same underground stream that had found expression in the Cathars, the Gnostic Christians, the Knights Templar, and the Essenes. Sadly the oracle failed to live up to expectation, giving answers that were all too often vague or contrary, speaking only in broad generalizations as spirit guides and ascended masters the world over are wont to do, avoiding specific data such as stock details, lottery numbers, or the secrets of free energy and eternal life, in short anything that might be of concrete use to mankind. Within a few months René Guénon and many of the other figures drawn by the initial divinatory sessions began to drift away, dissociating themselves from the movement.

Writing under his Zam Bhotiva pseudonym in *Asia Mysteriosa*, which appeared that same year, Cesar Accomani insisted the oracle was a form of *télégraphie télépathique* whereby the ascended masters directed their followers on the material plane. He claimed only one operator, namely Mario Fille, could be allowed to work the oracle in order to avoid creating mysterious "disturbances in the aether" that would garble or "negatively influence" the transmissions. Despite his privileged position as gatekeeper to the masters of the Orient, Mario Fille was, strangely enough, not the leader of the nascent fraternity. It is clear Accomani was the driving force behind the foundation of the Polaires, an occult hierarchy he hoped might one day reach across the world, moreover he had made up his mind the Grand Maître de L'Ordre Secret had to be "someone of a high rank or position," a decision that would cause the Brotherhood no end of teething problems. In the first two years of their existence, the Polaires inducted and were subsequently obliged to oust no less than three grand masters, none of whom were ultimately capable of negotiating the esoteric minefield of egos, aetheric beings, opaque mathematical transmissions, and transparent subterfuge that were apparently theirs to command.

The first grand master of the Polaires was a certain Monseigneur Lesètre, a canon of the Roman church who was forced to stand down after only a few weeks when his forceful style of leadership proved too much for Fille and Accomani to bear. Pierre Geyraud recounts a bizarre anecdote in his esoteric memoir *Les Sociétés Secrètes de Paris—Parmi les sectes et les rites, Les Petites Eglises de Paris* (1937) in which he describes Lesètre, garbed in a tuxedo and stylish yellow mask, attempting to question the otherworldly masters of the world through the intermediary of a trance medium. The dashing Monseigneur was rapidly succeeded by Henri Meslin du Champigny, a bishop of L'Église Gnostique Universelle, who proved equally incapable of juggling the complex balance of power between Mario Fille, Cesar Accomani, and the mythical Great White Brotherhood. Du Champigny resigned after less than six months in the chair, leaving the order in disarray. Fille and Accomani promised their confused adherents that a true master was on his way from the mountains of Asia to take charge and shortly thereafter the young heir to the royal house of Cambodia, Prince You-Kantor, was briefly sworn in as their third grand master. Despite his tender years, the twenty-five-year-old prince was a renowned student of the occult and, according to some, a practiced sorcerer in his own right, but again his personality proved too uncontrollable for Fille and Accomani's liking.

You-Kantor's abrupt departure coincided with another blow to the fraternity. The first issue of *le Bulletin des Polaires*, published on May 9, 1930, announced the death of the movement's "guiding light," Padre Giuliano, the former hermit of Bagnaia. Esoteric researcher Milko Boga, writing in a 2006 paper on the Polaire Brotherhood, points out this initial bulletin was published only two days after the death of the Italian alchemist and thaumaturge Giuliano Kremmerz (1861–May 7, 1930). Kremmerz, whose real name was Ciro Formisano, was the founder of the *Confraternita Terapeutica e Magica di Myriam*, or the Brotherhood of Miryam, and a key figure in the late nineteenth-

Fig. 7.3. Ciro Formisano, aka Giuliano Kremmerz (1861–1930).

and early twentieth-century hermetic revival. It is certainly tantalizing to imagine the aging Neapolitan alchemist may have been the same mysterious figure encountered by young Mario Fille on the balmy slopes of Monte Cimino.

Giuliano Kremmerz's work laid the foundations for transmitting the "underground stream" into the modern world by drawing on an archetypally feminine form of the mystery tradition that flourished as the Pythagorean School in Magna Graecia and resurfaced in the twelfth century with the *Fedeli d'Amore*, or the Brotherhood of the Faithful in Love, an order founded by the legendary Papa Nicetas, the same outcast bishop of Constantinople who sowed the seeds of Catharism in the south. This Italian branch of the hidden tradition subsequently informed such luminaries as the poet Dante, Renaissance philosopher and kabbalist Giovanni Pico della Mirandola, Giordano Bruno, Cornelio Agrippa, Paracelsus, and Count Cagliostro (Joseph Balsamo) who reformed French Freemasonry to admit the Egyptian Mithraic rite.

Certainly if Kremmerz was Mario Fille's initiator, as seems likely on the strength of the existing evidence, then it would tend to make sense of their claim that the fraternity of the Polaires was an expression of the same spiritual impulse that had given rise to the heretics of old

Occitania. While at face value it may seem difficult to reconcile the selfless gnostic dualism of the spiritually driven Cathars with Kremmerz's notion of sacred materialism, the two schools of thought are not necessarily at odds. Kremmerz argued that all was one, hence there could be no separation between spirit and matter. Moreover he believed our species must strive toward full integration of these two apparently opposing principles—spiritual origin and material manifestation, nothingness and form, emptiness and pleroma. This integration, synonymous with the Buddhist notion of Dharmakaya, is the ultimate goal of hermetic philosophy and the task that Kremmerz believed humanity must accomplish en masse if it was to fulfill its destiny on the planet. After all what does the Grail stand for, if not the harmonization of opposites, the symbolic marriage of the sun and the moon? Kremmerz used the word *matriarchy* to symbolize the achievement of this goal, albeit not in its usual, modern sense but in its original sense. Our modern word *matriarchy* is derived from the union of two older words: *mater*, "mother," or *matrix*, which has the same root as *matter*—the veritable prima materia of the alchemists—and *arché,* "commencement," "origin," or "essence" as in *archetype*. According to some period documents, Kremmerz and his followers apparently practiced a form of high magic known as Magia Avatarica in which members of the Order of Miryam's inner degrees underwent a magical ritual that bonded their soul to an otherworldly spirit referred to as a numen that subsequently served as their personal gateway to the astral planes. There were even those who implied that Giuliano Kremmerz, or "Kremm-Erz," was not just a pseudonym of Ciro Formisano, but the name of the numen, or walk-in, that inhabited his body.

With the passing of Padre Giuliano, the fraternity's father figure and guiding force, Fille and Accomani's leaderless, and increasingly rudderless, secret society found itself falling under the spell of a matriarchy of a different order. The wily Buddhist scholar and neo-Cathar poet Maurice Magre introduced them to a leading member of the French Gnostic Church, a remarkable woman Fille and Accomani took to be the immortal Cathar high priestess, Esclarmonde de Foix herself. Although the Polaires took pains in their bulletins to keep this woman's identity a secret it is easy to deduce their new spiritual figurehead was none other than the Countess Miryanne de Pujol Murat, Otto Rahn's patron who apparently believed she was acting under the spiritual guidance of her own ancestor on a mission to help bring about the revival of the heretical faith of the south.

While the countess was to become an influential figure in the order, there is no evidence to suggest she was ever its leader. Surviving records do not list the names of any further grand masters after the departure of You-Kantor. While it is within the realm of possibility the countess's favored neophyte, Otto Rahn, may have stepped into the young prince's shoes, as the article in *la Depeche* (March 6, 1932) suggests, it would seem unlikely, given Accomani's insistence on the role being filled by someone of high position, a candidate whose standing would lend the order easy access to the pockets of the great and the good.

The Rosicrucian historian Christian Rebisse records a meeting in the fall of 1931 between Accomani and H. Spencer Lewis, the grand master of the American Rosicrucian Order (AMORC), although the minutes of this summit have not come down to us. Both AMORC and the Polaires would later become affiliates of a federation of esoteric orders known as FUDOSI or FUDOESI (Fédération Universelle des Ordres et Sociétés Initiatiques), founded in Brussels on August 14, 1934, with a mission to "protect the sacred liturgies, rites and doctrines of the traditional initiatory Orders from being appropriated and profaned by clandestine organisations." This attempt to establish some sort of spiritual legitimacy for the signatories, if not an agreed dogma, foundered in 1951 after bitter infighting but by then the Polaires no longer existed, at least not in their original form.

Despite the faternity's leadership crisis, it is clear Accomani had not abandoned his dreams of projecting the order's power beyond Europe, into England and the United States. After receiving news of the death of Conan Doyle on July 7, 1930, Accomani wrote at once to the bereaved

Lady Jean Elizabeth, claiming he had an urgent message from her dead husband. Lady Doyle received this curious missive with due caution. In fact she refused to open the envelope until she had summoned Grace Cooke to "psychometrize" the letter. Grace, acting under her spiritual nom de plume, Minesta, had already been channeling Sir Arthur in a series of private sessions with the Doyle family that had commenced only ten days after his passing. Thus far the dead author's messages had consisted of the usual assurances of love and support that are the common currency of spirit mediums the world over. All that was about to change. Assuring Lady Doyle the letter was safe to open, Grace set in motion a series of events that continue to have repercussions to this day.

Grace Cooke claimed to have been unsurprised by the missive, having been warned of Accomani's coming by her spirit guide, White Eagle. Grace insisted she had been waiting for the message to arrive for several weeks. Assuming the guise of Zam Bhotiva, Cesar Accomani traveled to London in January 1931 at the behest of Lady Doyle and her family. The initial meeting took place in a crowded hall at the Stead library. When Grace Cooke entered the room, Accomani rose to greet her, effecting his practiced hypnotic gaze.

"Yes, I know you," murmured Accomani, looking into the young medium's dark eyes as if they were windows. "We have worked together before, long, long ago—in former lives in ancient Egypt." Accomani's fox-like smile broadened as he reached into the sinus of his turquoise robe, coming up with a tiny pendant.

"See—I have brought you this little star. It has been sent by the Wise Ones for you to wear."

Grace felt her mind swimming, the crowded room seeming to melt away, as if the two of them were someplace else, amid the sands of a forgotten world. The sight of that six-pointed star resting in the palm of the swami's hand, the interlacing triangles of the Polaires, conjured a maelstrom of emotions Grace could barely process. Silver Star was the secret nickname her spirit guide used for her, but how could this strange young man know such a thing?

Fig. 7.4. Grace and Ivan Cooke.

When Grace asked Accomani for an explanation he told her his mission was to free Sir Arthur's soul from its "astral limitations" so he might speak with the authority he had shown in life, to deliver his final message from beyond the grave and provide proof of the posthumous survival of consciousness.

"The spirit of Sir Arthur waits for the meeting of the red and violet rays, which will enable him to reveal himself and to speak to his friends," Accomani told the assembly. "We advise those who will participate to use during the séance a dark red light in order to aid Sir Arthur. The medium must carry a six-pointed star to give her the necessary strength!"

Grace's husband, Ivan, described what followed in a memoir that appeared in December 1933 under the title *Thy Kingdom Come* and was subsequently reissued by the White Eagle Publishing Trust in 1956 as *The Return of Sir Arthur Conan Doyle*.

"The group waited until the white light in the small chapel was switched off and the ruby light switched on," wrote Ivan. "By my side sat the medium, on my left was Miss Estelle Stead; the red glow fell on the earnest and reverent faces around the circle as the guide White Eagle rose . . ."

"The medium (Grace Cooke) went into a deep trance almost immediately," wrote Cesar Accomani in *le Bulletin des Polaires*. "She rose, crossed the room, and in a masculine voice recognized by several present as that of her guide, White Eagle, began a long conversation with Lady Doyle and her sons." On this occasion, "Sir Arthur" was speaking through the possessed medium's spirit guide, a not uncommon protocol. Grace rationalized this arrangement by explaining that White Eagle was the more practiced "control." "We shall not repeat the conversation, which was strictly personal," wrote Accomani. "After nearly an hour, the medium rose to search for someone else who was present. With closed eyes and firm step she approached Zam Bhotiva [here Accomani writes of himself—in his Zam persona—in third person] saying, There is a gentleman here whom I have not known during earth life, but with whom I am now linked in view of a common work." A long and low-pitched conversation then took place between the "dead" and the living. Conan Doyle made himself known to Zam Bhotiva as "Brother," and then, speaking again to those present, spoke of the Polaires as a "group destined to help in the moulding of the future of the world. . . . For the times are near!"

This was the first in a series of séances, held between January 27 and May 22, 1931, in which Grace Cooke and Cesar Accomani, allegedly channeling Sir Arthur, sought to reform Spiritualism in the hope of bringing the British movement under the direct control of the French occult fraternity. During this period, Accomani shuttled to and fro between London and Paris with alarming frequency, often showing up on Grace Cooke's doorstep without warning. Ivan Cooke claimed Grace could always tell when the "swami" was about as she could "smell the particular brand of cigarette he smoked." Accomani, operating in full Zam Bhotiva mode, seems to have made a powerful impression on

Grace and her husband, who describes their visitor standing out from the rush-hour commuters like an "eagle among pigeons." His English, Ivan recalls, "was of the sketchiest, so that it needed some concentration to follow him." At times, particularly when conversing with Grace, Accomani's predatory features would soften to an "almost Christlike expression; yet when he was stirred to anger he looked formidable indeed."

Cesar Accomani had good reason to be unhappy, for the Doyle sittings did not go as planned. Unimpressed by the séance at the Stead library, Lady Doyle was circumspect about further sessions. Taken aback by the impersonal and downright contradictory statements attributed to her late husband, she demanded tighter "Spiritualist controls" be placed upon subsequent sittings, a move Accomani indignantly resisted. The transcripts of these sessions, placed in print by Ivan Cooke and the White Eagle Publishing Trust, reveals the channeled "message" is a rambling, blend of New Age love and light, and vaguely understood Eastern mysticism, repeatedly stressing the importance of the Polaires while singularly lacking in either finite content or the rich turn of phrase we might have associated with Sir Arthur in life. As the sittings progressed, so the message unraveled, promising a major shift in global consciousness when the "red and the blue rays come into contact"—an event that stubbornly failed to happen.

While the Doyle family began to distance themselves from the transmissions, Grace Cooke and her husband, Ivan, continued to insist Sir Arthur's message was of tantamount importance to humanity, comparing it to the revelation of the Cathar *consolamentum*—the supreme initiation that promised instant enlightenment and liberation from the cycles of time and material incarnation. Those who held a vested interest in the neo-Cathar revival, notably Maurice Magre and the countess, undoubtedly saw the potential of the Spiritualist movement to reach across the centuries and restore the long-lost rite.

In *Thy Kingdom Come*, Ivan Cooke unambiguously states, "Certainly the complete ACD (Arthur Conan Doyle) message might be considered as something akin to the consolamentum, and as preparing for it someday to be restored to men."

Sensing the Doyle family were drifting away, Accomani decided to bring out the big guns. Ivan Cooke records that a pivotal sitting with Lady Elizabeth Jean Doyle on May 22, 1931, at Shenley Park, near Bletchley, was attended by no less a figure that the "Polaire chief" himself. Surprisingly this figure was not Mario Fille, the keeper of the oracle, but a young engineer from Bordeaux named René Odin. Whether this individual was indeed the latest grand master of the order cannot be verified, although a 1967 booklet, *Un Oracle Kabbalistique*, co-authored by Fille and Odin, confirms the engineer was one of Fille's associates who had been drawn into the web of occult intrigue surrounding the Countess de Pujol Murat. Odin seems to have believed the oracle and Sir Arthur's astral presence would guide the Brotherhood to uncover the tomb of Esclarmonde and the "treasure of the Cathars"—the Book of the Seven Seals or possibly even the Holy Grail itself.

Unmoved by Odin and Accomani's theatrics, Lady Doyle and her sons withdrew their support for these otherworldly sessions after the Shenley Park sitting, making it clear she did not want the transcripts attributed to her late husband in print. The White Eagle Publishing Trust responded by doing the next best thing, repackaging and reissuing Ivan Cooke's account of the sittings under the title *Arthur Conan Doyle's Book of the Beyond* with Sir Arthur's photograph prominently displayed on the front cover beside the six-pointed star of the Polaires. The Doyle estate, to the best of my knowledge, did not attempt to take legal action over this misrepresentation, presumably imagining the book would disappear into obscurity soon enough. The rift with Lady Doyle distressed Grace Cooke no end as she had lost both a friend and a patron. The young medium fell ill, discontinuing the sittings.

"My dear Bright Eyes," soothed Accomani, writing under his Zam Bhotiva pseudonym in one of the surviving letters from his correspondence with Grace, whom he refers to by his favored nickname. "Do not be downhearted, do not be worried. Everything is going on for the best. . . . Nobody can stop the march of the six-pointed star. You are at work, we are at work, for humanity and not for individuals. So I beg you, my dear sister, never mind about personal feelings."

Accomani had further news to communicate. The oracle had informed the Brotherhood it was their mission to master the so-called red rays that would soon be confronted by the blue rays, in a powerful battle between two opposing principles—a confrontation that would give rise to a Second World War that would change Europe forever. The French Polaires were destined to be destroyed in the conflagration but the Great White Brotherhood had chosen Grace Cooke to keep the faith and revive the order when the war was over and a new world come about. This baffling announcement must have given Grace and her husband pause, yet the young medium rapidly accepted the destiny thrust upon her. Booking passage to Paris, Grace and Ivan were duly initiated into the Brotherhood of the Polaires at their Montmartre headquarters and began to prepare themselves to assume stewardship of the movement. From then on, they too would wear the turquoise gowns and silver stars that would identify them as initiates of the order's inner circle.

In July 1931, Grace and Ivan Cooke (referred to in the Polaire's internal memos by his spiritual nom de guerre "Brother Faithful") traveled with the secret society's leading members to the mountains of Occitania to meet with the Countess Miryanne de Pujol Murat and supervise excavations on her property at Lordat in the Ariège where they believed the supposed treasure of the ages would be found. In typically flamboyant style, Cesar Accomani equipped himself with a magic wand he claimed was the dowsing rod of the Renaissance-era philosopher and kabbalist Giovanni Pico della Mirandola (1463–1494). The wand would tremble whenever it detected gold, Accomani insisted.

There seems to have been (typically) some disagreement over the nature of the treasure they sought. While Accomani was hoping for gold, there were others, notably the countess, who were concerned with a more spiritual treasure, with an impending revelation that would revive the forgotten faith of the Cathars.

178   Infiltrating the Order of the Polaires

Fig. 7.5. Grace Cooke and the Polaires in the ruins of Lordat, July 1931.

According to the article in *la Depeche*, the Polaires believed their excavations at Lordat might uncover the remains of the mythic founder of the Rosicrucian Order, Christian Rosenkreutz. Turning their attention to Montségur, the order hoped to locate the tomb of na Esclarmonda and the lost book of the Cathars.

Cesar Accomani set about vigorously dowsing the ruins of Montségur with his wand, instructing Grace Cooke and the others to sing traditional Occitan songs in order to create a spiritually harmonious atmosphere, one conducive to making the desired discovery. In 1931, Accomani had written a book, *la Magie appliqué à l'art du chant* (Magic applied to the art of singing), that discusses these notions and it seems he had some inkling of the keep's unusual acoustical properties, although clearly the order's questing raised more than a few eyebrows among the locals.

Otto Rahn wryly refers to these events in the account of his initial visit to Montségur:

On my first day here I met an engineer from Bordeaux (M. Arnaud) who is looking for the treasure of the Albigensians. He explained the castle is the property of the municipality and he obtained their permission in a written contract, which, if his project is successful, awards to him half the treasure (which he is convinced is gold and silver). Furthermore, he hopes to find the authentic Book of Revelations, the Apocalypse According to John, which contains the true message of Jesus Christ and was believed to be in possession of the Albigensians. The Cathars believed the Church of Rome wanted to destroy the only true message of the Son of God because the Catholics had falsified it. How does he know all this? I asked. He made it clear that he couldn't tell me because he belonged to a secret association that demanded silence from its membership (the Polaires?). Even though the Albigensians were exterminated by the Inquisition and its executioners, the true Book of Revelations was placed in a safe resting place inside the mountain, which is hollow. In addition, he told me that he knew the location of Esclarmonde's grave. A man with a divining rod had revealed the place to him, and thanks to the way the rod turned, he was able to describe the sarcophagus: It was stone with a golden dove decorating the top. I had to stop myself from smiling. (Otto Rahn, *The Court of Lucifer*, 1937. Author's translation)

In other respects, Rahn was more clearly in accordance with the order's views. British author Nigel Graddon notes that Rahn saw the pog of Montségur as "a sacred centre, an antenna of initiatory energy that transmitted its mystic rays to all those embarked upon a personal path"—a view that has much in common with the Brotherhood's perception of the pog as a sacred mountain that acted as a "substation" for communicating with the Great White Brotherhood in Agharta. Whether Otto Rahn's impressions of the magic mountain were directly informed by the Polaires and whether he became a member of the order or even its leader, as the article in *la Depeche* suggests, remains impossible to clarify at this distance in time.

The illicit excavations at Montségur and Lordat took place over forty arduous days in the summer of 1931. "The occult forces were strong," wrote Ivan Cooke in his memoir, recalling how one of the members of the secret society working on the excavations seemed to become possessed, attacking his companions with a knife. It was as if a demonic force was vested against them. Grace found herself falling prey to a "mysterious illness" and not long after her arrival in Montségur, grew so distressed she ordered a will to be drawn up. "I used to call upon Christ with all the strength of my soul," Grace wrote later. "The thought of the cross of light and of the Christ presence were ever with me through those hazardous weeks."

But there were other presences in the castle, what Grace referred to as the "unseen brethren of the heights." The disembodied Cathar adepts still watched over their shrine and, according to Ivan Cooke, made themselves known to Grace. "They came close and spoke to the soul of 'Minesta' [Grace Cooke], telling her whence they had come and what had been the faith for which they had died. . . . The secret of secrets which was theirs had been the consolamentum, which alone had power to lift men literally from earth to heaven by unveiling heaven itself before them; and this even by a word, a glance, a touch of the hand of an Adept."

Nor was Grace alone in believing they were in contact with the uncanny. The ruins seemed alive with unseen "presences" as if the castle's original inhabitants still existed in some other zone of time and were even now reaching out to the seekers, guiding them toward a goal they could scarcely comprehend. These disembodied entities were particularly strong when the skies were clear and the stars or the waxing moon shone down with preternatural brightness—or perhaps they were there all the time and moonlight merely made them more solid.

Otto Rahn's patron, the Countess de Pujol Murat claimed she could see the spirit of her own ancestor, na Esclarmonda, standing on "the wooden platform of the north facing tower of Montségur, reading the stars" as if silently guiding the destiny of the illusory waking world. The countess believed the immortal high priestess was the true guardian of the Grail, the sacred treasure she described as a "stone fallen from the crown of Lucifer"—a diadem that symbolized the lost link with the divine and which now lay hidden somewhere within the magic mountain. For a while the far Grail's beckoning light must have seemed almost within reach.

"Dressed in white and holding lit candles," Grace Cooke and the other members of the order sang songs in praise of na Esclarmonda in the keep of Montségur. At one of these neo-Cathar ceremonies, the Welsh medium prophesied the Book of Love would soon be found. Yet, despite her apparent optimism, Grace felt a growing disillusionment and alienation from the other members of the group. "They were hurried, over-eager to find the treasure," noted Ivan. "By now she was not convinced that any material treasure existed." After forty days in the Pyrenees, Grace and Ivan Cooke returned home, convinced the expedition had been a total failure, at least in its declared intention of finding a physical treasure left by the Cathars, yet the young medium felt changed by her experience, spiritually enriched by her encounter with the otherworldly adepts. "Hers had been a minor initiation into their mysteries," wrote Ivan in *Thy Kingdom Come*. "It remained to see what use she might make of it in the modern world."

Cesar Accomani continued to search the magic mountain but found nothing. The miraculous divining rod failed to tremble even once. Realizing the other members of the group were losing faith, Accomani broadened the scope of his investigation, crossing the border into Spain, yet his increasingly desperate questing failed to produce results. Disgraced and discouraged, Cesar Accomani, cofounder and instigator of the Brotherhood of the Polaires, was forced to resign from the secret society he once hoped would bring him fame and fortune. Broken by the experience, he dropped off the esoteric map. I do not know what subsequently became of him.

Incredibly, only a few days after Accomani's departure, the prophecy Grace Cooke made during the ritual workings was proven to be true. One morning while surveying the excavations, Mario Fille and René Odin

182   Infiltrating the Order of the Polaires

Fig. 7.6. The wooden book of Montségur.
Photo by Hamilton White.

noticed a section of the wall of the fortress that was a slightly different color than the rest of the citadel. Fille called for a pick and Odin struck at the wall, uncovering a niche in which they allegedly found a number of yellowing parchments. The upper pages had been destroyed by moisture and only one word could be read: *Fatalité*—Fate.

Commonly referred to as the *feuiles de bois*, the "wooden book of Montségur" consists of eighteen palm leaves inscribed with illegible characters, numbers, drawings of animals, and geometric figures. Fille and Odin swiftly concluded the mysterious book was a divinatory oracle and rumors of its discovery spread rapidly.

In Otto Rahn's *The Court of Lucifer*, the young SS officer recalls that many of the names in *Parzival* might reveal Iranian origins, musing, "I ask myself: Could that book found in the rubble of Montségur and written in an unknown alphabet be filled with Manichaean writing, perhaps even a copy of the original Iranian version of *Parzival*?"

At least six of these ancient palm leaves fell into the hands of noted anthroposophist, Freemason, and neo-Cathar philosopher Déodat Roché. Whether Fille and Odin deliberately passed these pages to Roché or whether they came to him by chance will never be satisfactorily cleared up. After Roché's death in 1978, the mysterious leaves passed into the keeping of his friend and former secretary, Lucienne Julien. They were subsequently photographed and reproduced in a number of French periodicals before finding their way onto the internet where they became the focus of the usual conspiracy theories. What did become abundantly clear was that the palm leaves were not of Manichaean origin, as Otto Rahn suggested, although they were indeed a divinatory system.

The cryptic characters inscribed on the leaves are written in Oriya, a language dating to approximately 1050 CE and closely related to a system known as Nadi astrology (or *naadi jothidam*) originally practiced in Tamil Nadu, India. According to esoteric researcher Philip Coppens, this system is based on the belief that the past, present, and future of all mankind was recorded in ancient times on palm leaves known as nadis by the Seven Sages of the Hindu tradition. These leaves, allegedly preserved by coating them in an oil extracted from peacock's blood, were stored in the Saraswati Mahal library of Tanjore where generations of astrologers made use of them to scry the future and penetrate the web of past incarnations. When consulting the leaves, seekers will apparently only ever pick out the pages that describe their own destiny, a similar catchall explanation that provides the basis for tarot reading and any number of other divinatory systems predicated on the notion that the future has already happened and we are essentially living in its backwash; moreover, on some level, we are already aware of what that future holds. In Tamil the word *nadi* betokens "destined to come of its own accord."

How the wooden book came to be hidden in the walls of Montségur did not become apparent until 1967 when a pamphlet written by Mario Fille and René Odin entitled *Un Oracle Kabbalistique* revealed these parchments were one and the same as the mysterious Oracle de Force Astrale bequeathed to Fille by Padre Giuliano. It would seem impossible not to conclude the palm leaf pages were planted in the ruins by Fille and Odin and then publicly rediscovered in a desperate attempt to bolster confidence in their secret society. If so, the ruse backfired. To what extent Grace and Ivan Cooke were willing accomplices or unwitting pawns in this subterfuge is impossible to know, although it is hard to imagine they were wholly innocent.

Shortly after her return to England, Grace Cooke founded a British chapter of the Order of the Polaires, adopting their regalia, the turquoise robes and six-pointed silver star. Following the astral guidance of the Cathar adepts she encountered in the ruins of Montségur and Lordat, Grace reformed the movement's rituals, bringing them in line with what she believed to be the rites of the mysterious twelfth-century heresy. In 1936 the White Eagle Lodge was established in a hall in west London, a somewhat cramped venue that was subsequently destroyed in the blitz. After this temporary setback, the group relocated to the lavishly appointed private chapel and healing center where I found myself a guest some sixty-seven years later. The original European Polaires did not fare so well.

Reeling from Cesar Accomani's departure, the order sought to reposition itself under René Odin as a more mainstream spiritual movement with "an emphasis on practical magic, astrology and herb lore." Odin seems to have had little time for the Oracle de Force Astrale, which was seldom mentioned again although Mario Fille did his best to maintain his influence over the order. While the fraternity had always admitted women to their ranks, a separate female branch was briefly established and faltering attempts were made to set up sister lodges in New York, Geneva, and Belgrade.

In August 1933, a year after the Montségur debacle, the Brotherhood

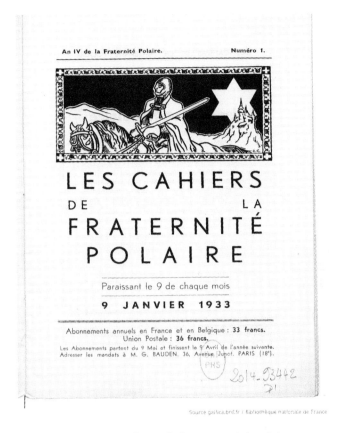

Fig. 7.7. *Les Cahiers de la Fraternité Polaire.*

was officially registered at the *bureau des associations de la préfecture de la police de Paris* in a deposition that lists a certain Victor Blanchard as president. This is doubly confusing, given the Polaires were not known to have previously had a president, although quite possibly the post was only created after Accomani's resignation. There is certainly no mention in any documents of further grand masters. Victor Blanchard was a known figure on the French occult scene, the leader of L'Ordre Martiniste et Synarchique and also a high-ranking initiate in L'Église Gnostique Universelle, L'Ordre Kabbalistique de la Rose-Croix, L'Ordre du Lys et de L'Aigle, and L'Ordre Hermètiste Tétramégiste et Mystique, as well as one of the founders of the FUDOSI federation. Blanchard would eventually be expelled from the federation after issuing an edict auto-consecrating himself as the "Universal Grand Master" of the Rose-Croix and all the initiatic orders of the entire world, a move that did not go over particularly well with the other members. Like several members of the fraternity, Blanchard was closely affiliated with the synarchist movement and an advocate of a united Europe. The synarchists would achieve a certain notoriety as a result of a formation known as Le Mouvement Synarchique d'Empire, a cabal of businessmen, bankers, diplomats, and other government officials who conspired to bring Europe together under the leadership of the Nazis, allegedly playing a key role in the preparations for the German invasion of France and the installation of the Vichy regime. The synarchists ultimately chose to support Hitler because they thought he was the only figure capable of unifying the continent. If the secret societies of the period played a role in helping bring the Nazis to power, then they also sowed the seeds of their own destruction.

Shortly after war broke out in 1939, all secret societies were prohibited by the Vichy government and the Brotherhood of the Polaires formally ceased to exist. Their records were relocated to the Theosophical Society headquarters in Paris and subsequently mislaid.

In 1967, his glory days long behind him, Mario Fille finally broke the promise he made to Padre Giuliano and publicly explained the workings of the oracle in the slender thirty-five-page pamphlet co-authored with René Odin, *Un Oracle Kabbalistique.* The booklet was reprinted in 1971 and briefly made available by mail order. Unsurprisingly, the revelation of this secret was met with a resounding lack of interest from a world that had long since moved on, changing in a manner the Brotherhood's cofounders could surely never have anticipated. The densely inscribed palm leaves of the Oracle de Force Astrale, allegedly retrieved from the walls of Montségur, continue to circulate in private hands and were recently offered for sale at a suitably extravagant price by a collector of rare esoterica in Rennes-le-Château. While intrigued to finally view these relics for myself, I did not bother putting in a bid.

"The old world passes, yet it will live again."

I nodded, blinking a little, the silver star on Jenny Dent's breast swimming in and out of focus.

"To such limited five senses as mankind possesses, this etherealized world of the future is intangible and invisible. Nonetheless that otherworld will embrace a greater measure of reality than time and sense can now unfold . . ."

It was a warm afternoon in the late nineties and I was finding it hard to stay awake, although I did my best to lend an ear as Grace Cooke's granddaughter held court over her followers in the inner sanctum of the White Eagle Lodge, somewhere just off Kensington High Street.

"While man dwells in lowly estate, he cannot recognize anything outside his own capacity. Like a fish in darkened waters he gropes, unconscious of any other sphere of life. So is he blind to these more beautiful and ethereal worlds."

I stifled a yawn and, politely excusing myself, left the high priestess to her address while I took the opportunity to investigate the small private library and reading room on the floor below. Browsing through the lodge's bound memos and copies of their bimonthly periodical *Stella Polaris*, it became apparent the archived material only covered the postwar years. I could find no reference to the events of the 1930s that presaged the lodge's foundation. Looking up, I noticed the high priestess's blue-robed husband, Colum, watching with suspicion from the doorway and deciding to brazen it out, broached my concerns directly.

"Uhm . . . I was wondering if either you or Jenny were familiar with the life and work of Otto Rahn?"

Colum looked a little blindsided by this. "Well, yes . . . that name does ring a bell."

I met his eyes, trying on my practiced Aleister Crowley gaze, just enough to show I meant business.

Colum looked away. "Actually it's ringing quite a few bells now. Maybe we should talk outside."

I waited with my buddy Andre until the high priest had the chance to change into his street clothes. When we met some fifteen minutes later, on the sidewalk outside the lodge, I proffered my hand to Colum and he immediately gave me a Master Mason's grip. He was visibly surprised when I returned the grip with interest.

"Who's your mother?" he asked, one eyebrow raised.

"New Camberwell 778." I smiled.

"How on earth did you find out about Otto Rahn? That's not a name you hear very often these days."

"It's a long story. But I'll try to be brief . . ."

Beside us, the early evening traffic continued to crawl by on the High Street but the present day seemed scarcely relevant. Once again I found myself drawn back into the immutable past, caught in a web that grew out of time. I explained to Colum that I had been conducting a study of the French Polaires. Not only was Otto's name linked to the movement by the article in *la Depeche* but he was alleged to have been the Brotherhood's leader during the period of the excavations at Montségur and Lordat. Colum was quick to dispel this theory, however, along with the persistent rumors of a physical treasure removed by Rahn from the caverns beneath the mountains.

"He wasn't an academic. I'm sure that any professional archaeologist would find the notion absurd."

I nodded. "Actually, I believe he did have a degree, but not in archaeology. His field was etymology. The study of words and word roots—essentially the study of language and its origins, something that ultimately proved useful when it came to tracking down the origins of the Grail."

Colum looked at me blankly. "Fascinating. I'm sure."

"He spent a lot of time in libraries and archives, sourcing the original records, the Inquisition registers and the surviving troubadour songs he believed held clues to the mystery."

I told Colum I had enjoyed visiting the lodge's reading room but had been unable to find any documentation extending back to the war years, let alone to what had come before. Hastening to set my mind at rest, Colum explained that earlier editions of the lodge's bulletins had been removed for safekeeping to their out-of-town headquarters. Then, urging me to get in touch by email, he politely took his leave. Putting the experience behind us, Andre and I picked up a couple of portions of fish and chips before joining the crowd trying to force its way into the maw of the nearest tube station, yet I was in too deep and had gone too far to let the story go. Despite the mystical posturing, the New Age doublethink, and the carny flim-flam of the Polaires, something still lurked amid the details, a "factor X" that refused to readily explain away.

I could tell my questions had rattled Colum, so it came as no surprise when subsequent attempts to contact him at the address provided drew a blank. The Rahn affair was toxic spiritual waste and the last thing anyone needed was for some smart-ass to forge a paper trail linking the burgeoning British New Age Spiritualist movement to Hitler's Reich.

8

The Methodology of Information and Disinformation

Europe Hypnotized

> *I can heartily recommend the Gestapo to anyone.*
> SIGMUND FREUD (1856–1939)

CAMP DE CREMAT: THE FIELD OF THE STAKE, MARCH 16, 1998

"I first came to Montségur to try to find the answer to one very simple question," said Guy Puysegur. "What would make a man of sound mind want to die by the worst kind of death? The death by the fire, you know?"

Monsieur Puysegur was strolling beside me across the site of the original thirteenth-century holocaust, the windswept field at the base of the pog. He was clad in a heavy woollen jerkin and an American cavalry officer's hat, a pair of U.S. Army field glasses dangling at his throat, which seemed almost sensible attire given the inclement weather. I had

Fig. 8.1. Otto Wilhelm Rahn.

timed my return to Montségur for the anniversary of the fall of the castle and the death of the martyrs and was wishing I had packed long underwear. The incline, halfway between the parking lot and the chateau, had become a wall of ice and the glacial wind whipping across the mountain barely allowed me to remain standing. In my black suit and tie I was definitely feeling underdressed for the altitude. Behind me rose the twin ramparts of the Throne of the Gods, Soularac, and the Pic de Saint Barthélémy, known collectively as the Tabor, or mountain of transfiguration, over which the Grail was said to have been carried on its passage to the caves of Ussat. Around its summit, nearly 9,850 feet up, danced a fiery halo of cloud.

"All they had to do was recant and they would have been spared. Instead they chose . . . this," Guy snorted, shaking his head in exasperation. He held some nebulous position with the United Nations and claimed to be a former administrator of the International Labour Organization but was a spook through and through. He had cold-called me at Maison Couquet and had been surreptitiously sounding me out ever since. Back in the '40s he had been an operative for the OSS, the wartime precursor to the CIA, at least until the Nazis caught him and sent him to Auschwitz. Since then, he seemed to have taken *Arbeit macht frei* (or "work sets you free") as a life motto.

Fig. 8.2. Montségur abides.
Photo by Richard Stanley.

"I spoke with a doctor in Geneva about it and he said that after a few minutes you wouldn't feel it anymore with the smoke and everything, but even for a few minutes! I couldn't stand it! I don't know what I would do! I think I would convert to any other kind of religion rather than die that way."

"Is that what happened to Rahn? Did he die that way? The death of a martyr?"

Guy Puysegur blinked, cautiously narrowing his eyes, a survivor to the core. He made no further effort to respond.

"He was certainly a believer."

Guy snorted, "Yes. But a believer in what? He wasn't Christian. At least not in any conventional sense of the word."

I shrugged, doing my best to roll a cigarette as I watched a small group of Occitan nationalists gathering around the stubby memorial.

The Methodology of Information and Disinformation

Red and gold flags fluttered in the icy wind as someone tried to read a poem.

"When I started looking for Otto Rahn, I was told he was still alive but now I'm not so certain," I mused. "If only we could find out what really happened back then, before the war, back in '39."

"Nobody knows and nobody will ever know because he disappeared," hissed Guy. "He's gone now, all right? It's finished." For a moment Guy started to look worried again, lines and creases appearing all over his face as if he were being sewn up from the inside with an invisible needle. I never did get to find out what his beef was with Rahn, but Guy did have a copy of a densely annotated first edition of *Crusade against the Grail* he claimed had been given to him by the vanished SS officer. The flyleaf contained a hastily scribbled dedication and a signature I figured might prove useful as a handwriting specimen further down the pike.

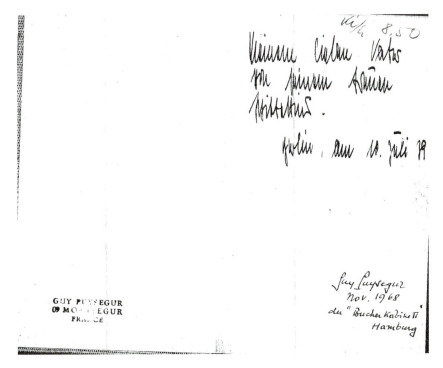

Fig. 8.3. Inscription on the fly leaf of *Crusade against the Grail*.

RENNES-LE-CHÂTEAU, SPRING 1998

All roads lead to Rennes. At least that's what they used to say, back in the day when the so-called Rennes mystery was still a thing.

Guy Puysegur referred me to one of his associates in the tiny village, a former OSS man he claimed had known Otto personally, but sadly this contact died of natural causes the very day I was supposed to meet him. His name was Ian Meadows. I spoke to his wife not half an hour after it happened. There had been no prior history of heart disease. Apparently Ian had been very anxious to tell me something. Too anxious perhaps. His widow referred me to a retired Egyptologist, a certain Dr. Graham Symmonds, who had apparently known Ian well.

Symmonds, an owlish former army officer gone to seed, had a lot to say about the corporate structures set up by the SS to channel the vast revenues generated by slave labor and the nationalized assets made available through the "final solution." A great many folks had profited from those structures, Dr. Symmonds warned, gently swirling a cup of tea with his spoon. So long as those who had succeeded in whitewashing their past were still alive, they possessed both the means and the motivation to derail my inquiries and stop the real truth, whatever that may have been, from coming to light. I shrugged off the old man's warnings, tired of being run in circles. Dr. Symmonds was a known quantity in Rennes-le-Château and I had received word he had been hiring hippie labor to dig beneath the plateau in the hope of breaking through to a cavity he believed was below the church of Marie Madeleine, furtively moving his rickety caravan from one patch of vacant ground to another to hide his illegal excavations in a ruse seemingly inspired by an old episode of *Hogan's Heroes*. Given Symmonds seemed to believe this physical treasure was the Ark of the Covenant, I took everything else the retired "Egyptologist" had to say with a pinch of salt.

I was starting to wonder if Cat hadn't been right and I really was wasting my time with this nonsense. I was getting tired of treasure hunters and conspiracy theorists, of the murky web of inference, innuendo,

Fig. 8.4. Montségur, midwinter.
Photo by Richard Stanley.

and outright myth. The only thing that kept me going was the memory of what I had seen on the mountain. The light that had all but blinded me and that strange bittersweet smell.

GENEVA, SPRING 1998

"I was born in 1900, in a hospital for the insane," rasped Paul Alexis Ladame. "My father was a doctor there and my mother was also a doctor, for eyes. And the patients there were my first teachers in life."

Paul, a former head of the Geneva chamber of commerce and professor of the methodology of information and disinformation at Geneva University, was seated beside me on a park bench in the Swiss capital. Before us the morning light fell cold and clear on the freshly cut grass and a bronze statue in the middle distance depicting two blank-eyed children standing hand in hand. A plaque at the base of the statue identified the figures as *les petits amis*.

"Every one of them thought they were absolutely sane. But the others in the hospital, maybe they had something a little wrong with them."

Fig. 8.5. Professor Paul Alexis Ladame at work in his study in Geneva. Photo by Richard Stanley.

Paul's voice was a hoarse whisper. He had recently had his left foot amputated and in a cruel twist of fate a tracheotomy had severed all but one of his vocal cords. A cartoonist, actor, journalist, and former radio man, Paul had lived at least nine lives but he knew his luck was finally running out. He seemed driven to tell me something first though, as if eager to make confession.

"I first met Otto Rahn in 1929. I'd just finished high school and I wanted to learn a trade with my hands, to become a painter, and I was told that in Berlin was the best school in Europe, der Reimannschule, so I went there. Berlin was a marvelous city. Very poor, but very gay. We were very young, dancing a lot, loving the girls and music and everything, enjoying life ten years after the end of World War I and ten years before started the Second World War." It was as if each word was costing Paul some terrible inner price. His eyes were upturned, hands clasped around an elegant cane bearing a silver eagle's head.

"One night I received a telephone call from one of my pals, telling me that he had the flu and that he couldn't go the next morning at five to play in a film for Pabst somewhere on the border of Germany and

Fig. 8.6. Paul Alexis Ladame on the set of *Westfront*, summer 1930. Courtesy of Paul Alexis Ladame.

Poland. Would I be kind enough to replace him? I said yes. I went there and I played there in the first film of Pabst, *Westfront*. We were what you would call extras, a group of about thirty young men in French uniform of the war of Verdun playing war against the Germans."

"One of my little pals came from Switzerland too and one of his great friends was a German four years older than we were who came to visit us on the set and his name was Otto Rahn. Why did he look at me and talk to me? For the very simple reason that I taught French to him and he had with me a good exercise. I don't see more than that at the beginning."

Around us normal life was continuing. Cyclists glided past, couples strolled, and mothers shook rattles at prams, yet somehow Paul's insistent whisper made even the open brightness of the park seem treacherous.

"At the time I met Rahn I looked at him with awe and interest and I thought, 'that's a man who has ideas about things I couldn't dream of.' He was obsessed with the agendas of past times and wished to write about those who had been crushed, about the minorities . . . called

Cathari . . . to write a mystical book, a mythical book but also a political book, to write about the search for the Grail and the wisdom of past centuries and he imagined that these times might one day come back! And so came the idea to Otto Rahn that someday Germany and France must be united with England and united also with Italy, united with all Europe . . . to form a united Europe."

Paul's daughter, Shiva, was strolling beneath the trees, just within earshot, trying to appear disinterested. Like Paul she was a Buddhist, convinced the answer to all of it lay in the mysteries of reincarnation. Weekdays, nine-to-five, she was a senior administrator for the Red Cross.

"On his first visit to Paris, Otto introduced me to a man who was a Frenchman from the south, with the accent from the south, who shared

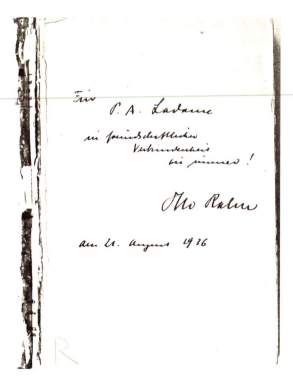

Fig. 8.7. A signed copy of Otto Rahn's first book, *Crusade against the Grail*, addressed to his best friend Paul Ladame.

his enthusiasm and this was Magre . . . Maurice Magre . . . who had already written books, *Le sang de Toulouse,* 'The blood of Toulouse,' telling about the crusade, about the suffering of the south and he says, 'Look Otto, go to Montségur and witness one thing, that the crusade went on for about a century, not a few battles. Not a few people vanquished but they fought on, fought on . . . all the time . . . and the last ones to defend themselves hid themselves in grottos.' Now I had a few years before accompanied my brother who was an engineer in mines and I had experience with all the instruments one has to have in a cavern, so suddenly Rahn tells me, 'Well Paul, you must come with me. You can go in these caves and help me with the lights and all that.' And I, as a feeble man, say, 'Yes, Otto, I'll come so long as you pay for the trip.' We happened then to go to Lavelanet in the French Pyrenees and to go up the road and then on the second or third turn you discover Montségur, a huge mountain watching you like it had never been touched by a human foot. First impression.

"Then, I met the people of Montségur . . . "

Paul's recollections of the village seemed a little shaky and while continuing to insist he had accompanied Otto in his explorations, he failed to recognize any of the names I threw at him, notably those of Nat Wolff, Habdu, Joseph Widigger, and the other members of the Grail hunter's entourage. He was equally vague when it came to what Rahn had been looking for in the caves, despite the inference in his correspondence that the young researcher had made some sort of breakthrough.

"I was not entirely mobilized with the enthusiasm of my friend, Rahn," Paul confessed. "He was in heaven but I thought all the time that I had a girl waiting for me in Paris so did not want to make it too long."

For a moment I found myself doubting whether Paul had ever really been in the caves. Then rummaging in a manilla envelope, he pushed a faded photograph across the desktop toward me. I squinted, holding the sepia image closer in the half-light. The photograph showed a young

Fig. 8.8. The initiation.

man in a beret, approximately my own age, standing in the octagonal depression above the altar in the Bethlehem Grotto, arms outstretched to form a pentagram "Gadal took this picture back in '33. It was his initiation."

"What about Beatrice?"

"Who?"

"The face he was supposed to have drawn on the cave wall?"

In truth, Otto Rahn's connection to the cave remained circumstantial and there was no evidence other than Christian Bernadac's word that he had ever drawn a mysterious woman's face on the rock. The

Dante reference, however, chimed with Rahn's penchant for alluding to the *Divine Comedy*. In a broadcast he made for Southwest German radio, Rahn describes a rock formation guarding the grotto of Fontanet that allegedly resembled a three-headed dog—and there is that numinous line in *Court of Lucifer*—"I was looking for divinity yet I find myself at the gates of Hell." Dante was said to have been a member of the Fedeli d'Amore, a secret brotherhood founded by the Bulgarian mystic Nicetas himself. Dante was allegedly initiated into the order by Guido Cavalcanti, who is depicted in the *Inferno* as a heretic burning in hell, the Bulgarian mystic who established the formal Cathar Church in the south. In fact it was Dante, in his monograph *On the Eloquence of the Vulgar*, who had initially coined the term *Occitan* or *Lenga d'Oc*, defining the all but forgotten language of Romans according to its positive particle *oc*, from whence the region drew its name—Occitania.

"Wasn't there a story about some girl who refused to marry him? He'd already sent out wedding invitations to his superiors in the Ahnenerbe SS, even to Himmler himself, but she apparently backed out

Fig. 8.9. "One of My Little Pals"—a sketch of Otto Rahn, drawn by Paul Alexis Ladame in 1936 and signed with his usual nom de plume, PAL.

Fig. 8.10. Otto Rahn at work on his first book, *Crusade against the Grail*, **1934.**

at the last minute. I mean there must have been someone in Otto's life? Someone special."

Paul thought it over for a moment. Then his expression abruptly darkened and he pushed back his chair as if to signify the interview was over.

"I won't play those games. He was a good man. He deserved better."

9
Pagan Imperialism
Europe 1932–1938

Take my hand, Faust and let us leave Rome and seek together the mountain of assembly in the most distant midnight. It is far better to be near a bearer of light than a dissimulator of light, a broken mirror stained with blood. . . . Still I may continue to walk, to fall, even in flames. If there exists a way towards heaven, then it crosses hell. At least it does for me. Well then, I dare!

OTTO RAHN, THE COURT OF LUCIFER,
AUTHOR'S TRANSLATION

Otto Rahn left the south of France in a hurry, hounded by financial problems and possible legal proceedings. On October 6, 1932, the commercial court in Foix declared Rahn bankrupt and for the next two years his movements are all but impossible to track. Evidently he did not depart the country immediately, as that same month the author and historian Isabelle Sandy mentions in a letter that Rahn is staying with her in Paris. According to Sandy's missive, "a valuable treasure has been returned to us, without diplomats and without fuss and that is the result of an incomparable success." Whether she is referring to a spiritual, literary, or physical treasure remains crucially unclear. Tensions were mounting between France and Germany, but Rahn seemed optimistic war could be averted. Isabelle Sandy allegedly told Christian Bernadac she believed Rahn's work had the potential to secure a Franco-Germanic treaty, bringing together a united Europe under the Grail.

Seemingly infatuated with Rahn, Isabelle Sandy continued to hold the Grail hunter in high esteem long after he was obliged to leave France. "Between the two wars," she wrote, "there appeared from the heavens a meteor over the valleys of the Ariège. He cut the firmament like a diamond cuts glass and then disappeared forever. He carried a human name: Otto Rahn. Who was he? One knew not. Where did he come from? From Germany, his homeland. He was a Tyrolean, pale with eyes like anthracite. . . . He intruded a little childishly with his mystery, which accompanied him in death and into the beyond."

Otto Rahn always hoped to return to the holy mountains of Occitania, to Montségur and his beloved Ariège, but there is no hard evidence to confirm he ever did. His subsequent visa requests to return to France were consistently denied and the bad debts left in his wake continued to dog him. He kept up a regular correspondence with Antonin Gadal, the original copies of which are now held in the archives of the Lectorium Rosicrucianum (LR). In one letter Rahn thanks his old friend for putting out a good word for him in Montségur and helping smooth the ruffled feathers of the villagers he quarreled with during his quest. As late as 1934, Rahn still talked frequently of returning to the caves of Ussat and expressed concern over whether the locals would accept him back into the community after the "awful things they did to me . . . and I to them." Quite what these awful things were will probably never be known, but for whatever reason, the Montséguriens had felt the need to drive the Grail hunter out of the village with whips and pitchforks. "These simple people can't understand that I advertised their country and that I will continue to do so," Rahn bewails in another message to Gadal. "They judge me by what they have seen. I can understand them. But we are even now."

Within a year of leaving France, Otto Rahn was back in Germany, residing in Berlin-Charlottenberg. One of Rahn's associates from this period, medical student Hans Grebe, recalls a bicycling excursion to Wilnsdorf, following the trail of the notorious thirteenth-century witch hunter Konrad von Marburg. On several occasions Rahn mentions he is drafting a new book on Marburg's crimes against the "old religion" but for whatever reason a completed manuscript failed to materialize. In other correspondence, he claims to be working on a novel, *Lauren*, concerning the mythical king of the Little People, but again this does not seem to have been completed although a draft survives among the effects in his niece Ingeborgh Roemer-Rahn's possession. Rahn sojourned in Switzerland long enough to catch up with his alleged lover Raymond Perrier and recorded a series of programs with Paul Ladame for Radio Geneva. Thereafter Rahn seems to have taken the countess's advice and decamped for Catalonia and the shrine of the Black Madonna of Montserrat, studying at the Benedictine library.

The Countess Miryanne de Pujol Murat continued to occupy a prominent place in Rahn's consideration. As late as 1935 his correspondence with Gadal expressed the hope he would soon return to the Ariège to pursue his explorations with her help and approval, joking about his plans to again borrow her chauffeur, Joseph Widigger, and "relieve her of a lazybones."

Otto Rahn's first book, *Crusade against the Grail*, appeared in the autumn of 1933 from Urban Verlag in Freibourg to critical acclaim and middling sales. Breaking seven centuries of silence, Rahn's opus was the first time the tragic history of the Cathars and the last crusade was brought to public attention outside of France. Otto Rahn was twenty-eight years old and by any critical yardstick his first book must be considered a groundbreaking achievement. Despite favorable reviews, only two thousand copies of the first edition were sold and before long Rahn found himself swapping autographed copies of his book for packets of

Fig. 9.1. The Benedictine monastery on the mountain of Montserrat where Otto Rahn completed his occult studies.
Photo by Richard Stanley.

Fig. 9.2. Inside the basilica of the Black Mother on the mountain of Montserrat. Photo by Richard Stanley.

Fig. 9.3. First edition of Otto Rahn's *Crusade against the Grail.*

cigarettes and other essentials. In a letter to Gadal the Grail hunter claims his shoes are worn out and he has been forced to leave his watch at a bakery in exchange for a loaf of bread. Rahn's enthusiasm for heresy, however, remained undimmed. His letters to Rausch from this period indicate a clear sense of mission.

"Must a Hessian journey to the Pyrenees to reveal that Montségur was Munsalvaesche, the grail-castle?" Rahn wrote to his literary mentor, Rausch. "Must a Hessian learn in southern France that Grail-Christians lived in Hesse? Is it not strange that I, the Hessian who so often as a high school student hiked those same trails where brothers of the Provencal Cathari were burned and must write books like *Crusade against the Grail* and *Konrad of Marburg*? The material lay before me. I was predestined for it, I believe."

The following summer found Otto in Italy, this time in the company of tantric magician and committed pagan imperialist Baron Julius Evola.

Fig. 9.4. Julius Evola, otherwise known as Baron Giulio Cesare Andrea Evola (1898–1974), occultist, philosopher, radical traditionalist, and anti-Semitic conspiracy theorist.

The eccentric Sicilian nobleman was at that time working on his magnum opus, *Rivolta contro il mondo moderno* (*Revolt against the Modern World*) (1934), a ringing denunciation of both democracy and socialism. In Evola's elitist worldview, capitalism and communism were twin aspects of the materialistic forces that had conspired since the dawn of time to subvert the spiritual ideals of the primordial Indo-Aryan tradition.

It is possible Otto Rahn served as a sort of esoteric diplomat, shuttling between the leading lights of the neo-Cathar and neo-pagan movements to see if they could be united in common cause. Some believe he sought to recruit the baron to the service of his Nazi paymasters, but it is unlikely his views were shared by Evola, whose anti-liberal interpretation of the "primordial tradition" essentially amounted to an unequivocal endorsement of divine monarchy and the absolute rule of a master caste, an authority to which the baron assumed he was entitled by dint of blood.

Perhaps unsurprisingly, something went awry with Otto Rahn's

Italian excursion. One of his associates, Dr. Adolphe Frise, describes in a letter how he was forced to rescue Otto from Milan and drive him hastily back to his home in Bad Homberg. Dr. Frise claimed Rahn was visibly upset and chain-smoked throughout the journey, muttering darkly about how he was caught up in something he was not at liberty to explain. The true import of his words is lost to us, but back in Germany the glacial forces of history were on the move. The German parliament, the Reichstag, had just been destroyed in a fire that would allow the National Socialist German Worker's Party to consolidate its hold on the levers of power.

It is difficult to know when Rahn's work first came under the aegis of the SS.

Christian Bernadac implied the young Grail seeker's quest had been funded by clandestine nationalist forces from the very beginning, yet there is no paperwork or prima facie evidence to prove this. A cloud hangs over the provenance of Rahn's funding during his sojourn in the Pyrenees but, given the bankruptcy proceedings filed against him, it is clear that source had run dry. Paul claimed Rahn had been back in Geneva by the tail end of 1935, taking time out with Raymond Perrier and counting his small change.

He was on the verge of returning to the Ariège when he received a telegram urgently summoning him to Berlin. An anonymous benefactor was offering to underwrite the young Grail hunter's continuing research. According to Paul, when Rahn reported to the address given in the telegram he was shocked to find himself in the presence of none other than Heinrich Himmler, the reichsführer of the SS.

His mysterious benefactor's Faustian offer, Paul implied, was one Rahn had no choice but to accept. "What was I supposed to do?" complained Rahn. "Turn him down?"

On February 29, 1936, Himmler's personal adjutant Karl Wolff sent an internal memo to the recruiting office requesting that Otto Rahn be inducted into the Allgemeine-SS on the reichsführer's personal authority. The application was duly processed and approved on March 12 and

Rahn was assigned the number 276 208. Just over a month later, on April 20, Rahn was promoted to SS-Unterscharführer and elevated to a privileged position on Himmler's personal staff. This new role came with perks including a luxurious basement apartment on Tiergarten Strasse and a personal adjutant-secretary, a male secretary, of course, who reported directly to Rahn's new masters. With the full support of Himmler's Black Order behind him, Otto Rahn prepared to continue his quest, believing his far-flung goals to finally be within reach.

To what extent Heinrich Himmler truly believed Otto Rahn knew the physical whereabouts of the Holy Grail remains a matter of speculation, but the young adept's subsequent rise through the ranks of the Schutzstaffel cleared the way for him to further his research and set in motion the macabre and tragic events that followed. To some extent, Himmler seems to have perceived Rahn as the ideal SS man, a Grail knight whose occult ideals embodied the ancestral spirit of Germany and the new gnosis to which the Black Order aspired. Rahn's books were made compulsory reading at a certain level of promotion within the SS, a key element of the doctrine that helped forge the myth of the "master race" and laid the ideological underpinnings of the holocaust.

Gay, bookish, and descended from Semitic ancestry, Rahn was far from an Aryan superman, yet for a while at least his newfound success and growing influence within the order seems to have gone to his head. His correspondence from the period shows a streak of arrogance that would prove to be his undoing.

On August 20, 1937, Rahn attended the wedding of a certain Mrs. Hartmann (née Gotz) in Hamburg. At the reception, Rahn, garbed in black, full-dress uniform, allegedly picked a fight with a young Wehrmacht officer, lieutenant Horst Buchrucker. Rahn was apparently upset over the seating arrangements, having been placed at the far end of the table among some of the younger guests. Rahn taunted Buchrucker, claiming he had powerful friends and the younger man would be sorry for his insolence. He spoke scathingly of the Wehrmacht and in a flash of sheer hypocrisy derided Buchrucker for not being a party member, an

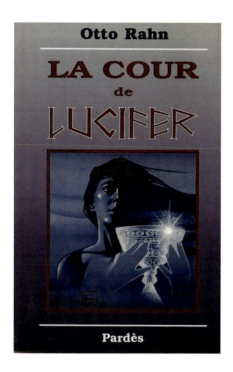

Fig. 9.5. *The Court of Lucifer* (1937), French translation, edition Pardès.

extraordinary choice of insult given Rahn himself never officially joined the Nazi party or carried a party pin.

Otto Rahn's sensational early work led to him being feted by the Nazi elite and for a few years his research was lavishly funded by the Race and Settlement department.

In April 1937, Rahn's second book, *The Court of Lucifer*, was published by Schwarzhaupter Verlag, Leipzig. Himmler showed his appreciation for the completion of the second volume in Rahn's projected occult trilogy by promoting the young Grail hunter to the rank of untersturmführer. While reviews were mixed and sales poor, the book was embraced by the Black Order as essential reading, assuming something of the character of a Nazi gospel.

To promote his latest book, Rahn toured schools and town halls, lecturing the baffled public on what he termed the "Lucifer problem." It's hard to imagine being lectured at school by a uniformed SS officer banging on about how Lucifer had been misunderstood, but by all accounts, Otto was a charismatic speaker and Germany was a very strange place in those days.

In January 1938, Rahn traveled to Dortmünd to address the Dietrich-Eckart Rote Erde Society whose cultural director Kurt Eggers was believed to have been one of the Grail hunter's closest friends. Eggers was a fellow writer and SS man who had written a book, *The Birth of the Century*, that was known to have influenced Rahn, who quotes from it in *Court of Lucifer*. Eggers, who will resurface later in this narrative under less convivial circumstances, would eventually die in Russia in a burning tank and earn the dubious honor of having a present-day neo-Nazi formation named after him—leibstandarte Kurt Eggers. It is clear Kurt and Otto were cut from the same cloth. Whether or not they were lovers we will never know for sure.

An article in the *Westphalia Landezeitung* gives us some sense of what the evening might have been like. The *Landezeitung*'s journalist Dr. Wolff Heinrichdorf writes:

> Otto Rahn the young poet and researcher read and lectured on Friday night at the Dietrich Eckart Verein [club] in front of a rather large and highly captivated audience. Kurt Eggers, the person in charge of cultural events for the Verein, made a few introductory remarks, greeting Rahn as a comrade and briefly outlining the "Lucifer problem," which Rahn would talk about. Rahn quickly sketched an image of Lucifer in such emphatic and compelling language that it could not be thought out in a more moving and explicit manner. The author read from his newest work, *Lucifers Hofgesind*, which tells of his travels and findings in Southern France, where he followed the traces of the Grail and the Albigenses [Cathars], the pure and true heretics. Developing this theme, Rahn also drew a picture of how this anti-Roman movement had also spread through Germany at the time. The lecture covered difficult material and required a very high degree of discipline and alertness from the audience. It was a good sign for the symbioses of lecturer

and audience that no word was lost, and that the image of Lucifer, which Rahn celebrated with the Albigenses as Bringer of Light was most effective.

Two parts of the evening can clearly be differentiated: the first, where Rahn reported on the research and current status of the Grail and Lucifer problem—here the most powerful words and the most exciting creativity came into play—and a second, which the lecturer based on concrete examples, drew conclusions from his new points of view and teachings and arrived at a largely convincing reevaluation of historic events. With true excitement he led us back to the source of the origins of our desire for freedom and closeness to nature. The Albigenses have been exterminated. In southern France, 205 leading followers of Lucifer were burnt on a gigantic stake (March 16, 1244) after a great crusade led by Dominican priests in the name of Christian mildness. The teachings of Lucifer, the Bringer of Light, and his followers were persecuted with fire and sword. The Albigenses are dead but their spirit is alive. Christ's representatives could burn people but they were wrong when they thought they could burn their spirits, their passion, and their desire. This spirit became alive again yesterday, took its effect on the many people present and was visible in Otto Rahn—a descendant of the ancient Troubadours. Rahn negated Yahweh and the Jewish teachings, and proposed the truth of Lucifer's Hofgesind in whose name Kurt Eggers closed the evening with the following salute, "Lucifer, who has been done wrong to, we salute you!"

10

Dark Camelot

Castle of the SS Order

Hell is the place of those who have denied; They find there what they planted and what dug,
A Lake of Spaces, and a Wood of Nothing . . .

       W. B. Yeats, *The Hour-Glass*

Tourist maps of Germany make no mention of the SS order castle, which was allegedly all but obliterated at the end of World War II. It was only with the aid of a large-scale map of Westphalia that I managed to find the initials "Schl" (oss) next to the tiny village of Wewelsburg. It was the better part of a day's drive on the autobahn from Frankfurt, then a zigzag course, through ashen, withered fields and thick forest, traveling on ever smaller back roads. Mostly I remember sleet blowing through the headlights and sunlight glinting on black ice.

 The town of Wewelsburg seemed as sleepy as any other German hamlet and we had to drive through it twice before we caught sight of the castle looming from the dark. While remarkably well preserved, there were no signposts to indicate the structure.

Fig. 10.1. Schloss Wewelsburg—the SS order castle.
Photo by Richard Stanley.

Fig. 10.2. The *mittelpunkt der welt*: architectural plans for the SS order castle showing the north-facing tower at the apex of the triangle and the center of the circle—the axis of Heinrich Himmler's empire.

Fig. 10.3. Defaced SS runes on the Wewelsburg guard post. Photo by Richard Stanley.

Viewed from above, the walls of the schloss form an isosceles triangle with the keep at its northern apex and the other two towers at the southwest and southeast corners. Passing a small guardhouse, which bore a defaced but still legible SS insignia atop its gate, I tiptoed over the drawbridge to discover a party in progress within. I swiftly learned the order castle was owned and maintained by the international youth hostel movement, itself an offshoot of the Wandervogel, whose members had serenaded us in the ruins of Wildenberg. There were lights glowing in the windows of the Wewelsburg this evening and laughter trickled out into the cold night air. Deciding not to alert the partygoers to our presence, Mr. Horn and I walked stealthily past the moldering ping-pong tables propped against the outside wall to peek though the windows of the tower that once housed the castle library and its legendary round table. In dividing the SS into twelve departments the reichsführer probably saw himself as the living symbol of the sun, surrounded by the houses of the zodiac. Of course, thirteen is also the number of the traditional coven. Twelve witches and a high priest.

We worked our way toward the base of the tower, frost crunching

Fig. 10.4. The North Tower.
Photo by Richard Stanley.

beneath our feet, to find an open door leading to a small, dark room that reeked of raw sewage. A hole had been cloven through a concrete wall dividing the room, apparently to deal with recent plumbing problems and squeezing through the gap we found ourselves in the castle sewers. The darkness was so thick it was almost palpable and, casting about ourselves with our flashlights, we caught sight of a weird arched annex leading deeper into the fortress, its walls lined with chipped and discolored tiling.

In the Dark Ages, the castle cellars were used for the incarceration and torture of witches and heretics. The torture chamber, known as the *hexenkeller*, was still there, its racks, chains, and iron maiden preserved as a monument to the malignant traditions of the past. All told, it was hard to comprehend just how much suffering had been poured into this place. The pain seemed to have curdled the air itself. Even the trees surrounding the Schloss appeared stunted and somehow pain-wracked, their trunks twisted as if bowed under by the sheer horror of what they had been forced to witness.

There were dark smudges on the tiling, shapes, swimming in my flashlight beam. I realized it was just my imagination, but the eerie sensation that we were somehow not alone in that tunnel was hard to shake and the back of my neck prickled with the sensation of being watched by invisible eyes.

The way into the Hall of the Dead was blocked by a barred gate. We thrust our flashlights through the bars to illuminate the beehive-shaped room beyond, glimpsing a ventilation hole shaped like a rune-accented swastika cut into the apex of the domed roof. On the floor of the Hall of the Supreme Leadership, immediately above us, was the mysterious rune wheel made of green stone with its central disc of dark marble commonly known as the Black Sun. Each one of the twelve runes pointed to one of the columns forming the arris vaults above the windows with their green sandstone frames. At the center of the hall was a shallow pit containing a disused gas faucet surrounded by twelve unoccupied pedestals. This was the center of the web, all right. The gas faucet had probably been intended to feed some sort of "eternal flame" but it seemed an appropriate enough symbol of the Reich's grisly, dysfunctional legacy. The acoustics of the chamber were such that, standing upon a pedestal, one's whispered voice could readily be heard in any other part of the room. The central pit placed one at the acoustic focus of the chamber, as well as at Heinrich Himmler's hypothetical *mittelpunkt der welt*, the physical axis of his evil empire.

Heinrich Himmler was a former chicken farmer and fertilizer salesman whose role as the head of the SS, the black-garbed "guard unit" established to maintain order at the Nazi rallies, had such a deleterious effect on his ego that he eventually came to believe he was the reincarnation of Heinrich of Saxony. He purchased the sixteenth-century castle, the former seat of the bishops and witch hunters of Paderborn, under the direction of his resident rune mage, deranged Brigadeführer Karl Maria Wiligut-Weisthor, who prophesied that the Wewelsburg and the nearby pre-Christian sacred site known as the Externsteine would

Fig. 10.5. The Black Sun.

one day be the principal battlefield in an apocalyptic final conflict between the east and west.

Wiligut-Weisthor was one of the most bizarre and colorful figures to have been drawn to the black flame of Himmler's Nazi Camelot. Born as Karl Maria Wiligut in Vienna in 1866, he believed himself to be the "secret king of Germany," the last descendant of an extinct line of royalty stemming from the ancient Germanic sages, the Uiligotis of the Asa-Uana-Sippe. He not only claimed to have been tutored in the runes and initiated from an early age into the secrets of his family, but to also possess clairvoyant abilities. By faith he was an Irminist, an adherent of the pagan deity Krist, whose worship he believed had been hijacked and ruthlessly distorted by the Christians.

Following a family tradition, Karl Maria Wiligut joined the Austro-Hungarian army at the age of fourteen and held a series of commands spanning a good forty years of loyal military service. He was repeatedly decorated for bravery in World War I during which he was gassed and wounded several times. After being demobbed, he seems to have suffered from an unusually acute form of post-traumatic stress disorder, developing the conviction he could remember all of his past lives, experiencing total recall of over 8,000 years of Germanic history. His subsequent desire to father a son who might inherit his ancestral memories placed his marriage under considerable strain. Wiligut blamed his wife's inability to conceive a healthy boy child on a Zionist Masonic-Catholic conspiracy, which he also believed was responsible for the collapse of the Habsburg dynasty and his homeland's ignominious defeat in the war. He grew increasingly violent and after repeatedly threatening to kill his wife, was confined to an asylum in Salzburg where he was diagnosed as a paranoid schizophrenic with megalomaniac tendencies.

On his release, Wiligut managed to emigrate to Germany where he found friends and like-minded comrades among the volkisch groups of the day such as the Free Sons of the North and Baltic Seas and the Edda society. In 1933, his old friend Richard Anders, who was now serving as an SS officer, introduced him to Heinrich Himmler who was deeply impressed by the weird old man. Wiligut was duly recruited into the Ahnenerbe SS under the pseudonym *Weisthor* (literally "wise Thor" or the "wise warrior") and installed as the head of a newly created Department for Pre and Early History within the Race and Settlement Main Office in Munich.

Dark Camelot 221

Fig. 10.6. The rune mage—Karl Maria Wiligut aka "Weisthor."

Fig. 10.7. SS Brigadeführer Karl Maria Wiligut aka "Weisthor" (1866–1946).

There is no doubt Wiligut-Weisthor, dubbed "Himmler's Rasputin" by popular historians, served as an occult mentor to the reichsführer and came to wield considerable influence within the Black Order. He was rapidly promoted from the rank of SS hauptsturmführer (captain) to SS brigadeführer (brigadier), playing an instrumental role in the design of the SS uniform and *totenkopf* (or death's-head) ring, which bore his family seal. He encouraged the reichsführer to purchase and restore the schloss that was to become the seat of Himmler's nascent warrior knight dynasty, over whose quasi-pagan birth rites Wiligut-

Fig. 10.8. Totenkopf ring. Design by Karl Maria Wiligut—a silver death's-head flanked by two sieg runes, a hagal rune, and a swastika. On the back of the ring is the bind rune Wiligut-Weisthor drew from his own family crest.

Fig. 10.9. Totenkopf ring bearing Himmler's signature on the inner band. Photo by Hamilton White.

Weisthor presided like some deranged cross between a Nazi Aleister Crowley and Uncle Fester from the Addams family.

The death's-head rings were not the personal property of the SS elite to whom they were issued but were literally designed to bind them to the order. The bind rune positioned on the backs of the rings testifies to this occult purpose. After the deaths of the men who wore them, the rings were collected and returned to the Wewelsburg for symbolic interment in the Hall of the Dead, like some ghastly real-life equivalent of Tolkien's "crack of doom." Indeed, it is hard not to imagine the celebrated author of *The Lord of the Rings* (1954) drew direct inspiration for his ring wraiths from Himmler's inner circle and the twelve dark knights whom the reichsführer believed were destined to rule the "new earth," a world redesigned and repurposed according to his own apocalyptic neo-pagan fantasies.

It comes as little surprise Wiligut-Weisthor adored Rahn's first book, *Crusade against the Grail*, which was recommended to him by his young driver-secretary Gabriele Winckler-Dechend. Wiligut-Weisthor passed the book on to Himmler who swiftly summoned Rahn to Berlin, recruiting the young Grail historian onto his personal staff as a junior noncommissioned officer. It is not hard to see Otto Rahn as a sort of gothic Parsival to Wiligut-Weisthor's malignant Merlin. While he was never a card-carrying member of the Nazi party and, according to Ingeborgh, found the uniform he was forced to wear "faintly ridiculous," Rahn was clearly elated at the prospect of pursuing his quest in France, Italy, and Iceland. He was only too aware of the Faustian nature of the bargain and paraphrases Goethe in his second book, *The Court of Lucifer*, "Give me your hand, Faust! Let us leave Rome and seek out together the mountain of assembly in the most distant midnight."

Throwing himself wholeheartedly into his continued pursuit of the mysterious Cathar treasure he believed to be the Grail, Otto Rahn communicated his further findings to Wiligut-Weisthor in coded dispatches that were to be shared with no one else but Himmler, so secret were their contents.

In a message addressed to "Weisthor" in October 1935 and signed with a hearty "heil Hitler," Otto Rahn requests permission to travel to Odenwald, Westerwald, Sporkenburg, Drutgerestein, Steimel, Hellenborn, Wilderstein, and the ruins of Wildenburg castle near Amorbach, where Wolfram first penned his Grail romance. In the same missive Otto mentions his pressing need to visit the stone circles of the Dornburg and Willendorf, the former seat of the German heretics and birthplace of the mythical Christian Rosenkreutz, along with several other locations so secret that they could "only be communicated orally." Weisthor signs his response in runes as was customary for the aging magus. Otto's subsequent journey is noted in a report to Himmler dated October 19, 1935, and Himmler's journal for November 3, 1935, remarks, "Report back and to be kept secret."

It is difficult to know what could have been so essential about these

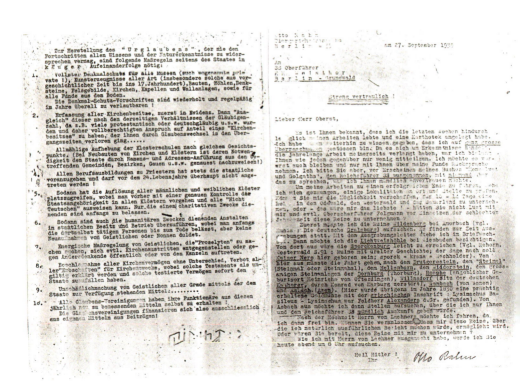

Fig. 10.10. Correspondence between Weisthor and Rahn.

neolithic sites that the reichsführer considered it necessary to stress the secrecy of Rahn's mission. British author and researcher Nigel Graddon suggests it may have concerned sacred geometry and the manipulation of the subtle currents of geo-telluric energy commonly believed to be focused by these alignments. Surviving documents imply the Black Order may have been experimenting in geomancy as Graddon believes, but without further data it would be unwise to speculate about just what Rahn and his superiors hoped to achieve.

Rahn, like Wiligut-Weisthor, saw the rise of the Hitler dictatorship as a means to an end, a golden opportunity to avenge his ancestors and oversee the destruction of organized religion and even Christianity itself, clearing the way for a new pan-European paganism designed and directed by his black-garbed masters, whom he imagined to be the servitors of an unknown god whose messiah was Lucifer rather than Jesus.

The reichsführer's chief architect, a diabolic little man named Bartels, intended the redesigned order castle to be the center of a new world, with the Grail chamber in the north tower of the Wewelsburg as its axis. The establishment of a local concentration camp provided the necessary manpower for the huge renovations envisaged. Between 1939 and 1943 the inmates of the camp at Niederhagen had to perform the necessary work on the castle in line with the principle of "extermination through labor." During the refurbishment of the north tower alone 1,285 people perished—1,285 souls.

Later, in the holocaust museum, I found the testimony of Joachim Escher, a former inmate of Niederhagen, who had been assigned to the North Tower Labor Unit that performed the excavation work. "We had to lower the floor which was made of rock. We worked with drills at times but also with crowbars, spades and pitching tools and then everything was put onto hand barrows and tipped out. The rock was pretty hard. There were only a dozen prisoners working there—a small unit."

I admit the recurrence of the number twelve gave me goose bumps. Further investigation indicated the practice of assigning twelve men to a group was commonplace within the SS, an order presided over by twelve ubergruppenführers, whose ashes and ceremonial rings were intended to rest someday on those twelve vacant plinths in the circular chamber at the very center of this unholy web of power.

W. Jordan wrote the following rather chilling poem about Bartel's grand design. It appeared in the *Julfest Zetitung*, the festivity newspaper of the SS Castle Unit issued on Christmas Eve:

> And now in the architect's brain shines a new and brighter flame. If our tower is to stand forever more, we must remove the evil at its core. And is the tooth with cavities, helped by fillings, tell me please, when it stands loosely in the bone with no support, no stable home? And thus it was not so insane, to dig around the tower again. Day and night they drilled around, creating thus an awful sound, so that not a soul could sleep within an hour of the keep.

W. Jordan was an SS officer. What became of him, I don't know.

Wolfram von Sievers, another Nazi monster working under the guise of the Ahnenerbe would have been known to Rahn through Wiligut-Weisthor. He was appointed by Heinrich Himmler to the role of general secretary with the specific task of administering the Exernsteine-Stiftung—the Exernsteine Foundation. Here, he manipulated many of the excavations and faked finds used to demonstrate mendacious racial theories supporting Hitler's Reich. In 1943 he was placed in charge of the organization's military-medical research. In this capacity Sievers came to play a major role in the infamous Jewish skeleton collection—a pseudo-anthropological idea to demonstrate the racial inferiority of the Jewish race through skeletal displays destined for Strasbourg University.

Evidence of the murder and dissection of eighty-six selected Auschwitz inmates was found by allied forces at Natzweiler-Lager. At the "Doctors Trial" in 1947, Sievers and four others were convicted of their crimes and sentenced to death. Wolfram von Sievers met his end on the gallows at Landsberg Prison in 1948 and was buried in an unmarked grave.

Fig. 10.11. Wolfram von Sievers (1905–1948). United States Holocaust Memorial Museum, Photograph #07320.

Some believe that Rahn's Grail was secretly transported to the Wewelsburg where it was allegedly exhibited to Himmler's inner circle, the twelve knights who administered this dark Camelot.

Fortunately for the world, Himmler and Bartel's grand scheme was never fully realized before the sky came crashing down about their heads. For all the pomp and ceremony, only one meeting, during operation Barbarossa, was ever held at the order castle's round table.

At the bitter end, his empire in ruins, Himmler dispatched his surviving knight, Captain Heinz Macher, to blow up his beloved castle so it wouldn't fall into Allied hands. Macher, like the warrior ordered by Arthur to throw his sword back into the lake, botched the job and hence the castle stands. Macher reported a successful mission and was promoted to major on the spot. As he already wore the Knights Cross with Oak Leaves, his word was never doubted and Himmler never knew the mission had failed.

As soon as Macher's team departed, the looters swarmed in and began to strip the castle of its furnishings. On April 12, 1945, when the first American soldiers arrived, they released a number of inmates from Niederhagen concentration camp, Joachim Escher among them. The former prisoners and U.S. soldiers completed the task of picking the castle clean. Among the items that disappeared were literally thousands of priceless medieval manuscripts, paintings, statues, rugs, tapestries, porcelain, silverware, coats of arms, a solid gold bathtub, Samurai swords, antique armor, firearms, fine furniture, and other precious objects. Thus Himmler's personal treasure passed out of his control.

Brigadeführer Karl Maria Wiligut-Weisthor's loyal secretary, Gabriele Winckler-Dechend, kept her children up late the night the reichsführer SS fled the Wewelsburg so they might be able to see their uncle Heinrich one final time. She later told me they were so sleepy that by the next day they had forgotten he had ever been there. Himmler had been thoughtful enough to leave a staff car behind at Gabriele's house so that her husband could sleep with her one final time before hurrying to catch up with his master.

Within a month, disguised as an ordinary Wehrmacht soldier, Heinrich Himmler would give himself up to a GI guarding a bridge who stubbornly refused to believe that this nondescript, bespectacled man could really be the leader of the dreaded Black Order. A day later the reichsführer SS committed suicide by taking a cyanide capsule in his cell. Conspiracy theories began to spring up almost immediately, hinting that the man who gave himself up to the Allies was really Himmler's double and that the true reichsführer was really still alive and at large, but I think this simply reflects the public's inability to accept that such an enormous evil could have come to so shabby and ignominious an end.

Some claim Otto Rahn's mysterious Pyrenean Grail was among the treasure hidden in the nearby salt mine at Merkers, while Colonel Howard Buechner insisted it had been smuggled by U-boat to a secret base at the pole. Either way it was clear that Elvis had left the building.

We stuck our 16 mm camera through the corroded bars, lighting the Hall of the Dead with our flashlights so that we could commit what we could to film before making tracks. Neither Mr. Horn nor I had the stomach to spend a moment longer in that place than we had to, retreating to a nearby guesthouse to recharge our batteries and regroup.

It was probably just another coincidence, but it was strange how swiftly our batteries seemed to discharge themselves in those subterranean passageways, as if the power was being sucked right out of them.

And when sleep finally came, I was troubled by a dream.

In the dream I was lost in a frozen landscape, somewhere in the far north, walls of ice rising on all sides—and there was blood everywhere. So much blood. Red rivers frozen into the ice, pouring down the rocks in suspended cataracts. I was searching, turning in circles trying to find where all that blood was coming from, wanting to know and not wanting to know at the same time. A breathless, awful sense of expectation hung in the thickening air.

I turned a corner in my sleep and realized I was not alone.

Twelve naked men were seated at a long table facing me, their bodies entirely covered with crimson ichor, and on the table lay the remains of the human being they were feeding on. I had interrupted their meal. As I looked into their eyes I realized at once they were dead and this was hell. Then, I woke up—at least I think I woke up—to find my body again, still on earth, which could well be a place in hell too. And hell was cold. Hell was beyond zero, beyond hypothermia. Hell was a place without love—and isn't evil at the end of the day only the absence of love?

A void.

11

The Fear

Germany 1938–1939 and Geneva 1998

Fear eats the soul. . . .

RAINER WERNER FASSBINDER

"Then comes the fear," muttered Paul. "At first a nagging fear and then the deep down fear that you are being followed. You pick up the phone and sometimes you hear a noise as if someone might be listening to you. You are in a café. At another table there is a man reading the newspaper. Then suddenly the newspaper goes down and he looks at you. Ah . . . he is a spy . . . and you are afraid and you stop talking with your friend. So comes the fear."

The sun had already settled over Lake Geneva and the office was vanishing into shadow. Paul Ladame's face was almost lost in the darkness. He had been talking for almost two days now. A long, difficult story rife with contradictions.

"I didn't return to Germany until I was sent to report on the Olympic Games of 1936 for French radio. During the games the town

The Fear 231

Fig. 11.1. The Fear, winter 1998—Mr. Horn sets up a shot outside the Schloss Wewelsburg, doing his best to ignore the two burly Germans of a certain age who were clearly tailing us.
Photos by Richard Stanley.

was lovely to look at, clean everywhere, everywhere flags, everywhere flowers, everywhere smiling people meeting foreigners and asking them, 'Are you are a foreigner? Welcome to Berlin during the games. You will see how happy we are.' And then comes September and the whole picture changes. Suddenly the people look at you and ask: 'What does that bloody foreigner do in Berlin? Why don't they just go home?'"

For a moment I thought about turning on the light but then decided against it, not wanting to break the spell.

"I was walking on the Kurfurstendam, the greatest street in Berlin, when suddenly, by chance, I meet Otto Rahn in SS uniform, in black uniform, in the uniform of Himmler—and I ask him in German, 'Mein lieber Otto, what are you doing in this uniform?' And he answered, looking to the right and to the left, as if to make certain no one was listening to what he said, 'My dear Paul, one has to eat.'"

Rahn had been mobilized as part of Operation Smile and, possibly because of his command of the French language, found himself press ganged into forming part of the reception committee laid on by the Nazi brass to greet the foreign teams and their supporters at the games. He apparently considered himself to be among the elite of the Nazi party because he had carried out the research on Heinrich Himmler's genealogy to provide proof of the reichsführer's Aryan ancestry and had come to believe he had direct access to the levers of power. In the hierarchy of the Third Reich however, he was, at best, a marginal figure, a mere cog in the machine.

"I had planned to take a flight to Leningrad or Moscow" continued Paul, choosing his words with care. "I went to the Russian embassy to get a visa. When I returned to my lodgings my aunt told me, 'Your friend Rahn has phoned several times.' So I ring back and he gives me the order, 'Paul, come as quickly as you can to meet me.' So I took the car of my uncle and drove through Berlin to his apartment where I discovered Rahn in uniform. He had a flask of French cognac and was quite a little bit drunk. He said, "Paul, you have been at the Russian embassy at ten minutes to twelve. You were allowed to bypass the queue and were out again ten minutes later. Proof that you are a spy. I have been asked to follow you and to report on who you meet, what telephone calls you get and what mail you receive. Paul, I can only give you one advice—get out of Germany as quickly as you can.'"

The aging expert in the methodology of information and disinformation insisted he had fallen under suspicion because of a series of unflattering cartoons he had drawn of the Nazi leadership he met during the games. Although I have not been able to access the relevant tailing report, I imagine the SS may have had good reason to be wary of Paul Ladame. His mother was born in Russia and his political leanings before and after the war betrayed deep-rooted socialist sympathies.

Paul shrugged. "What could I do? Just run away before I myself was taken prisoner or maybe even sent to one of the camps. He saved my life but who could help him? Who could help Rahn? Who could save him from what he had become?"

For a moment Paul met my gaze and I could tell the tone of regret in his rasping voice was real, even if the facts of his story may have been blurred and softened a little over the years. It was as if Paul felt compelled to somehow set the record straight while he still had the chance.

"That was the last time I was in Germany during the Hitler dictatorship and I have never seen Otto Rahn again" He abruptly looked away, turning his pale, watery eyes toward the dossier lying before him on the desktop. "Then in the spring of 1939, I received an anonymous letter addressed to me at the radio station in Paris. Inside the envelope was this obituary cut out neatly with a pair of scissors, saying that Otto had died in a snowstorm high on the Kufstein. They say he deliberately sat on top of the mountain until he froze, until his heart had finally turned to ice."

I shivered, squinting in the half-light at the simple, black-rimmed obituary written by Himmler's personal adjutant, a man whom Christian Bernadac insisted had been one of Otto's guests at the Hotel des Marronniers in Ussat-les-Bains back in '34—the lupus in fabula.

"In a snowstorm in the mountains in March, SS Obersturmführer

Fig. 11.2. The obituary of Otto Rahn.

Otto Rahn tragically departed this life. We mourn the loss of our comrade, a good and decent SS man and writer of notable historical, scholarly work—Chief of Personal Staff Reichsführer SS Karl Wolff SS Gruppenführer."

"What did you feel when you saw this?"

"I felt nothing," Paul murmured. "War had just been declared and there were other things on my mind. Otto had, you must admit, a very terrible life. A few years when Himmler protected him. And then came the day when Himmler could no longer protect him and that was the day he made the decision, when the war broke out, to take his own life. In the midst of the winter he died the death of a Cathar." Paul took off his glasses, polishing them on his plaid shirt and I saw at once his eyes were full of tears.

"That was my friend . . . Otto Rahn."

"The Cathar rite of endura. The death of a martyr." I shook my head, trying to make sense of Paul's words. It had not escaped my attention the date given for Rahn's alleged suicide (March 14, 1939) was just forty-eight hours shy of the anniversary of the fall of Montségur. "Perhaps it was the only way he could make his peace with God and escape the cycle of incarnation?"

Paul blinked. "He never used the word *God*. For him Lucifer might be something like God. God could be anything to anyone. God is a chemical in which we swim."

"If only we could find out what happened to him in that final year, what he experienced while he was still attached to Himmler's personal staff and then later in the camps, in Dachau and Buchenwald."

Paul shook his head slowly, scowl deepening. "I'm sure that it would be fascinating, but who could tell you that? Who the hell could ever know a thing like that?"

CARCASSONNE—SPRING 1998

Suzanne Nelli drew herself a little closer to the fire, petting her trembling chihuahua, the fourth dog she'd owned named Leika since the death of her husband, René. I was back in the south of France and while it was a few degrees warmer than Switzerland, it was still too early in the year for summer to have dropped the other shoe.

"We don't know for certain what became of him. Did he disappear in the snow and the fog? Well, valleys, snow, and fog often mean death. Or was he killed because they found out about his Jewish ancestry?" She looked at me closely, a little puzzled by my lack of visible response. "Otto Rahn was a Jew. Didn't you know?" There was a gloating, half-mocking tone to Madame Nelli's voice. "Through his mother. Clara. Clara Hamburger. It's possible he didn't even know until it was time for him to submit his Ahnenpass."

The Ahnenpass was one of the most grotesque forms of bureaucracy ever devised, a complex genealogical document that all German citizens were required to fill out in order to prove their racial purity. Curiously I later discovered that a copy of Otto's completed Ahnenpass was indeed on file at the Bundesarchiv in Berlin, confirming Madame Nelli's suspicions, but quite how it had ended up among the other public records remained a mystery. While the document had clearly been completed in Otto's familiar wilting hand, it had never been stamped or approved. Certainly to have deliberately submitted such a form, containing clear

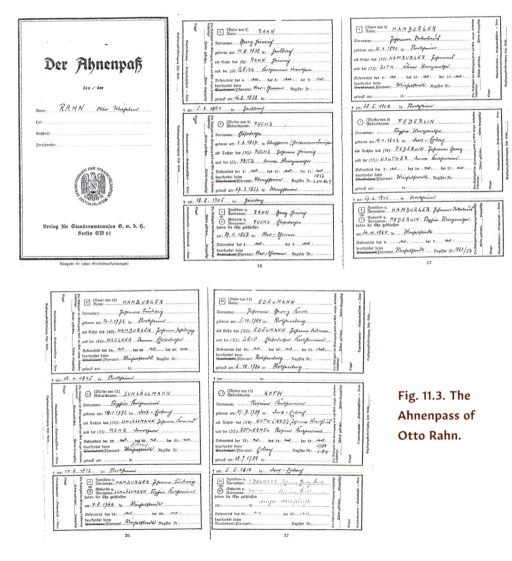

Fig. 11.3. The Ahnenpass of Otto Rahn.

proof of his Semitic ancestry, would have been tantamount to suicide. But why had Otto filled in this murderous document to begin with?

"Isn't truth the most important quality of knighthood?"

Madame Nelli gave me an appraising look, nose slightly upturned as if there was something about me that didn't quite come up to standard. "He was true to his ideals. In the end perhaps he died for them. His political and philosophical convictions were modulated by the visionary passion that characterized him, but also by the restraints of the official propaganda of the regime. His second book, *The Court of Lucifer*, may have contained Nazi propaganda but those who knew him agreed he was never an anti-Semite and with very good reason. In the end his disillusionment with the regime must have been complete."

"Then they killed him. It's obvious."

She shrugged, in that inimitably gallic manner that signifies so much more than just a shrug. "Could he have changed his identity? It was said he assumed the identity of his deceased brother and I think I should mention it was Christian Bernadac who told me this story. That he became a diplomat, in the Vatican, Lebanon, and different places."

"Christian told me that story too," I admitted. "But I don't think it's true. The consensus seems to be that he died in the spring of '39. Just like Paul Ladame says."

Madame Nelli sighed, long-sufferingly. She was once a great beauty but now as the head of the Centre for Cathar Studies in Carcassonne, she had become a kind of a right-wing dragon lady, notorious for getting up the noses of everyone who had dealings with her, myself included. In the course of befriending her, I had my tolerance tested to its limits.

"The problem of Otto Rahn is very complicated. He is an enigma. An enigma wrapped up in a mystery. I think I was alone in really understanding his sensitive side. He had the soul of a poet but he eventually had to prove himself to Himmler. First, by taking part in the Lebensborn program—the experiments into genetic engineering that Himmler had initiated in an attempt to breed a new race—a Fourth

Reich. Otto had this certificate so we have proof that he spent two weeks in this special clinic and left behind some essence of himself. There are probably twenty or thirty young Otto Rahns out there, somewhere, and the biggest joke of all is that they'd all be just as Jewish as he was."

I had been in Carcassonne for a week now, spending my days with a group of knights who were holding jousting tournaments on the patch of land between the city wall and the tower of the Inquisition, where the last of the prisoners from Montségur had been interred alive some seven centuries ago. For anyone seriously interested in chivalry, sword, lance, or bow—those maniacs were the best tutors one could hope to find and I was duly grateful to be back under blue Occitan skies, although this was tempered by my irritation at having to endure Madame Nelli's foibles and thinly veiled insults.

"Those employed by Himmler had to give him guarantees. These pledges weren't only spoken, they consisted of deeds as well. Deeds, in Otto's case, meant the writing of his second book. After this the best proof that he could give was to accept the crime. I'm not saying he killed with his own hands—but Otto Rahn agreed to serve with the deaths-head in the concentration camps. Buchenwald may not have been Auschwitz, but people died there. People were killed and he witnessed that. On the initiatory journey Otto Rahn passed through all the stages—and for him that journey ended in a precipice."

Beyond the shuttered windows, real life continued, but seated in Madame Nelli's library, we seemed set aside from time. The whole house felt like a museum, dominated by photographs of her late husband René, one of the co-founders of Déodat Roché's Society of the Remembrance whose books *La Philosophie du Catharisme* and *Ecritures Cathares* (1969) had revolutionized research into the so-called Albigensian heresy, going a long way toward establishing it as a form of gnostic dualism.

René Nelli's work in bringing together the surviving Cathar rituals and establishing the central archive in Carcassonne had clearly been invaluable, but he had also translated Otto's work into French, adding several anti-Semitic passages to the original text in the process. There were clear discrepancies between the original German edition of *The Court of Lucifer* and the later French publication that had been pointed out to me by Paul Ladame back in Geneva, all of which seemed to indicate that René, for all his erudition had drunk somewhat more deeply from the right wing Kool-Aid than Otto. I discretely set aside the notes on his translation I found folded into the presentation copy of the first edition I admired in the Nelli's private library, furtively passing them to JB who hurriedly photocopied the relevant pages while I kept Madame talking.

"Otto Rahn arrived in Montségur around the time of the first neo-Cathar conferences with Déodat Roché and truly at these conferences there was an atmosphere of fraternity," continued Madame Nelli. "We had the impression that the people present had common interests, something that mattered to them, something important. The Countess de Pujol Murat served as a mentor of sorts. She united friends and sympathizers with regard to archaeology, with regard to religion, and with regard to the Grail and spiritism. They held séances in those days. La Comtesse was a spiritist. Do you know what that is?"

I nodded. "As far as I remember it's an offshoot of the nineteenth-century spiritualist movement that, stop me if I'm wrong, embraced the theory of reincarnation. I believe the term was coined by the esotericist Hippolyte Rivail, who wrote under the pseudonym Kardec. Like Conan Doyle, I think Rivail was searching for a form of scientific spiritualism building on the work of Swedenborg."

For once Madame Nelli looked impressed and I felt duly grateful that in this respect at least, I had done my homework, delving through dozens of turgid late nineteenth- and early twentieth-century texts in the hope of gaining a better understanding of the shadowy context of Rahn's life and work.

"A science that deals with the nature, origin, and destiny of spirits, and their relationship with the corporeal world." Madame Nelli nodded. "Rivail rejected Mesmer's theories of animal magnetism as an explanation for the phenomena he witnessed in the séances of the time and sought demonstrable proofs for the survival of consciousness outside the body. I believe his teachings are still popular in Brazil and Vietnam where they form the basis of a syncretic faith known as *Dao Cao Dai*, or Caodaism, that actually hails Kardec as a prophet of a new religion."

"And the countess, you say, was one of his disciples?" I frowned, taking this detail on board. "A spirit medium or a channeler?"

"I think la Comtesse believed she was in contact with the spirit of her own ancestor, Esclarmonde de Foix, a figure Otto Rahn identifies in his first book as the guardian of the Grail."

I raised one eyebrow. "She was channeling Esclarmonde? The thirteenth-century high priestess? Like some sort of past-life thing?"

Suzanne Nelli's comment pricked my interest. From what I could gather there had certainly been a whole lot of "channeling" going on at Montségur over the years. It seemed the mountain had lain dormant for centuries only to stir with the birth of a linguistic recovery movement known as the Felibrige, who set about trying to preserve and revive the Occitan language in the late nineteenth century.

The story of the last and greatest of the Cathar high priestesses was first popularized in a fanciful account entitled *Histoires des Albigeois* (History of the Albigensians) written by baptist pastor Napoleon Peyrat in 1870, allegedly to counter the Catholic cult of Joan of Arc. Operas were written about her and in 1911 there was a move to erect a statue to na Esclarmonda in Foix, the administrative capital of the Ariège. Somewhere around this time, the disembodied Cathar high priestess began to appear as an increasingly popular guest in séances as far afield as Paris. In keeping with the theosophically fueled mystical revival sweeping *fin de siècle* France, Esclarmonde and the Cathar perfecti were repositioned as ascended masters generally espousing a sort of woolly blend of proto–New Age anti-materialism and preclassical Eastern mysticism.

"I don't think *channeled* is quite the right word," mused Madame Nelli. "I don't think the countess believed na Esclarmonda had ever really died. She was supposed to have transcended this world and the cycles of time, attaining, as was taught in their faith, that abode where fire has no heat, water no fluidity, and matter no substance."

"I'm afraid you're getting a little ahead of me there."

"La Comtesse claimed to be in direct contact with the immortal chatelaine of the castle—*la dame blanche*, na Esclarmonda. She gave the impression she had met the Good Lady many times on the mountain, in the north-facing tower. She talked about how proud it made her feel to see her own ancestor standing before her in the starlight."

I shivered.

"And the other members of the group? Did they also believe in these ascended masters?"

Madame Nelli narrowed her eyes, not understanding where I was going with this. "La Comtesse was the last of an ancient line. Perhaps she was the recipient of some hereditary transmission, if not the second sight. She certainly inherited a great deal of property, including a castle on the Black Mountain outside Carcassonne and the ruins of Lordat in the Ariège and could afford to indulge her fantasies. Otto Rahn saw her as a potential patron. A patron and a financier. By the late 1920s she was almost single-handedly supporting the whole neo-Cathar revival."

"I don't know what was going on on that mountaintop seventy years ago," I mused, "but from the sounds of it, this countess not only had an open checkbook but deliberately surrounded herself with some pretty unsavory characters who had ample incentive to provide the phony evidence she was looking for. Even Rivail admitted a great many mediumistic phenomena could be explained by fraud, hallucinations, or unconscious mental activity. Egregores and tulpic projections aside, how do we know the countess wasn't being gulled by someone tricked out in a medieval veil and Scooby-Doo skin paint?"

"Scoo-bee-doo?" Madame's frown deepened, not getting the reference. She didn't have any appreciable sense of humor and my attempts at levity only baffled her.

I knew my skepticism was a knee-jerk reaction but the notion that Rahn's patron believed herself to be in direct contact with na Esclarmonda, the immortal high priestess of the Cathars, rattled me. Could the spiritual exercises of the Albigenses have allowed them to reach across the centuries to fulfill Bélibaste's prophecy? But even if the last high priestess of the Cathars had been able to transcend the material world and gain nonlinear access to the program, why would the saint of saints of a pacifist religion that revered all living things choose to manifest herself to a motley assortment of crypto-fascists and Nazi fifth columnists?

"I'm not sure la Comtesse shared Rahn's dreams of reviving an authentically European, essentially Western spiritual tradition—a pan-European neo-paganism, you could say—but it is certain she deliberately brought him to Montségur, and when she told him it was the chateau of the Graal it fired his imagination with all the phantasmagoria of the Round Table. Like the countess, he lived in legends and it was with a chimeric imagination that he saw Occitania." Madame Nelli leaned closer, hands weaving more fiercely as her expression hardened. "Besides, he was apparently haunted by demons. When he was alone he would cry out. He had presences, things like that." She wrinkled her nose as if at an intolerable smell, the look of disgust deepening in her eyes. "For me he was a little like the Antichrist, a prisoner of the forces of evil. He acted the way he did because he was looking for a form of purity. A purity of race perhaps? But to the extent of exterminating them? All he had to do was exile them, send them back to their own country. But to make them die, in the manner he made them die was terrible. There's nothing more terrible than that."

Leika IV, the chihuahua, gazed at Madame Nelli blankly, ears quivering as her mistress subsided back into her chair, apparently spent. For a while we were both silent. Then, she spoke again, more softly this time.

"But he recounted that one time he had met some Cathars. It was a dream, he dreamt while awake, that he had met these Cathars, what they had told him and all that. It stirred up his profound thoughts. He started to think this world was an illusion, the shadow of another reality, a game, and then he realized that he could no longer accept what the Nazis were saying. He threw himself headlong into poetry, the songs of the troubadours, his childhood under the apple trees where he took his siestas. But he was still an SS man. He made reports. He certainly carried out his duties. So you can't forget he was a Nazi with all the consequences such an attitude carries."

Fig. 11.4. Esclarmonde, depicted on Opera Romanesqeue poster.

12

Summer Solstice at Montségur

Midsummer 1998

You cannot hope to penetrate the labyrinth by moving in a straight line.

URANIE, THE SORCERER OF THE RIVER OF COLORS

By the solstice we had come full circle and Mr. Horn and I found ourselves back on the summit of Montségur, none the wiser. We sat with our cameras on the steps of the chateau's north-facing tower, where the countess claimed to have once encountered the specter of her own ancestor, nor were we the only ones waiting for the dawn. At least a thousand pilgrims had gathered at the base of the mountain, divided into three camps, Occitan nationalists, Catalan separatists, and for some incomprehensible reason, French Legionnaires. Their fires burned through the night and from the keep we could hear their voices drifting up to us, raised in curious songs, peculiar to their regions and dialects.

Toward morning a procession wound its way up the west face toward the tower, a formation of approximately twelve young men in short-

Fig. 12.1. Montségur, midsummer.
Photo by James "JB" Bourne.

sleeved khaki uniforms and flat military caps, burning brands held aloft in their right hands. Their leader was about my age, a paunchy individual with close-cropped, bleached hair. He was distinguished from the others by a single fingerless glove on his right hand. Lacking a proper introduction, we took to calling him "Black Glove" and his companions "the boy scouts." They were the first real neo-Nazis we had encountered since setting forth on Otto's trail and they were clearly none too pleased to see us.

Black Glove came up the steps first, his eyes meeting mine. In that instant, in the flickering firelight, I found myself face to face at last with a tangible nemesis, if not with the devil, then the naked face of intolerance—puffy features surrounding piggy, blue eyes like I'd seen a thousand times before back in South Africa and other places south. We resolutely stood our ground, refusing to vacate the tower to allow them to perform whatever ritual they might have had in mind. Wary of our cameras, Black Glove and his whelps decided to forgo their ceremony and sullenly settled down outside the tower to wait for dawn.

By morning there were approximately three hundred people crowded into and around the keep and as the first sliver of the rising sun showed above the rim of the earth everything happened just the way that it was supposed to.

Somehow the east-facing embrasures caught and focused the first faint rays, marking out a rectangle of light on the inner side of one of the slits in the opposing wall of the keep. As the sun climbed higher, its rays intensified so the colors visible within the west-facing slit deepened and brightened, taking on a vibrant hue like blood or fire, like no stone I've ever seen before.

The fortress of Montségur is oriented toward the cardinal points of the compass and built on such a strange plan that close study has led to numerous theories, including the notion that it is a solar or lunar temple. The ground plan of the castle mirrors the shape of the constellation Arcturus, known colloquially as *la bouvier, lo boier*, or simply the "shepherdess." There is no documentary evidence, however, of any connection between Catharism and sun worship, any more than there is with visiting extraterrestrials. Moreover, the castle we see today cannot be as it was in 1205 when Raimond de Pereilha, at the request of Esclarmonde de Foix, the venerable high priestess, fortified the existing ruins of what was, in all likelihood, a former pagan temple.

After the siege of 1244 the castle was granted to the de Levis family and the structure underwent a number of changes. Despite the passage of more than seven centuries, the mysterious solar phenomena have continued to manifest every year, weather allowing, with stubborn regularity. Indeed, you could practically set your watch by them. The annual light show in the north-facing tower is one of the few "supernatural" phenomena on this haunted Earth courteous enough to not only be repeatable, but to stick to a regular timetable. Strangely enough, the report filed by GRAME, who conducted the only detailed archaeological survey of the fortress in 1969–1976, glibly slides around the issue, insisting the "alleged solar phenomena in the donjon keep have not been

Fig. 12.2. Summer solstice at the keep. Photos by Richard Stanley.

scientifically documented, witnessed or verified"—whatever the heck that means.

According to Otto Rahn's field notes, the citadel of Montségur was in ancient times a sanctuary dedicated to the goddess Belisenna or Belisama, the Astarte-Artemis-Diana of the Celto-Iberian folk. Astarte was the Paredra de Baal in Phoenician theogony, Artemis was the sister of Apollo in Greek mythology, and Belisenna (the moon) was the wife of Abellio (the sun) in the Celto-Iberian cosmos of divinities. Accordingly, it made perfect sense that the keep on the mountaintop was aligned to the seasonal positions of the sun and the moon. Indeed it was not beyond possibility the mythic Grail was really nothing less than the geometric construction of the castle itself, the "marriage of the sun and the moon" symbolizing the harmonization and reconciliation of opposing principles, something that by its very nature is an impossibility.

By approximately 6:10 a.m. a second rectangle had appeared in one of the adjacent embrasures while three squares of light began to smoulder on the upper reaches of the chamber's western wall.

Fig. 12.3. The keep at 6:10 a.m.
Photo by Richard Stanley.

For a moment it was as if the whole castle were awakening, glowing portals opening in the stone, the rays of light criss-crossing the keep. Everyone assembled—young and old, Occitan and Catalan alike—seemed intent on reaching into the beams, trying to touch the light as if hoping to suffuse themselves with its energy.

"*Putain Américains*," hissed Black Glove, misjudging our nationality. He spoke in French, underestimating our ability to understand his every word. "*Ils ne comprennent rien*. It's the secret of the Gods but only we know."

The scene was strangely dreamlike and I couldn't help but feel as if Mr. Horn and I were adrift in an esoteric aquarium in which the only other fish were plainly piranhas.

Normally for this kind of thing you need a prism. So what gives?

The intensity of the colors visible in the keep's embrasures are in all probability achieved by the castle's long-forgotten architects making use of the density of the Earth's atmosphere as a natural prism. Air molecules in the atmosphere, while invisible to the naked eye, have relative substance and reflective qualities similar to more substantial objects

Fig. 12.4. The keep at 6:13 a.m. Photo by Richard Stanley.

250   Summer Solstice at Montségur

**Fig. 12.5. The keep at 6:14 a.m.
Photo by Richard Stanley.**

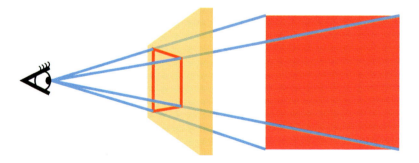

Fig. 12.6. Prism diagram.

on the Earth's surface. At dawn on the summer solstice, the rays of the rising sun have to pass through a greater amount of atmosphere before reaching the east-facing arrow slits than at any other time, filtering out all other parts of the light spectrum save for those jack-o-lantern oranges and richly infernal reds.

We watched in silence, documenting the ghostly display on 16 mm, realizing we were receiving a garbled message from the other side of time whose true meaning we would never understand.

After approximately twenty minutes, sharp black shadows began to edge into the fiery rectangles like fangs or the blades of a closing portcullis and by 6:30 a.m. the infernal glow had dwindled to nothing. Almost at once the crowd began to disperse. I would later learn from firsthand observation that the solar phenomena are visible for approximately seven days on either side of the solstice before going dark for another twelve months.

**Fig. 12.7. The keep at 6:15 a.m.
Photo by Richard Stanley.**

Fig. 12.8. The keep at 6:16 a.m. Photo by Richard Stanley.

Summer Solstice at Montségur 253

Fig. 12.9. The keep at 6:25 a.m.
Photo by Richard Stanley.

I was told by one seasoned solstice goer, a bearded old Catalan gentleman, that since the industrial revolution, the smog accumulating over the flatlands had begun to interfere with the intensity of those first rays, and coupled with the shifting weather patterns, had caused the yearly light show to grow somewhat erratic. It had apparently been four years since it last took place with the same intensity as we saw that morning and it might be another four years before it happened again. What any of it meant was beyond me, although I realized things do tend to come in cycles—moons, times of the month, reincarnation, wars, the whole damn thing. I only wished I had the smarts to calculate what those stars might have looked like a thousand years ago when the foundations of the keep were first hewn from the raw bedrock of the mountain.

The castle's alignment to the sun and the moon has led historians and New Age gurus alike to lazily identify the keep's builders with the heliocentric Celts. In point of fact, the building has little or nothing in common with the megaliths of Stonehenge, Avebury, or Newgrange. Its construction is without precedent and we have no clue as to its purpose, only a series of vague conjectures regarding the citadel's function as a vast stone calendar, regulating the planting of crops or whatever seasonal rites the ancient inhabitants of these high valleys celebrated.

I learned from the old Catalan mountaineer we spoke to in the tower room that a similar, albeit less visually spectacular, alignment occurred at the other end of the year, on the morning of the winter solstice. Subsequent firsthand observation confirmed that the rising midsummer moon was directly in line with the almost vaginal south-facing embrasure in the tower and the mysterious platform immediately beneath it. The sun and the moon switch azimuths between one solstice and another, a difference of 33 degrees, so in midwinter the sun aligns with the southerly embrasure and the moon rises in line with the eastern apertures. This measurement, known as the "goose foot" is a key proportion in gothic architecture and is reflected in the remains of the north-facing tower's arched ceiling. This apparent alignment to not only the moon but the stars as well dispels the notion that a purely heliocentric culture was at work, hinting at a far more complex understanding of the physical universe.

An unsubstantiated account claims that during the celebration of the spring equinox shortly before the castle's capitulation in 1244, a message was sent to the leader of the besieging crusaders dug in about the mountain's flanks that read something like, "The body of our lord has become flesh. Please come and take a look"—an offer the prelate nervously declined. Was it possible that "smoke and shadow" could be woven together to create an illusory egregore miraculous enough for its adherents to go willingly to the stake and convert other onlookers in the full knowledge their lives too would be forfeit? Given what I'd heard about Pierre Roger de Mirepoix's penchant for phosphorescent

Summer Solstice at Montségur   255

Fig. 12.10. The sun's rays enter the keep on the morning of the winter solstice, December 21, 2001. Photo by Richard Stanley.

paint, the notion that it may have all come down to some form of medieval sleight of hand was not entirely beyond thinking. Yet could such an apparition, artfully conjured by the castle's occult geometry, still be so potent after seven centuries to inspire Otto Rahn and his shadowy cohorts to wage a secret war against the forces of the one God, against the Christians and Jews whom the young SS officer perceived as the descendants of an alien, usurper tradition?

I certainly wasn't prepared to consider that a genuine supernatural force might be at work, let alone that the last high priestess of the Cathars might still be alive and covertly directing an otherworldly rearguard action against "consensus reality." If I was going to get any answers, I knew I would have to penetrate the shadows of those prewar years.

13

The Stones from the Sky

They live from a Stone whose essence is most pure. If you have never heard of it I shall name it for you here. It is called "Lapsit exillis." By virtue of this stone the Phoenix is burned to ashes, in which he is reborn—Thus does the Phoenix moult its feathers!

WOLFRAM VON ESCHENBACH, *PARZIVAL*

The summer of 1998 was almost over and the end of the century was in sight. The knights had ridden their last joust in Carcassonne by the time I found myself standing on the curb outside the gutted shell of the Hotel des Marronniers. I had passed through Ussat-les-Bains half a dozen times before but always the silence and dereliction of its streets caused me to hurry by. The tiny settlement, really just a cluster of houses surrounding the abandoned spa, had seen better days, its mock-Bavarian rooftops warped with age. There were no signs of children or household pets although here and there were traces of habitation, a twitching curtain in a closed window or the occasional battered vehicle rusting silently at the curb. The exterior of the church was pockmarked with what appeared to be bullet holes, possibly damage incurred during the war and the locked door didn't look as if it

Fig. 13.1. The Stones from the Sky.
Photo by Hamilton White.

had been open to the public in many a moon. Peering through the keyhole I noticed the pews had been removed and the interior piled high with old hose pipes, rusting lawn mowers, and other disused municipal equipment.

The premises seemed utterly abandoned, clearly lacking any congregation or continuing relevance as a place of Christian worship.

A short walk from the locked church, on the banks of the icy Ariège stands a curious monument, commonly known as the Galaad memorial, which was erected by Antonin Gadal and his followers in the Lectorium Rosicrucianum shortly before the old man's death in 1962. A granite block, a replica of an ancient altar unearthed by the former minister of tourism in the nearby Bethlehem Grotto, stands in the center of a ring of twelve marker stones while a plaque at the base of the altar bears the sign of the pentagram and a dedication to the "Threefold Alliance of the Light, the Cathar Grail, and the Rosy Cross." The monument, referred to by Gadal as the "Rock of

258 The Stones from the Sky

Fig. 13.2. As above, so below—the Galaad memorial, or the Rock of Testimony, on the banks of the Ariège. Photo by Richard Stanley.

Fig. 13.3. Plaque on the Galaad memorial—the threefold alliance of the Light, the Grail, and the Rosy Cross. Photo by Richard Stanley.

Testimony," bears silent witness not only to the secret societies of the past but to the continuing influence their adherents still wield over the area, given that these ersatz megaliths were evidently far better maintained than the all but forgotten church.

The hotel that once served as Otto Rahn's headquarters had long since fallen derelict and was marked for demolition, its interior walls stripped back to yield up copper wire and anything else of value. I made my way cautiously up the sagging stairs, finding little that was helpful. Since the war the building had been repurposed to serve as the offices of the local electricity board before being summarily abandoned and left to rot. The attic was hot and airless, filled with cobwebs and just for a moment I thought I caught the faint tang of darkroom chemicals, but it was probably only my imagination and the smell of the old paint, peeling and blistering in the meridional sun. The broken windows in the master bedroom still opened to a view of the Tabor, the mountain of transfiguration, and that at least gave me pause for thought, knowing Otto must have woken to that sight every morning. I stood staring at the massif's brooding outline, wondering what secret the young Grail seeker had pried from the mountain's depths and what that moment of discovery might have been like.

Leaving the condemned hotel to its slow decline, I doubled back across the river to locate the home of the late Antonin Gadal, a controversial figure whom Paul Ladame described to me as the "master, the meister, the guru of Rahn."

The deceased patriarch's ramshackle two-story cottage looked like something out of a fairy tale, only the kind of fairy tale that doesn't have a happy ending. The windows were boarded up and the garden a jungle of untended weeds. The sun-bleached porch creaked beneath my feet as I tiptoed around the side of the house, searching for an open window. Just then one of the shutters burst open and I realized to my shock the dilapidated building was still inhabited, catching a smell of stale air and sour wine. An unkempt, middle-aged man, with bloodshot blue eyes, glared fiercely out at me, his face almost hidden by a long,

Fig. 13.4. The Gadal house, Ussat-les-Bains.
Photo by James "JB" Bourne.

silver-streaked beard that grew high on his cheeks. He initially took me for a thief or a prowler, which I guess I was, but mellowed somewhat as I haltingly explained I was researching the life of the house's former occupant.

Uttering an irritable grunt, the hermit pointed me in the direction of the neighboring property and its owner, a man named Christian Koenig, whom he insisted was the only one left who could tell me about the time before the war.

Later I learned the grizzled recluse had in fact been Gadal's grandson who apparently made a point of never speaking about the past or what exactly had gone wrong for Ussat-les-Bains.

It took the better part of a week to track down the enigmatic Monsieur Koenig who turned out to be the former curator of a museum Gadal established in the neighboring town of Tarascon to house the relics retrieved from the caves in his original prewar excavations. The museum had been shut down a couple years ago, after the regional government had begun to take an undue interest in some of the items on display. The artifacts had since been dispersed into private hands, presumably to prevent them from being confiscated by the authorities. I suspected the lion's share of those enigmatic relics were probably still in Monsieur Koenig's possession. At first we traded messages through the office of a local psychiatrist, Valerie Tercine, who was a personal acquaintance of the former curator and tried to broker a meeting. Monsieur Koenig however grew reticent when he learned I was a documentary filmmaker. While I omitted any direct reference to Otto Rahn or the Nazis from our initial correspondence, he nonetheless feared I might be trying to forge a link between the apparently benign Rosicrucian movement and the then-current Solar Temple murders. This caught me by surprise as I had not been hitherto aware of any such linkage. Subsequent research, however, turned up a slew of surprises.

The initial excavations at Montségur and on the countess's property at Lordat had been conducted by the Brotherhood of the Polaires, which ceased to exist at the onset of World War II and whose leadership had long since been discredited. There are those, however, among them French esoteric researcher André Wautier, who claim that some of the former members of the Polaires joined forces with the remains of the German Thule Society to found a new order in 1945, known as *L'Ordre Vert*—the so-called Green Order—that continued its activities well into the 1960s. This Green Order supposedly merged in 1976 with the German *Luzifer Gesellschaft*, or Lucifer Society, whose rites, based on the so-called Red Mass, were, according to Wautier "less demonic than those of the Satanic Gnosis." The Lucifer Society's adherents apparently honored Mithra, Kali, and Lilith, as well as the light bringer, and successfully established lodges in Cologne, Belgium, and France, where they became known as L'Internationale Luciférienne. One of their foremost initiates was a French neo-Templar grand master named Julien Origas (1920–1983), a right-wing political activist and known wartime collaborator. Origas had been a prominent figure in L'Ordre Martiniste Traditionnel as well as a member of AMORC, the American Rosicrucian Order founded by H. Spencer Lewis. In the early '70s, Origas launched a group known as *L'Ordre Renové du Temple*, or "Renewed Order of the Solar Temple" (ROTS) that included among its core membership, the homeopath and neo-Nazi sympathizer Luc Jouret (1947–1994) and Rosicrucian initiate Joseph Di Mambro (1924–1994), a duo who would eventually achieve infamy as the leaders of L'Ordre du Temple Solaire, the notorious Sovereign Order of the Solar Temple (or OTS), whose grisly history of mass murder and ritual suicide continues to defy easy comprehension or analysis.

The OTS was founded in 1952 by French author Jacques Breyer who based his plans for the order upon the modern myth of the continuing existence of the Knights Templar. The order's aims were apparently to prepare humanity for the Second Coming of Christ as a solar god-king. The movement's activities were a mix of early Protestant Christianity and New Age philosophy, using adapted Masonic rituals and drawing further inspiration from the teachings of Max Heindel's

Rosicrucian fellowship, the Hermetic Order of the Golden Dawn, and British occultist Aleister Crowley, who headed the Order of Oriental Temple (Ordo Templi Orientis, or OTO). Joseph Di Mambro and Luc Jouret revived the order in 1984, shortly after Breyer's death, establishing lodges in Switzerland, France, Austria, Quebec, and Martinique. In its early years the order attracted a number of wealthy and influential patrons, including Princess Grace of Monaco who was reputedly initiated into the movement shortly before her death. The order's leadership was known as the Synarchy of the Temple and its top thirty-three members were referred to as the Elder Brothers of the Rosy Cross.

Their quasi-Masonic ceremonies required adherents to make expensive purchases, including jewelery, costumes, regalia, and the payment of hefty initiation fees. During these rites members wore crusader-type robes and revered a sword that Di Mambro claimed was an authentic Templar artifact, given to him in a previous incarnation a thousand years ago.

In October 1994, an infant, Emmanuel Dutoit, barely three months old, was killed at the group's center in Morin Heights, Quebec. The child had been stabbed repeatedly with a wooden stake. Apparently Di Mambro ordered the murder, having identified the baby as the Antichrist, whom he believed had been born into the order to prevent him from succeeding in his spiritual aims.

A few days later, Di Mambro and twelve followers performed a ritual last supper before embarking on a spate of simultaneous murders and mass suicides in Switzerland and Quebec. Fifteen inner-circle members committed suicide with poison, thirty were killed by bullets or smothering, and eight died by other causes. Autopsies later indicated many of the victims had been drugged, possibly to prevent them from objecting. The buildings where the mass murders took place were then set on fire by timer devices, purportedly as one last symbol of the group's purification.

In total, forty-eight human beings perished in the wholesale slaughter that took place in Sion, Switzerland, where a number of the dead were found in a secret underground chapel lined with mirrors and other elements of neo-Templar symbolism. The bodies were dressed in the order's ceremonial robes and laid twelve to a circle, their feet pointing outward like the spokes of a wheel. Most of the dead had plastic bags tied over their faces before being shot in the head. It is believed that the plastic bags were a symbol of the ecological disaster that would befall the human race after the OTS members moved on to Sirius. Farewell letters left by the deceased cult members stated that they believed they were leaving to escape the "hypocrisies and oppression of this world."

I couldn't help but think of those twelve skeletons found arranged in an identical pattern in the mass grave on the countess's property, the twelve marker stones surrounding the Galaad memorial, the twelve little pips surrounding the Croix Occitan, the so-called Cathar cross—and those twelve empty plinths in the Hall of the Dead in the north tower of the SS order castle, the ceremonial chamber that Heinrich Himmler had intended to form the symbolic mittelpunkt der welt and the center of the Nazi Grail cult.

A mayor, a journalist, a civil servant, and a sales manager were among the victims in Switzerland and records seized by police in Quebec indicate that some OTS members had personally donated more than a million dollars to the group's leaders. Another attempted mass suicide of remaining OTS members was thwarted in the late 1990s. All these suicide/murders and subsequent attempts occurred around the dates of the equinoxes and solstices in accordance with the beliefs of the group. In 1997 a small house exploded into flames in Saint-Casimir, Quebec, leaving a further five charred corpses for the police to pull from the rubble. Three teenagers aged thirteen, fourteen, and sixteen, the children of one of the couples that died in the fire, were discovered in a shed behind the house, alive but heavily drugged.

Michael Tabachnik, an internationally renowned Swiss musician and conductor, was arrested as an alleged leader of the revived Solar Temple in the late 1990s and indicted for "participation in a criminal organization" and murder. He came to trial in Grenoble, France, during the spring of 2001 only to be acquitted.

French prosecutors appealed the verdict and an appellate court ordered a second trial beginning on October 24, 2006. He was again cleared on December 20 and rumors began to circulate shortly afterward that the movement had purchased land in the Rennes-les-Château area where they had allegedly made common cause with the OTO, who had come into conflict with the stringent new anti-cult legislation passed into French law as a result of the killings. The OTO's activities in the region drew the attention of the Assemblée Nationale, who described the formation as a "proscribed cult" in report number 2468. Regardless of whether the original death cult was still in business or not, it was clear I was going to have to treat my informants with kid gloves if I was going to have any chance of coaxing the truth out of them.

After several weeks of circling, Christian Koenig finally agreed to meet Mr. Horn, JB, and myself in a cave just outside Ussat-les-Bains. The Grotto of Ornolac, or more commonly, the *eglise*, or church, had apparently served as a place of worship for the fugitive heretics in days of old.

Fig. 13.5. Christian Koenig, master troubadour and neo-Cathar patriarch. Photo by Richard Stanley.

When we arrived at the stipulated locale, I was surprised to find it was the very same cavern where Cat, Mike Dee, and I had encountered the hermit, Uriel, on the night after the storm four years previously.

Christian turned out to be younger than I expected for a museum curator, a tall, elegant man dapperly dressed in a tailored black suit that seemed at odds with the prehistoric location. His high, balding forehead spoke of a keen intellect and unusual sensitivity while his full beard was vaguely suggestive of an Old Testament prophet. About his neck he wore a simple, yet curious pendant—a gleaming, black stone, the like of which I had never seen before. It was Christian's very calmness and the stillness of his gaze that made the deepest impression. Placing an unusually shaped black case on one of the limestone boulders, he popped its clasps to reveal a set of pan pipes. Then, settling himself on a rock in the center of the grotto, he confounded me further by casually continuing where Uriel had left off, picking up the same melody that had followed me into my sleep and haunted my dreams all those years ago—a tune I now recognized as the "Shepherdess song," allegedly a Cathar hymn to the constellation of Arcturus, known in the Occitan dialect as Lo Boier or Le Bouvier.

I listened, transfixed. It seemed beyond reason, beyond coincidence, whatever a "coincidence" may be. I recalled the look in Uriel's eyes, the figures I had seen in the courtyard during the storm, and the manner in which they seemed to touch fingers and form a circle in the very midst of that incandescent vortex.

Fulcanelli, the master alchemist, discussing the initiatory ladder depicted in the central bas relief on the great porch of Notre Dame de Paris, suggests that for an initiate to become an adept one must literally climb an analogic ladder of correspondences, in other words—follow the coincidences, the incongruous links and sympathies that led us from one seemingly unrelated idea and apparently random experience to the next—or as Agent Cooper puts it in *Twin Peaks*, "When two things happen simultaneously pertaining to the same object of inquiry we must pay special attention."

Christian Koenig smiled, a strange, humorless smile. The caves, he told me, were well known for their "unusual acoustic properties." I glanced about myself at the arched ceiling and those notches cut into the rock that had once served as sconces for candles. "Words and echoes linger for longer here than anyone might normally think possible," he offered, as if this explained everything.

Something ancient was reawakening in these mountains, Christian told us. Something that never really died but lay dormant for seven centuries. According to Christian, the Inquisition succeeded in destroying the written records of the Cathar faith—and any historical accounts that had come down to us were contaminated by their perverted ideology. The true faith survived only as an oral tradition—in the folklore of the region and in the songs of the troubadours and *minne* singers, literally the "seekers" and "memory" singers. He suggested that Antonin Gadal had been the recipient of just such a tradition, passed down to him by Papa Garigou, the old blind man he had cared for in his youth.

"I think on his journey through life, Gadal attained a certain illumination, and he reached that through the caves," Christian continued, deeply at ease in our timeless, albeit somewhat tenebrous surroundings. "He believed these caves played an important role in the formation of the Cathar spirit. He said there are places here where the Spirit still whispers."

"And the Grail?"

Christian nodded slowly. "Gadal sometimes spoke of a cup or a bowl." That fleeting smile came again—and then just as suddenly it was gone, Christian's expression hardening once more. "He described it as the object of a cult—the 'Graal Pyrenean' and even spoke of the 'Sangraal.' For some it is pure esoteric delirium . . ." Christian's voice tailed off and for a moment I thought he was going to leave it there, but he must have seen the look in my eyes. This wasn't answer enough. "However, it is curious," he added. "If we look more closely at the manuscript of Wolfram von Eschenbach, who was himself a troubadour traveling Europe, we can see in his text the Grail is a stone, *Lapsit exillis*, the "stone from the sky," and it is said that one who sees the stone or comes close to it will have eternal life and will be healed. That's how the fisher king, the guardian of the castle of the Grail, was cured from his wound." He paused as a swallow circled us before disappearing into the shadowy eaves of the grotto where it made its nest.

"Otto Rahn believed it was a stone," I mused, slipping the German Grail seekers name into the conversation. "The crown or diadem of Lucifer. If Gadal fancied himself as Galahad, then Otto was certainly a latter-day Parsifal—a twentieth-century quest knight."

"Perhaps he saw in Rahn, a fellow spirit," Christian concurred. "And a possible successor."

"A successor?"

"Someone has to guard the mystery." Christian fixed me with his gaze as if looking into the narrows of my soul. "Someone has to transmit the flame to the ones that come after."

I shivered.

"In the Cathar rites it is clearly stated their tradition comes from the apostles and is transmitted from bonhomme to bonhomme, and it will always be that way," he continued calmly. "One cannot influence anyone to believe in something they do not discover for themselves. Truth has to be born inside one, in your soul, in your body, in your spirit. It's like a flower that needs to open itself through another dimension. You cannot force that flower to open."

Speaking slowly, in an even tone, Christian confirmed that in the early 1930s Otto Rahn and Antonin Gadal collaborated on a series of unofficial digs, unearthing a plethora of artifacts that would later form the basis for the collection housed at the museum in Tarascon. Otto found clues in Wolfram's text, Christian suggested, particularly when it came to the character of the hermit Trevrizent who was said to live in the "grotto of the wild fountain," *Fontanet de Savage*. Otto believed this hermit to be a Cathar adept who could "eat neither flesh nor fowl" and who initiated the young Grail seeker into the mysteries of his faith. Christian pointed out that we stood not 500 meters (less than a third of a mile) from the mouth of a cave known locally as Fontanet where Otto and Gadal had allegedly discovered something unimaginable. According to Christian they had unearthed, from within a hollow stalagmite surrounded by the blackened bones of former knights, an ancient meteoric artifact that never tarnished yet somehow secreted a substance almost identical to human blood, a vessel dubbed by Gadal the "Graal Pyrenean."

I gazed at Christian Koenig, incredulous.

"You're telling me this thing exists?"

"I knew this vase well. It was fashioned from the concavity of a broken stalactite," continued Christian calmly, a tone of utter conviction to his voice. "It was exhibited in the Salle Gadal in Tarascon for many years. A vessel containing a hyperdense meteoric aerolite that had magnetic properties."

I shook my head, wishing I could light a cigarette, although I knew

Fig. 13.6. Antonin Gadal with relics removed from the caves. Courtesy of Hamilton White.

Fig. 13.7. The Graal Pyrenean displayed in the Salle Gadal in Tarascon. Courtesy of Hamilton White.

full well my informant didn't approve of such things. "You're suggesting they not only found the blessed cup but that it came from outer space? Like some sort of extraterrestrial power object?"

"It came from the outside," Christian nodded.

"It's just a reach." I turned in a semicircle, gazing out over the silent valley. "I mean it's a lot to take on board. Lucifer's diadem. The stones from the sky. This thing, they call . . ."

The former museum curator watched placidly as I struggled in vain to find words. It all sounded so absurd. Words simply couldn't encapsulate it. Human words anyhow.

". . . the Grail."

Christian nodded. "The ancients prized such stones, not because they came from the heavens but because this substance is a very beautiful, very pure form of iron. It never rusts but bleeds. They say the black stone of the Ka'bah is made of the same substance, the stone Muslims the world over face when they kneel in prayer. It contains an extraordinary power. The first light. The primordial light. The essence of the immaterial made manifest, drawn into the dense vibration of being."

"Then there's more than one of these objects?" My eyes fell to the pendant at my informant's throat.

Christian nodded. "Rahn and Gadal removed hundreds of meteorites from the caves. The largest of those stones now forms the centerpiece in the altar of the Rosicrucian Temple in the Netherlands."

I took a deep breath, sensing the outlines of another deeper mystery wrapped like a chrysalis within the shadowy folds of the Rahn affair. Christian turned away, eyes unreadable.

"Of course, the Grail is the symbol of an interior process, yet if we accept the material world is merely the physical manifestation of a spiritual reality, the three-dimensional shadow of an ultradimensional truth, then it is possible such an interior process might find exterior expression. A hard dark symbol of humankind's suffering. I believe the Dalai Lama has a dorje fashioned from the very same substance. A symbolic lightning bolt, similar to a sieg rune, forged from meteoric iron. In Malaysia they apparently make ceremonial knives from them." Christian shrugged.

"Otto Rahn described these relics as the stones that had fallen from Lucifer's crown when he was cast out of heaven, that symbolized the fall of man, the fall of matter, and the fall of Satan."

And I thought once again of that lightning flash on Otto's pullover, the same knitted sweater Ingeborgh had inherited and made into a pair of play trousers for her son. I thought of the seething rivers of white-hot plasma that had played about the castle walls during the storm and the name of the Cathar high priestess. For a moment I felt as if I had been struck by lightning myself.

Otto left France immediately after the excavations, returning to Germany and the waiting arms of the SS. Antonin Gadal, rather more wisely, stayed put, living out his remaining days in that little cottage near the river. In 1957, the aging self-proclaimed patriarch of the Sabartés assumed spiritual leadership of the Lectorium Rosicrucianum, or LR. He proceeded to reform the movement along his own neo-Cathar lines.

As the former minister of tourism for the area, Gadal ensured that all future members of the society had to make the pilgrimage to Ussat-les-Bains at least once in their lives, to be duly initiated in the stone pentagram in the Bethelehem Grotto that is still used for their rituals to this day. Quite possibly the meteoric vessel Christian described to us still played a vital role in those rites.

Colonel Howard Buechner insisted Otto's Grail had been transported back to Germany and later smuggled to Antarctica by U-boat, either that or blast-sealed into a glacier near Hitler's Obersalzburg complex. In truth, I was starting to suspect the blessed cup had never left France but had remained in the hands of the LR all along. There were a million questions buzzing through my mind, but Christian was already starting back toward the car, making it clear the audience was at an end. Pausing to indicate the plants growing at the mouth of the cave, he offered me another one of those oddly open smiles. "See how the leaves reach toward the light?"

We dropped Christian at his home, a rambling old building next to Gadal's residence, and to my surprise he invited us in for a cup of tea. It was immediately apparent that his musty lodgings had become the repository of a number of relics from the museum. Gadal's Graal Pyrenean had allegedly been on public display until just a few years ago and it was easy to imagine that the most sacred relic in all Christendom might be stashed away somewhere beneath that very roof, where we now sat, politely sipping chai.

MAISON COUQUET, MONTSÉGUR— AUTUMN 1998

"What the hell was that thing behind him?" JB seated himself on the end of his bed as we checked the camera equipment. We were back in Otto's room at Madame Couquet's auberge where all hell had broken loose on my previous visit. The room seemed tranquil now in the early evening, like any other hotel room.

Fig. 13.8. Living in a ghost town—the shadows over Ussat-les-Bains. Photo by Richard Stanley.

"What thing?"

"That big gold candelabra thing that was standing right behind Christian's chair while he was talking to us?"

I cast my mind back to the plethora of artifacts that filled every square inch of Christian's living room. "It looked like the menorah of the temple."

"What?"

"The menorah. That big six-branched candlestick thing from the shrine of Moses and later from Solomon's temple. It was supposedly part of the sacred treasure of the Jews."

As the words left my mouth the handle on the bedroom door rattled unexpectedly and began to turn. We both froze, exchanging an uneasy glance. Neither of us was expecting company, not at this hour in a village where folks hit the hay at sundown and any form of nightlife was wholly unheard of.

The door slid silently open and getting to my feet I realized there was no one on the threshold, at least no one I could see. I blinked. Then, taking my hat off, I placed one hand to my heart, thumb at a right angle to my palm, bowing deeply.

"You're most welcome," I offered.

And at that the door was sucked violently shut, slamming with sufficient force for the echo to reverberate through the sepulchral household. I turned to see JB staring at me, eyes wide as saucers.

"Told you this place was haunted."

"The fuck was that?"

"Some dead treasure hunter hanging about on the landing, I guess. Either René Odin or M. Arnaud, I imagine."

"Who?"

"The engineer from Bordeaux. Probably heard us mention the menorah. I mean don't you get the impression time works differently here? Like things that were supposed to have been over and done are somehow still happening on another channel. Perhaps those channels overlap sometimes."

But JB just kept on staring.

"Ah hell, I don't know. It was probably just a draft."

I wasn't sure whether I believed in ghosts. Certainly if they existed they seemed more active in Montségur than the outside world. What Christian had said about the original light, the primordial light of creation contained within the stones had set my mind racing. What if there was another component to this mystery? One I had never guessed at before? A military-industrial application to Lucifer's diadem?

THE GROTTO OF FONTANET—AUTUMN 1998

The grotto of Fontanet has been a sacred place since time immemorial. The river that flows through its stygian galleries has an irregular phreatic source controlled by a subterranean syphon that causes the water level to rise and fall unexpectedly, bringing to mind the menstrual cycles of the Goddess and linking the site in Otto's imagination to the mythical cave of Wolfram's hermit, Trevrizent—Fontanet de Savage, the wild fountain. The cavern's significance in ancient times was clearly illustrated by the terraces surrounding its entrance and the remains of a stone circle that was torn down when the site was Christianized in the eighth century.

Otto Rahn described his first visit to the site in dramatic terms in a broadcast recorded by Southwest German broadcasting, a show provocatively entitled "What Happened to Me in the Pyrenean Cave!" I had hoped Paul Ladame might have kept a copy of the recording in his collection as, apart from anything else, I was keen to hear Otto's voice, but sadly all that remained on file was a typed transcript, enough at least to get a sense of the long-lost broadcast's content, which largely concerned itself with the tale of how Habdu, his Senegalese bodyguard, had saved him from the rising floodwaters. According to Otto's account, they had been forced to retrace their steps through the cavern's galleries in total darkness, a distance of nearly two miles, recalling the initiatory ordeals of the Eleusian mysteries. Knowing this account, it took either bravado, stupidity, or blind obsession to willingly follow in their steps.

Fig. 13.9. Pre-Christian standing stones near the mouth of the grotto of Fontanet in the Ariège.
Photo by Richard Stanley.

Fig. 13.10. The author in the grotto of Fontanet.
Photo by Hamilton White.

Fig. 13.11. Beneath the Tabor.
Photo by Richard Stanley.

Following Otto's lead, we penetrated as far as we could into the mountain only to find access to the lower depths barred by a locked gate and a corroded sign warning prospective treasure hunters they faced a 300,000 Franc fine for venturing farther. I would later learn from

The Stones from the Sky   **277**

Fig. 13.12. In places deep, where dark things sleep . . .

Fig. 13.13. The altar of Fontanet, summer 1932. Photo by Otto Rahn.

the local authorities that Fontanet is considered an important prehistoric site and is still being excavated by French archaeologists who have apparently identified the footprints of children and wolves preserved in the sand from the Magdalenian period, suggesting ancient interaction between the species.

Unable to reach the underground stream or the initiatory chamber containing the natural rock formation described by Otto as the altar, we set about a careful fingertip search of the upper galleries. I was unwilling to take Christian's word for what Otto and Antonin Gadal had really found in those lightless gulfs beneath the mountain any more than I had been prepared to accept Colonel Howard Buechner's claims concerning the "treasure of the ages" falling into Nazi hands. Gadal was hardly the most credible of witnesses, having been publicly humiliated a few years later trying to pass off funerary ornaments purchased by a friend during a holiday in Egypt as artifacts exhumed from one of the caves in Ussat, apparently in a desperate attempt to shore up his theories linking his beloved Cathars to the science and sorcery of ancient Khem. Given the earlier, equally embarrassing efforts of the Polaires to plant a book of Nadi astrology in the walls of Montségur and the murky rumors concerning the provenance of the mystical graffiti on the walls of the Lombrives, it was only natural I had come to take tales of spectacular archaeological discoveries in the Zone with a pinch of salt. Neither Otto nor Gadal were trained archaeologists and the stories surrounding their discovery and the alleged properties of the so-called Graal Pyrenean seemed fantastical to say the least.

In truth, I didn't believe a word of it until I saw the stones bleed for myself.

We never reached the sunless banks of the river that flowed beneath the mountain, but we did retrieve something from within those folds of rock, departing the cave system with a number of mysterious stones in our possession that I had no doubt were identical to the ones referred to in Christian's account.

Without recourse to spectrographic analysis, we couldn't be sure

Fig. 13.14. The bleeding stones.
Photo by Momo Milla Gross.

whether they were really meteoric debris as Christian suggested, or tektites thrown up from somewhere deep within the earth's mantle. The only thing we could tell with any certainty was that the samples that came into my possession were a form of hyperdense iron, and it did not take us long to figure out that they did indeed possess curious electromagnetic qualities.

JB was wearing a biomagnet around his neck, a curious doodad marketed by one of Cat's friends, Carole Caplin, New Age guru and "lifestyle advisor" to Tony Blair, the then-incoming British prime minister. By the time we had hiked back to the car, the swinging talisman had inadvertently magnetized the stones he was carrying, causing all the small change in his pocket to adhere into a solid lump. Nor was this the relic's only remarkable property.

They say you can't get blood from a stone, just like you can't fly or breathe underwater.

But it's not true.

While the "stones from the sky" never rust or tarnish, when agitated their surface secretes a bright red ferrous solution, 99 percent pure iron. This at least goes some way toward answering how the meteorites might have found their way into the cave system to begin with, iron oxide being one of the principal ingredients in the prehistoric rock art that stampedes across the ancient limestone walls of the Ardeche and the Ariège. It is not hard to see how a superstitious mind might be affected by the sight of that blood, seemingly springing from nowhere. It is iron oxide after all that gives the Ganges its sanguine tint at source, identifying it as the lifeblood of the Goddess.

The possibility that the mythic black stones, the *Lapsit exillis* of Wolfram's *Parzival*, might be tektites rather than aerolites was further raised when we retrieved more of the precious samples from a second location, a deep gorge below the so-called Devil's Bridge, a thirteenth-century fortified causeway that spans the Ariège just outside Foix. Wherever they came from originally, from outside the earth or within, it was clear the blessed stones had lain undiscovered in some deep strata, buried for millions of years until being plowed to the surface by the passage of the glacier that cut the valley of the Ariège during the last ice age. The only way to ascertain the provenance of the ore samples would be to gain access to a laboratory equipped to perform a credible analysis, something that sadly proved a taller order than we might have imagined. Until then, the true nature of the samples obtained from Fontanet would remain just one more unanswered question in a story already bristling with loose ends.

"So where does that leave us?" Mr. Horn scratched his head, turning two of the precious stones in the palm of his hand. "Like we're supposed to live forever now?"

I shook my head. "I don't think its that simple. At least it didn't work out that way for Otto."

"How do you know?" Mr. Horn returned his attention to the river below. There were a bunch of local kids farther down the bridge, young teenagers daring each other to clamber onto the parapet and tombstone into the icy waters below. The day was still warm, but it looked too dangerous for us to want to join them. "I mean we haven't exactly seen any graves, let alone an autopsy report. There doesn't seem to be a death certificate on file for Rahn so, technically at least, he's still alive."

"Technically."

There was a shriek and a splash as one of the kids plunged from the bridge, followed by the jeers and hoots of his companions.

"Isn't that what Marius and the others told you the first time you came here?" continued Mr. Horn. "That Otto was an old man now but still visited the area?"

"I think they only said that because they were hoping to get themselves on television," I rationalized, watching to see if the kid resurfaced. "I was still working for Channel Four back then, so it was a big ticket for them. I suspect Madame Couquet and Marius got together behind our backs and agreed on a story to attract custom to the auberge. Otto and the goddamn cup are the closest thing they've got to their own Loch Ness monster. Of course they're going to say the monster's still around."

"I wouldn't put it past them," Mr. Horn concurred. "But what else is a Grail good for, if not eternal life?"

"Beats me." I shook my head again. "I read somewhere the black stones were important because they contained the Green Ray, whatever the hell that is. The condensed light of the Black Sun according to Serrano."

Miguel Serrano (1917–2009) was a Chilean diplomat and tantric yoga enthusiast perhaps best remembered for his memoir *C. G. Jung and Hermann Hesse: A Record of Two Friendships*. He served as Chile's ambassador to India from 1953–1962 and achieved notoriety when he declared Adolf Hitler to be the Tenth Avatar of Vishnu in a misguided attempt to reconcile his religious views with his political sentiments. According to Serrano, Hitler was the Kalki Avatar, incarnated to bring an end to the Kali Yuga and usher in the New Age.

Serrano's 600-page thesis, "Adolf Hitler, el Ultimo Avatara" (Adolf Hitler, the last avatar) (1984), dedicated "To the glory of the Führer,

Adolf Hitler," was memorably described by esoteric scholar Joscelyn Godwin as "probably the fullest modern statement of the Thulean philosophy in any language."

"Yeah. But Serrano's batshit."

"True." The shadows were lengthening and I cast about myself, searching for JB who was still scrambling between the boulders beneath the Devil's Bridge, trying to see if he could find any more of the stones before the light deserted us. "What I don't get is how the black stones and Gadal's Graal Pyrenean can be the same thing as the emerald cup or the emerald diadem," mused Mr. Horn. "I mean they're hardly green."

"Yeah. That's been bugging me too," I admitted. "Maybe the emerald thing doesn't refer to the physical substance but some kind of energy contained within. Y'know, like the *visio smaragdina*?"

"The emerald vision?" Mr. Horn nodded, getting my drift. "As in the Emerald City or the Emerald Island where the hidden Imam dwells?"

"Or the Emerald Tablet of Hermes Trismegistus, for that matter. The Iranian theosophers constantly refer to the color and I don't have to remind you how often green lights, green rays, and green children turn up in Hollow Earth literature. What if it's referring to some other plane of consciousness? Something we can't see with the naked eye. The energy contained within the stones, rather than the stones themselves. I mean they're obviously some form of heavy metal and heavy metals are generally pretty limited in their application."

"Yeah," murmured Mr. Horn darkly, attention returning to the stones, which did seem to sparkle oddly in the westering sunlight. "I mean, immortality would have been nice."

"In point of fact, Wolfram actually doesn't say anything about immortality. I think the gods have that one pretty much sewn up."

"What does Wolfram say?"

"That 'however ill a mortal may be, from the day on which he sees the Stone he cannot die for that week, nor does he lose his color.'"

"That week, huh?" Mr. Horn shrugged. "Well, I suppose that's something. Do you think it's any good when it comes to dealing with bullet wounds?"

"I doubt it. But Wolfram does go on to say, "if anyone, maid or man, were to look at the Graal for two hundred years, you would have to admit their color was as fresh as their early prime, except their hair would be grey'—so I guess extreme longevity is part of the deal, if not actual life eternal. You noticed how Christian was wearing one as a pendant."

"Better safe than sorry, I suppose." Mr. Horn delicately replaced the stones in his breast pocket.

A dragonfly silently circled us and then went flitting away, riding the lazy late afternoon thermals. JB was already working his way back up the path between the rocks and I shouldered my camera bag, getting ready to head for the car. "We've got our work cut out, all right. If we can just figure a way of measuring the abundance of gas-phase ions in these things or at least get a handle on their mass to charge ratio."

"You said it." Mr. Horn's scowl deepened as he considered the implications. "I do have one question though."

"What's that?"

"Why is this place called the Devil's Bridge?"

The bridge spanning the canyon had been constructed in the early thirteenth century and fortified with a garrison of troops to extract tithe from farmers and merchants taking their goods and livestock to market in Foix. Despite the passage of more than seven centuries, its crumbling arches remained undeniably impressive, if not a little otherworldy in the golden light.

"I mean, there's some tosh about the devil building it in one night, in return for the soul of the first person to cross but the real deal is that it was built before the fall of Montségur, when Occitania was still in its glory and Esclarmonde and her brother Roger Ramon were still running the show."

Mr. Horn raised one eyebrow. "You mean it was built by heretics?"

"I wish it were that simple. It probably got its nickname two to

Fig. 13.15. The Devil's Bridge (Pont du Diable).
Photo by Richard Stanley.

three centuries later, by which stage the Holy Roman Church had put an end to education and the Dark Ages were in full swing. They not only destroyed the books but the culture that produced them. Science and medicine more or less ceased to exist, and the Occitan language was criminalized. Within a relatively short time, a couple of hundred years, people had become so stupid they no longer understood how the

Fig. 13.16. Gateway to Elsewhere—the Devil's Bridge. Photo by Richard Stanley.

engineering works of the past could have been achieved and, concluding they were beyond human needs or ability, figured they had to be the work of the devil, a view the church actively encouraged. That's what happens when you lobotomize an entire civilization. There are hundreds of Devil's Bridges all over Europe, most of them originally of Roman construction. Let's just hope it never happens again, huh? That folks never look at the remains of our century and draw the same conclusions."

Mr. Horn was silent. I reached into my pocket, closing my hand around the two Grail stones I had placed there earlier when we divided the spoils from the cave, finding them oddly warm to my touch. "For some reason, I'm reminded of that dodgy Einstein quote," I added. "Y'know, the one about how he didn't know what weapons would be used to fight the Third World War but the Fourth War would be fought with stones?"

"I don't think Einstein actually said that," replied Mr. Horn at length. "It was misattributed." He glanced back at the silent causeway.

"I thought it was more about how you should never make deals with the devil. Like never bet the devil your head."

"There's that too." I tightened my grip on the stones, wondering if they really functioned as superconductors.

Yet, it turned out that for whatever reason, placebo effect, call it what you will, the stones really did seem to possess a healing virtue.

My first guinea pig was Andy Collins, a production assistant on *The Secret Glory* (2001), the feature-length documentary that would eventually spring from my obsessive quest for SS Obersturmführer Otto Wilhelm Rahn. The film was shot over a period of several years by Mr. Horn and his assistant Pascal Laugier, a young southerner who would eventually achieve notoriety as the director of the horror film *Martyrs* (2008). In a bid to evoke the stylistic tropes of Nazi propagandist Leni Riefenstahl, we decided to light several sections of the film with distress flares, a tactic that led to Andy picking up a nasty burn on the palm of his hand. The wound, treated with meteor blood, closed and healed over in a matter of days, leaving scarcely a trace.

The second beneficiary of the extraterrestrial artifact's mythic virtue was Beltane Fire Society founder Mark Oxbrow's then-girlfriend, Liz, who was struck on the head by a bottle flung by a drunken yob during one of the yearly Walpurgisnacht gatherings on Carlton Hill. We were in the midst of a crowd of a good ten thousand tripping revelers and while Mark set off as swiftly as he could to find a paramedic, it was clear it would take them vital minutes to reach us through the jam. Liz was lying at my feet in a state of concussion, a lump the size of a goose egg growing on her forehead, and I feared her skull might have been fractured. I had served as a torch bearer in the parade the night before and my skin had been painted for the occasion, black with an overlay of silver runes and knot work. Feeling the rising May Day sun at my back, I whipped out the stones I had taken from Fontanet and rubbed them together to make them bleed. By the time Mark returned with responsible adult help, the paramedics were no longer necessary. At first I told myself it was just a little old-fashioned shamanic sleight of hand, but the swelling retreated as if it had never been there and even a few days afterward Liz still claimed to feel no side effects.

Mark, the co-author of several popular history books, notably *Cracking the DaVinci Code* (2005) and *Rosslyn and the Grail* (2006), was an ardent Grail scholar in his own right and had spent years tracking down the dish described in Chrétiené de Troyes's twelfth-century saga, *Perceval, le Conte du Graal*, the immediate precursor to Wolfram's epic. He had eventually located the fabulous dish, complete with the decorative Christian fish symbol, the vesica pisces mentioned in de Troyes's verse, among the Louvre's permanent collection, just one of many magical items bobbing around Europe that might rightly answer to the description of a Holy Grail.

Mark found Otto's black stones just as fascinating as I did, the more so after Liz's miraculous recovery. I recall him carefully examining my samples with his magnifying glass, searching for the names of the guardians of the Grail physically written in the stone as Wolfram promised. Weirdly, there did seem to be tiny glyphs and cyphers scored into the blessed things although perhaps by then our minds were simply playing tricks on us, attempting once again to impose patterns on the chaos of the unknown.

"Such powers does the Stone confer on mortal men that their flesh and bones are soon made young again," Wolfram insists. "This stone is also called 'The Graal' . . ."

Despite the misleading statements given by Marius Mounié and the other good burghers of Montségur, it seemed increasingly probable that the real Otto Rahn had perished in 1939 on the German-French border, either murdered by the Nazis or deliberately relinquishing his life in a form of ritual suicide suggestive of the Cathar rite of endura. Christian Koenig had described Rahn as a potential successor to Gadal, but if that were the case then surely the secret of the Cathars and their Pyrenean Grail would have died with him.

In the course of my research I collated, translated, and compiled hundreds of pages of testimony, documents, and journal entries charting the elusive SS obersturmführer's quest for the roots of an authentic European "ur-religion," a body of invaluable folkloric data from a prewar Europe now lost to us, but despite my best efforts to coerce or cajole the secret of the Pyrenean Grail's current whereabouts from Christian Koenig, I failed to get within striking distance of the relic, although I had good reason to believe it was still somewhere in the vicinity of Ussat-les-Bains.

After four years on the trail, I knew we were still only beginning to understand what the story was really about. I knew the stones had been prized since time out of mind, and men might kill or die for them, yet without analysis we had no way of determining their actual density or the true nature of the properties attributed to them.

According to our current understanding of physics, chemical density is determined by the conditions prevalent during the first few nanoseconds of the big bang. On Earth, the heaviest element in our periodic table is uranium, which can be artificially enriched to form plutonium—and of course there's really only one thing plutonium is good for. In deep space, far heavier stable elements are known to exist, some of them dense enough to bend light or literally fold space-time, each one containing the latent energy of the original light, the big bang, still trapped within it, awaiting some future redemption, like the Cathar notion of souls being imprisoned in "tunics of flesh," trapped in the dense vibration of solid matter. The Cathars accepted Christ only as a prophet and awaited the coming of a true messiah, who would incarnate not as a human being but as pure light, a light that would liberate us from the "sin of matter," cleanse the earth, break the cycle of incarnation, and bring all of us back to God.

Delving deeper into the dismaying literature of crypto-fascism and Aryan identity, I found further references to the emerald cup and the unsettling suggestion that it was so named, not because of its shade but because of what it contained, a force indetectable to mortal eyes. There is some unsubstantiated evidence to suggest several artifacts from Otto's initial excavations were shipped to the United States just before the war, where they came to the attention of one of Einstein's associates, a young physicist named Dr. Herbert Fleischmann who had a particular interest in superconductivity, supercooling, and covalent bonds. The military applications of this work remain classified, along with the details of the SS polar expeditions, in which Otto Rahn certainly played a role. It is well documented that after his time exploring the caves of southern France, he undertook an expedition to Iceland and the Arctic Circle underwritten by Wiligut-Weisthor's department. The purpose of this mission remains unknown with theories ranging from an obscure male-bonding exercise based on the Eddas to an investigation into the remains of a lost Hyperborean civilization hidden beneath the ice mantle and speculation over secret experiments into the Earth's magnetic fields. Rumors, possibly deliberate misinformation, abound concerning ice caverns, warm water lakes, and even dinosaurs. Several sources repeat the story of deranged Nazi scientists setting up radar transmitters at the pole that pointed skyward, allegedly trying to bounce signals back off the concavity of the "hollow earth" but couldn't this have simply been a convenient cover story, dreamed up for the same reasons U.S. intelligence promulgated the myth of the flying saucer to act as a smoke screen for their own dirty work during the cold war?

Murky 16 mm footage exists from the 1930s, depicting some sort of primitive radar apparatus reminiscent of the modern day arrays at the HAARP (High Frequency Active Auroral Research Program) installation in Gaakon, Alaska, that has become the focus of considerable speculation by uninformed conspiracy theorists who believed it was capable of causing earthquakes or weaponizing the weather while some insist similar research is still being conducted at an American airbase in Thule, Greenland, a location said to have been a former Nazi installation, which apparently came over to Allied administration after the war under Operation Paperclip. But it's all speculation and without tangible evidence will remain so. Like Fulcanelli's incomplete trilogy, the notorious *verbum dismissum*, or the missing word, of the alchemists, Otto Rahn's work remains unfinished. He speaks of three stones, after all.

In the final pages of *The Court of Lucifer*, written in 1936, three years before his lonely demise on the Kufstein, Otto describes three manuscripts resting before him on his writing desk. On the first pile of handwritten pages, the notes that comprised the substance of *Crusade against the Grail* (1933), rests one of the stones he brought back from the Pyrenees. On the second, the text of *The Court of Lucifer*, rests a fragment of the frieze from the temple of the Oracle at Delphi, the very temple that was once looted by the Visigoths who allegedly cast its cursed treasure into the Devil's Lake. On the third pile of pages that Otto promised would constitute the final part of his trilogy, a book supposedly entitled "Orpheus—A Jouney to Hell and Beyond," rests a "lump of amber, golden yellow," reminiscent of Masonry's three degrees and the transition from the nigredo to the whitened final substance of the alchemical great work.

In the last of his words to have come down to us, Otto describes how the window beside his desk stands opens and a violent electrical storm rages outside. A small Empire clock, a gift from the late Countess Miryanne de Pujol Murat, who had become one with the Spirit some two years previously, rests beside Otto's desk, measuring out the hours remaining to him as he works feverishly into the night, mindful of the promise he made to his former mentor, trying to order and set down all he had learned while there is still time.

"My little Empire clock will soon strike seven times," writes Otto cryptically. "At nine o'clock, it will be dark. I will leave the house. Very near here, I know a forest path bordered by majestic pine trees. It begins in a place called the 'Free Man,' then passing through the Dornberg, it rejoins the Ransberg. There is a meadow there—the rose garden. The path is called the 'Path of the Thief' [*Diebsweg*]. I will carry with me the key, the Dietrich. I am going to follow the ancient path of the thief, eyes constantly fixed on the great Bear. In the Nordic sky, in ancient times, the constellation bore the name Arktos . . ."

After that, there is only silence and the mystery that would grow around his passing. The manuscript of "Orpheus," the third book of Rahn, begun in the Arctic Circle, is missing, either seized by the Nazis when Otto fled the SS, or as his niece, Ingeborgh Roemer-Rahn, would have us believe, burned by his mother at the end of the war. I had vainly hoped to find a copy of the precious text lying about her house in the Black Forest and while I turned up the lump of amber that Otto used as a paperweight, the pages it formerly held down were long gone. Ingeborgh did have a copy of an unpublished novel written in high German in Otto's familiar hasty hand and the text of a mercifully unproduced SS Yuletide play entitled "Endless Christmas" that sounded like something Mel Brooks might have dreamed up, but of the third and final part of his vital Grail thesis, I could find no trace, not even a top sheet.

The only way to learn the truth about what Otto Rahn was doing in the Arctic, not to mention Dr. Fleischmann and the potential military-industrial application of those blessed black stones, would be to either track down the missing manuscript or access the redacted files relating to the SS polar expeditions, all reference to which seemed to have been tidied into a locked cabinet someplace that neither I, nor any other Reich historian I subsequently contacted, can access.

14

The Face in the Pentagram

Autumn 1998

Sometimes the underground stream ducks out of sight. Sometimes the trail peters out and so-called real life takes priority. It's just the way of things. There can be no other. I kept going until I ran out of funds and film stock, and when we were done with shooting the documentary that would become *The Secret Glory* (2001), we divided the artifacts recovered from the caves equally between myself, Mr. Horn, JB, and the other Shadow Theatre irregulars who had given freely of their time and energy, before reluctantly winding down the operation and going our separate ways.

Alone once more, I stood before the stone pentagram in the Bethlehem Grotto, trying to put the pieces together in my head. If Gadal had initiated Otto Rahn in this place, anointing him as his official successor, then why had the young German felt compelled to draw a woman's face on the cave wall? In any case, who on earth could that woman have been? Presumably it was just another shaggy dog story dreamed up by the first of the two Christians who had acted as conflicting advisers on my circuitous journey through the mirror maze of

Fig. 14.1. The black Dominican. Immo Horn and the author on Otto Rahn's trail, autumn 1998. Photo by James "JB" Bourne.

the Western esoteric tradition, crazy old Christian Bernadac with his vintage jeep, who insisted Rahn had survived the war, faking his own death in order to rise to power as the head of Coca-Cola Europe.

Feeling a little worn out by it all, I lay down on the stone altar, watching the swallows nesting in the eaves of the cavern roof.

Autumn was drawing in and the last remaining chicks were trying to gather the courage to leave the nest. I watched for a while, waiting to see if they would take the plunge and find the nerve to push themselves off into empty air. It was a hot early September afternoon and without realizing it I must have drifted into sleep.

When I came around, the birds were gone. I remember hoping those tiny chicks would somehow be all right, that they would have time to develop the strength and confidence to follow their parents on the yearly migration south. Then, returning my gaze to the pentagram, I felt a sudden, giddy rush of déjà vu.

Fig. 14.2. The face in the pentagram.

I hurriedly scaled the wall, finding worn handholds so I could draw myself up to the same height as the center of the pentagram. Reaching for the water bottle clipped to my belt I poured its contents over the stone, washing away the dust of decades and there, exactly where I had dreamed them to be, were the outlines of a partly obliterated face. A single angelic eye stared back at me out of time, drawn with what appeared to be a thick black crayon. The image of a hope that never quite dried up. The face of a lost love, perhaps the mythical Mountain Mother herself, the goddess of the caves or as Christian Bernadac suggested, a representation of Beatrice, whose memory led Dante like a guiding star on his journey through the seven circles of hell.

After passing through the ritual caverns of the Ariège and their attendant trials and mysteries, the initiate is said to emerge from the stone pentagram as a new man. I had stood in that same pentagram and emerged with one clear thought in my head. The depression in the wall was somewhat smaller than I had expected. Indeed it had been a rather awkward fit. There was a minimum height requirement in the SS and that figure in the faded snapshot Paul Alexis Ladame had given me would surely never have made the cut. In fact the more I looked at the man standing in the pentagram whom Paul had identified as his friend, the less he resembled the other images of Otto Rahn that had come into my possession. In the end I relayed a copy of the photo to Rahn's niece, Ingeborgh in the Black Forest, who confirmed my suspicions, casually passing her pendulum over the picture before pronouncing her verdict: "Otto would never wear tennis shoes."

It took another nine months to conclusively prove the individual in Paul's snapshot was in fact a little-known esoteric researcher named Karl Rinderknecht who, not unsurprisingly, turned out to be an adherent of Gadal's Lectorium Rosicrucianum. Rinderknecht had presumably made the initiatory pilgrimage to Ussat and stood in the pentagram as Gadal directed, but why had Paul Ladame gone to such trouble to lie to me?

The British author Nigel Graddon and various internet conspiracy theorists suggest that Rinderknecht and Rahn were the same person, shoring up the theory that the notorious Nazi Grail hunter returned to the Ariège incognito after his alleged demise. Surviving documentation however puts the lie to this theory. Rinderknecht's own investigations, detailed in an October 1941 edition of *Koralle Magazine* under the heading "In Quest of the Grail," mark the young Rosicrucian scholar as one of the first to follow in Rahn's footsteps. He would not be the last.

Paul Ladame's recall of events in Montségur and Ussat-les-Bains was suspiciously sketchy, and had made no mention of the bleeding stones, leading me to suspect he had never known about them, all of which called his claims of having accompanied Rahn on his exploration of the caves into question. Unfortunately I had no way of challenging Paul as he had passed away only a few days after our previous meeting, making further queries impossible. What baffled me most about the whole fandango was why this former professor of the methodology of information and disinformation had been so keen to convince me, with virtually his dying breath, that Otto Rahn had been a fully initiated Rosicrucian?

Antonin Gadal did not assume leadership of the European Rosicrucian movement until 1957, long after Rahn was dead, although some version of the secret society already existed in the prewar years. The true secret Rosicrucian Order and its messianic founder, Christian Rosenkreutz, are probably little more than myth or, in all likelihood, an elaborate seventeenth-century hoax. The order owes its origins to two anonymous manifestos, the *Fama Fraternitatis RC* (Fame of the Brotherhood of RC), and the *Confessio Fraternitatis* (Confessions of the Brotherhood of RC), which first appeared in Germany between 1607 and 1616. The influence of these documents, describing a secret order devoted to the "Universal Reformation of Mankind," spread through western Europe, giving rise to a sort of esoteric mania not dissimilar to the modern New Age movement, a popular fad largely confined to the middle classes that was later defined by historian Dame Frances Yates as the Rosicrucian Enlightenment.

The *Fama Fraternitatis* outlines the life and travels of the movement's founder, a learned doctor and philosopher who was said to have been born in the thirteenth century, at a time when Germany was devastated by the black-garbed Dominican Inquisitors and the fanatical witch hunter Konrad von Marburg, who, curiously enough, had been the subject of Otto Rahn's doctoral thesis. The *Fraternitatis* describes how a community of Albigensians had been discovered in the castle of Germelhausen, one of the locations Rahn later requested permission from Wiligut-Weisthor to investigate as part of the inquiries he carried out under the auspices of the Ahnenerbe SS. The castle had been duly besieged and its inhabitants put to death, including the noble Germelhausen family who were allegedly adherents of the Cathar doctrine, practicing its austerities and rites such as the consolamentum that promised deliverance from the cycles of material incarnation.

The last surviving member of this vanished line, the youngest son of the Germelhausens, then five years old, was said to have been carried out of the blazing castle by an anonymous monk, apparently an adept from the Languedoc who had instructed the family. The last of the Germelhausens came to be known as Christian Rosenkreutz (literally "rosy cross") and was raised and educated in secret in a remote monastery where he founded the fraternal order that bore his name. When he was fifteen years old Christian Rosenkreutz allegedly embarked on a journey to the east in search of a secret initiatory center hidden somewhere in the mountains of Asia. According to the *Fraternitatis* the order's founder was accompanied on this journey by his best friend, a figure described in the text only by his initials, PAL.

It did not escape my attention that Paul Alexis Ladame styled himself as PAL in the letters exchanged before our meeting and the signatures that appeared on his satirical cartoons. Another example of the mysterious mirroring that haunted this affair from the very beginning, like the two Wolffs, the two Christians who had guided me through the caves, the two Esclarmondes, and indeed the two Rahns—a series of goofy coincidences that only added to the lattice of confused identities. Paul had arranged to meet me beside a statue in the park named *les petit amis* (the "little friends") and when first speaking of his friendship with Otto had introduced the subject with the phrase "one of my little pals back then." Of course, in the world of electronic data the initials of these two thirteenth-century traveling companions, CRC and PAL, could just as easily be taken to stand for Cyclical Redundancy Check and Phase Alternating Line, but this was pure delirium, that point where, having stared too long at the text, all the facts start to join hands and dance in circles in one's head, singing funny songs.

PAL had allegedly perished in Cyprus, but CRC had somehow gotten across the water to Damascus where he was said to have made contact with the mystery schools of the East. Under these enlightened Sufi masters he was familiarized with the sacred book of their order, the Masnavi that mirrored the mystical pantheism of his forefathers. He immersed himself in the alchemy of Gazali, the poetry of Omar Khayyam, the algebra of Geber, and Euclid's discourses. After studying for several years in this secret Sufic center, CRC is said to have traveled on to Egypt, before crossing the Mediterranean to Fez, the city of the 600 fountains, which was then at the height of its glory. It was here Rosenkreutz allegedly learned the powers of divination by the stars and was initiated into the true secrets of magic and the occult laws that govern the hidden forces of nature. In Spain he became a close associate of the Alumbrados, a neo-Platonic order that had come into being under the influence of the Arabs and who were engaged in the search for the philosopher's stone in accordance with the discipline outlined in the secret book of Artephius. Crossing the Pyenees, CRC sojourned in the valley of the Ariège at the castle of Lordat, the same fortress that, according to the March 1932 edition of *la Depeche*, had been excavated by the Polaires under the auspices of Otto's mentor, the Countess Miryanne de Pujol Murat.

Returning at last to the monastery in Thuringia, Rosenkreutz was reunited with three of the original members of his order, the monks he studied with in his youth, and set about the reformation of mankind. During Rosenkreutz's lifetime the order was said to consist of no more than eight members who took an oath to heal the sick without payment and maintain their secret fellowship. Each had to find a spiritual heir before dying so the knowledge handed down from the elder times might be transmitted to the generations to come. Christian Rosenkreutz allegedly lived to 106 years of age but seems to have failed in his mission as humanity remained stubbornly unreformed.

The appearance of the Rosicrucian manifestos in the early seventeenth century caused a fever of occult excitement, prompting the hasty publication of countless imitations. Between 1614 and 1620 alone more than 400 books were printed addressing the theme. In 1622, at the height of the furor, two mysterious posters appeared on the walls of Paris. One read, "We, the Deputies of the Higher College of the Rose-Croix, do make our stay, visibly and invisibly, in this city," while the second concluded, "the thoughts attached to the real desire of the seeker will lead us to him and him to us."

The manifestos were not meant to be taken literally, directly stating, "We speak unto you by parables" and were assumed by many to be a hoax. Johann Valentin Andreae (1586–1654) claimed in his autobiography that he had been the true author of one of these manifestos, which he described as a "ludibrium"—a word derived from the Latin *ludus* (plural *ludi*), meaning a "plaything," "bauble," or "trivial game," an object of fun, scorn, and derision. It is easy enough to imagine that the high history of the Rosicrucian Order and its miraculous founder might well have been a literary concoction that simply got out of hand, catching the popular imagination in much the same manner as Lovecraft's Cthulhu mythos or the equally fictional Priory of Sion dreamed up by synarchist Pierre Plantard and twentieth-century pataphysician and practical joker par excellence Philippe de Chérisey.

The public seems to have an inexhaustible appetite for this sort of thing and numerous philosophers and scholars, as well as frauds, imposters, and mountebanks, were attracted to the mythical Rosicrucian movement, each reinventing it in their own image. Virtually all the alchemists either claimed to be Rosicrucians or were posthumously associated with them, among them Paracelsus, Francis Bacon, Spinoza, and the Count Saint-Germain. Rene Descartes tried in vain to establish contact with the genuine brotherhood, searching across Germany, Belgium, and the Netherlands, but on his return to France was forced to admit he had been unable to find any trace of their existence. Not so, Harvey Spencer Lewis, the founder of the Ancient and Mystical Order Rosae Crucis (AMORC), essentially the American Rosicrucian movement, notorious for advertising in *Popular Mechanics* and other periodicals. Lewis insisted he had been initiated in 1909 in Toulouse, France, by the hidden masters of the "true secret order" whom he claimed had granted him a mandate to establish his American branch.

I couldn't help but wonder who those mysterious southern French Rosicrucians described by H. Spencer Lewis might have been and whether Antonin Gadal, self-proclaimed patriarch of the Ariège, might not have been a part of the equation. Certainly the European

Rosicrucians looked down on their American counterparts, assuming themselves to have a monopoly on the truth as secret societies the world over are wont to do. In truth, there was about as much evidence for the existence of the true Rosicrucian Order as there was for the Illuminati, Blavatsky's ascended masters, or any of the other "secret rulers of the world" spoken of in hushed tones by wistful New Agers and paranoid conspiracy theorists in their tireless efforts to order the chaos of human history and rationalize the misery of mortal experience.

I had gone looking for Shambhala, for Gurdjieff's secret Sufic initiatory center in the mountains of Asia, and had found little more than a few horse-head markers, a handful of totem poles, spiral jewelry, and carved roof beams, all but lost in a fug of war and death. In my years of searching, I had followed a shining thread of synchronicity that had led me around the world without leaving me any wiser. I had burned credit cards and relationships and sacrificed the chance to start a family or even own a dog—and all I had to show for it was a pocketful of bleeding stones.

On my return to London, things began to slip. I tried to patch myself back into the normal flow of human life but a state of anomie prevailed. I found myself falling prey to the uncomfortable suspicion that people were watching me or even following me on the streets and public transport system. I thought I could hear strange clicking and switching sounds on the line when I placed calls to Mr. Horn and my other associates, just like Paul Ladame had described, and I began to develop the impression my phone was tapped. On one occasion black-garbed "electricians" with foreign accents demanded admittance to my apartment, insisting they had been called out to check the lines when no such calls had been placed. They seemed too well groomed to be servicemen and failed to present ID when challenged.

Not long after getting back into town, I received a frantic late-night telephone call from JB informing me that Christian Koenig's home in Ussat-les-Bains had been broken into. Although the house had been utterly ransacked, the only things Christian claimed had been stolen were his precious meteoric stones. Given that almost no one in the world knew about the blessed things, Christian immediately assumed JB and myself were the culprits and deeply regretted inviting us in for that cup of tea. JB had a story of his own to tell, claiming a stranger on an intercity train had tried to steal the bag containing the stones he'd received when we divided the specimens at Fontanet. He'd been asleep at the time and using the bag as a pillow when the man tried to sneak it out from under his head. Fortunately JB had woken in the nick of time and the "well-dressed" stranger had hurried away, getting off at the next stop.

I'd been having a devil of a time trying to get the stones in my possession analyzed. Without access to a mass spectrometer my inquiries had effectively hit a brick wall. Even when I managed to get through to a seemingly sympathetic expert in meteoric debris at the British Museum, he somehow succeeded in mislaying my samples before the tests could be carried out. I didn't trust him with my remaining stones, which I took to carrying on my person at all times, hidden inside a Kinder Surprise egg container in my jeans. I didn't expect them to make me immortal, but I figured that way round they were less likely to go missing.

We were eyeball to eyeball with the new millenium. The apartheid era, smoking in cinemas, Margaret Thatcher, the Peace Convoy, and the Stonehenge Free Festival were all ancient history now, gone as if they had never existed. The Russian bear was on its knees and the global economy was in free fall. Clinton's presidency had hit the skids and rogue construction engineer Osama bin Ladin, had declared a holy war on the West, determined to overthrow the corrupt Saudi leadership and drive America out of the Holy Land, all for the sake of the Ka'bah, the black, meteoric heart of Mecca that the royal house of Saud was bound to protect as the "guardians of the faith." Rumors abounded that the end of the world was coming but by now I didn't believe them.

15

Searching the Ends of the Earth

Iceland 2005

Very far north, in the country of Fritjof Fritjofson, is a mountain of granite, one thousand meters high. Once in a thousand years a little bird lands on top of the mountain to sharpen its beak. When that mountain is finally worn to the ground one second of eternity will have passed. And this is the spirit in which to understand the story of Otto Rahn. . . .

PAUL ALEXIS LADAME (GENEVA 1998)

The glacial wind howled like the furious breath of an ice dragon. Born in a cyclonic whirling of cloud in the North Atlantic a thousand miles to the south of Reykjavik, it spun poleward in a wave-flattening thrust of freezing air, gathering momentum as it roared across the wilderness of moss and broken lava to beat against the impassive face of Mount Krafla. In winter these storm winds, moving in an unfaltering blast across the frozen rocks can touch velocities of

Fig. 15.1. The *Schwabenland*, North Sea, 1936.

100 miles an hour or more. Human flesh exposed to it would simply crystallize and turn to ice.

Even now, in the late summer, the temperature could drop to 7 degrees below, numbing my flesh and causing my nose to run uncontrollably as I forced myself forward, one step at a time, toward the great dark pyramid of the volcano and its smoldering cone that dominated the barren skyline ahead.

Despite the sub-zero temperatures the black rocks that surrounded me were too hot for the snow to settle and the ground beneath my feet thrummed with incessant geothermal activity.

"This is no place for a human being," I told myself. "So why am I here? What can I possibly hope to find in this wasteland?"

I allowed my mind to wander, returning to the summer of 1936 and the events that led me here. It had been a giddy year for Otto Rahn. He was planning to collaborate with the composer Hans Pfitzner on a new opera telling the tale of the Cathars and that July he had embarked on his most ambitious expedition to date, setting sail with a team of fellow SS men for the Arctic Circle. Women had not been allowed on the *Schwabenland*, which apparently flew a mysterious blue swastika rather than the familiar black and red sigil of Hitler's Reich.

Fig. 15.2. The crew of the *Schwabenland*, summer 1936.

This voyage to the far north, to the Ultima Thule of his ancestors, was to form the final passage in Otto Rahn's second book, *Luzifers Hofgesind* (*The Court of Lucifer*), a rather insubstantial travelogue thrown together under the aegis of his Nazi supervisors and delivered just in time for a numinously chosen deadline of October 31, the pagan festival of Samhain.

Typically, Otto Rahn's text is less than clear about the true purpose of his journey to the Arctic Circle and speculation has been rife as to whether he had hoped to find some sort of Nordic Mount Sinai, the vestiges of a long-lost Hyperborean homeland hidden beneath the ice or the gateway to the Hollow Earth. Perhaps it was all just an obscure, occult bonding exercise based on the Eddas.

Mr. Horn and I retraced Rahn's steps to Laugarvatin and Reykholt, taking time out in Snorri Sturluson's hot tub, the oldest surviving man-made structure in Iceland. Rahn and his comrades had been here in midsummer, 1936. Then we headed north, playing "Stairway to Heaven" over and over on the car stereo, snow and lumps of ice pattering ever more thickly against the windscreen as we wended our way toward the desolate shores of the Greenland Ocean. After a blowout we were forced to stop at Akuriri to purchase snow tires before continuing as far as the steaming slopes of Mount Krafla where we struck out on foot.

A great crack ran across the mountains' flanks where the earth had subsided in a titanic upheaval some years before. Pale, sulphurous vapors whirled up from its abyssal depths, rising about me like reaching, tortured wraiths as I skirted the jagged edge of the fissure. The cave mouth lay in a barren valley just below the rift. It looked pretty nondescript from the outside and was easy enough to miss on the first pass. Hunkering down, I eased myself into the gloom, shinning down a mound of rubble to the miasmal shores of a superheated subterranean lake where Rahn's trail finally petered out.

Curious pictoglyphs swam in my probing flashlight beam and I could make out distinctly elfin faces carved into the volcanic rock. Their stone features were oddly reminiscent of Clak Ashton Smith's Hyperborean carvings or the notorious face on Mars. Whether or not they constituted material proof of the young SS officer's claims or were merely vestiges of another elaborate hoax was impossible to say. The Icelandic people place more credence in the existence of the otherworld of trolls, elves, and faeries than folk in the warmer, more clement countries to the south, but here in the veritable back of beyond it was easy to see how such whimsical notions might retain their hold on the popular unconscious.

One of Rahn's Nazi peers in Heinrich Himmler's Black Order once remarked in an internal memo that he "half suspected Rahn of being in league with the Little People." But if anything, it was the odd pragmatism of Otto's quest that had kept me on the trail all these years. Otto hoped to find, if not the crown of Lucifer, then at least the stone that fell from it. I had several specimens of those extraterrestrial artifacts in my possession now, yet I still couldn't see how the young Grail hunter had intended to join the dots in his third book, "The Testament of Prometheus: A Journey to Hell and Beyond," a final magnum opus whose opening pages were written here on the Icelandic north cape.

Fig. 15.3. From the land beyond beyond. Mysterious carvings surround a subterranean warm water lake a hundred clicks from Akuriri. Photo by Richard Stanley.

Fig. 15.4. Toward Agharta. Photo by Richard Stanley.

The manuscript of "Prometheus" was in all likelihood lost to us now, although Colonel Howard Buechner had referenced it as a primary source in his self-published tome *Emerald Cup, Ark of Gold* (1991), the first account of the Rahn affair to have surfaced in the English language. In his mendacious reordering of the facts, Buechner told how an

SS expedition had discovered a mysterious cavern at the pole. Beyond the warm water lakes, the floor of the cavern had allegedly given way to a bottomless abyss spanned by an emerald ice bridge. On the far side, according to Buechner, could be seen the mouths of a number of tunnels from whence emanated "strange whispering sounds resembling human voices."

In Buechner's fantastical account, the Pyrenean Grail had been sealed within a specially constructed basalt obelisk designed by Karl Haushofer, director of the black lodge known as the Vril Society, and deposited in the mysterious ice cave to mark the entry point to the lost kingdom of "Agharta" and the world within.

Agharta, first described by French colonial magistrate Louis Jacolliot in his book *Le Fils de Dieu* ("The son of God") (1873), as a prehistoric City of the Sun and the seat of the Brahmatma, chief priest of the Brahmins, the visible manifestation of God on earth, was a sort of mythic spiritual twin to Shambhalah. After an Ahnenerbe SS expedition led by German naturalist Ernst Schäfer succeeded in penetrating Tibet and establishing diplomatic ties between Lhasa and the Reich it became increasingly clear there was no trace of the mythical initiatory centers of Shambhala and Agharta to be found in the mountains of Asia from whence the hidden masters supposedly directed world affairs. Rather than accept these cities had never been anything more than a myth to begin with, popular imagination had simply shifted their location, first to the poles and then into the Hollow Earth itself, a wholly fictional realm first charted by Verne, Lovecraft, Edgar Rice Burroughs, Halley, Agrippa, and Klim. To this day, right-wing occultists and UFO freaks continue to insist the reptilian skeletons of an elder race who first colonized Earth in the time of Mu and Gondwanaland, might still be found moldering in the farthest, secret mazes of the cavern system, in the very womb of the Magna Mater, the cthonic backwaters of Mahar haunted Phutra, the lightless labyrinths of Agharta and the black flame-lit caverns of Atvatibar and Kôr.

While I found these conceits entertaining enough, I couldn't help

Fig. 15.5. Gateway to the Hollow Earth—the shores of the warm water lake beneath Mount Krafla. Photo by Richard Stanley.

but suspect the truth lay closer to the surface. If the meteoric chalice really existed, then it had probably never left Europe, its continued presence an open secret, known only to an initiated few. When I first set out on the trail, I would have doubtless found this suggestion almost as ridiculous as the notion of Agharta and the Hollow Earth but I had seen too much by now to dismiss the rumors.

Clambering back into the car I turned up the volume on the stereo, the keening wind buffeting the vehicle as we headed south into a waiting darkness that seemed to stretch away and away to the ends of the earth itself.

Shortly after I got back to my apartment in River City, my mother, Penny, called to calmly tell me she was dying.

The first symptom she had noticed was that her eyes had grown sore. A visit to the doctor had confirmed she needed more than eye drops. In fact she had terminal lymphoma. There were cancerous tumors surrounding her optic nerves that were pushing her eyeballs slowly forward in their sockets so that, without realizing it, she had taken to sleeping without closing her lids, which was a freaky enough thought to begin with. She believed the lymphoma was a complication of an extreme allergic reaction to the epoxy resin she had been using to make the molds for her puppets, the tiny, lifelike figurines with which she had surrounded herself in her dotage.

My mother, Penelope Elton Miller, was an author and illustrator by trade, but an artist to the core and an extremely talented one—some would say a genius—possessed of a rare creative gift, a talent for imbuing even the basest of raw materials with character and life. Knowing that further attempts at surgery would inevitably destroy her eyesight, I resorted to the only cure I knew. Telling her to lie down and rest, I put meteor blood in her eyes.

Penny had been so knocked out on her meds she didn't really know what was happening and later told me she dreamed there were angels standing around her bed, healing her eyes, a particularly strange admission given that she had always claimed to be a die-hard atheist, who had little time for the Rahn affair, believing, like most folks, that the Holy Grail should stay in the Monty Python movie where it belonged—which tends to rule out placebo effect as a logical explanation. Call it coincidence then, but over the weeks that followed she was to make a full and dramatic recovery. I had spoken to the doctors and been fully apprised of their diagnosis. There had been no doubt in our minds that my mother had been at death's door. Perhaps it had been that first round of chemotherapy that had caught the lymphoma in time and knocked the ball right out of the park, but there was no denying her subsequent return to health was little short of miraculous.

Wolfram von Eschenbach had put it more baldly, simply stating that whoever had the stones or came into contact with them, "will have eternal life and will be healed." Yet if those blessed bleeding stones really did contain the key to the elusive secret of the gods, to immortality itself, then why hadn't it worked for Otto?

16
The Death and Transfiguration of Otto Rahn

Germany 1938–1939

It is no longer possible for a tolerant individual to live in the country my homeland has become. On my return to Munich it all came back to me. The bloody events to which I had borne witness. I could neither sleep, nor eat. It was as if a nightmare lay upon me . . .

OTTO RAHN

Fig. 16.1. Otto Wilhelm Rahn (1904–1939).

Midsummer found me at the Externsteine, a natural sandstone formation consisting of several fingers of oddly weathered rock that rise above the waters of a shadowy lake in the Teutoberg forest near the town of Horn-Bad Meinberg in the German state of North Rhine Westphalia. Archaeological investigation reveals the site has held a ritual significance since at least the Upper Paleolithic period with findings dating to between 10,700 BCE and 9,600 BCE. According to popular tradition, the stones were sacred to the pagan Saxons and the mythical location of the Irminsul idol destroyed by Charlemagne. As with the Cathar stronghold of Montségur, the chambers carved into the spires of the Externsteine are clearly aligned to the seasonal positions of the sun, moon, and stars. The circular hole above the altar stone in a chamber known as the *Höhenkammer*, "high chamber," is precisely aligned to the position of the rising sun on the summer solstice. An arched alcove with an open stone sarcophagus has been hewn out of the sandstone beside the lake, a structure known as the *Sargstein*, "tomb stone," which is used by the German neo-pagan movement for initiatory rituals to this day.

The modern German pagans were more discreet than their British counterparts who would have been gathering that same morning in the chilly predawn mists of Salisbury Plain. The stigma of the war and Heinrich Himmler's SS, to whom these stones had been beloved, cast a long shadow over their continued reverence. For a while I thought I might be the only one to turn out for the occasion, so it was an eerie sensation to see the candlelit procession that wound its way through the aisle of trees at the edge of the lake shortly before sunrise. The bobbing lights had a spectral, otherworldly beauty when they first appeared, weaving through the haze between the shadowy tree trunks, their reflections dancing like will-o'-the-wisps in the inky water. Then as they came nearer, I realized that, rather than woodland elementals, the candles were held by dreadlocked New Agers, no different from the sort of folks I had rubbed shoulders with at Stonehenge and Glastonbury.

Under the Hitler dictatorship, the Externsteine had become

a symbol of Nazi propaganda. The stones were excavated by the Ahnenerbe SS under Karl Maria Wiligut-Weisthor, who had placed great store in their significance to German volkisch identity. Indeed, I was only in Westphalia that summer in order to meet with the surviving members of the reichsführer's inner circle. I was no longer carrying a camera or working for any recognizable production company or television station. I simply wanted to know what had really happened back then, in the days when Otto Rahn and his dark masters had drawn their plans to overthrow the edifice of the Judaeo-Christian tradition and restore the old religion of their pagan ancestors.

I spoke briefly by telephone with Heinrich Himmler's daughter, which was about as close to the center of the surviving inner circle as I ever got. She put me on to one of her friends, a stern-faced elderly woman named Gabriele, who knew a lot more about the workings of the Ahnenerbe SS and its malignant legacy than herself.

Gabriele Winckler-Dechend was still an unreformed supporter of the Third Reich and remained a close friend of the reichsführer SS's surviving family. During the latter part of the 1930s and throughout the war she had acted as the driver and personal secretary to Karl Maria

Fig. 16.2. Heinrich Himmler and his daughter Gudrun. Courtesy of Germany Bundesarchiv.

Wiligut-Weisthor, the rune mage who headed up Himmler's Race and Settlement Office (RUSHA). I had to practically shave my head to get an interview with her, posing as an academic researching the symbolism of the Holy Grail in Germanic culture. I had been on Otto Rahn's trail for more years than I cared to remember and I still didn't know whether he was a Nazi who had infiltrated the pagan underground or vice versa, a neo-pagan who had infiltrated the SS and sought to turn the Hitler dictatorship to his own ends. Back in Carcassonne, Suzanne Nelli had told me about Rahn's Jewish roots and there was that Ahnenpass in the Bundesarchiv, filled out in the rogue SS obersturmführer's own hand to provide conclusive proof that his inspired efforts to bring down the old world order had gone very, very wrong, yet Christian Bernadac implied Rahn's superiors had conspired to give him a new identity, keeping the door open on the faint, yet distinctly chilling possibility the Nazi Grail hunter might still be alive.

"Of course, the story that he was on the run from the SS is completely untrue. This is something his family has put about since the war when it was not so fashionable to hold the views that were so widely held back in the '30s." Gabriele lit another cigarette, regarding me coldly. She claimed to have been especially fond of Otto, going as far as to flirt with him in those far-off days before the war. Gabriele had been barely out of her teens at the time, an elegant blonde who must have looked quite the part in her black uniform. It was well known that she had been the one who first recommended Otto's book *Crusade against the Grail* to her boss, an action that led to the young Grail historian being taken onto the department's payroll. She reminded me that Otto had apparently inherited some form of sixth sense from his father and claimed he could speak to her without moving his lips.

The story matched what I had already heard from Ingeborgh, but there were other details that didn't rest quite so easily with the broader picture.

During our luncheon Gabriele regaled me with a charming anecdote about how Otto had accompanied her to the premier of Ernst Schäfer's

SS-produced Tibetan documentary, *Geheimnis Tibet* ("Secret Tibet"), shot on hand-cranked 16 mm cameras during the celebrated Ahnenerbe expedition to the Himalayas in 1938. She claimed Otto was inspired to reproduce the mental feats of the Lamas shown in Schäfer's film, proving his point by telepathically communicating with her from the opposite side of the street on their way home. I didn't have the heart to point out that *Geheimnis Tibet* premiered in 1942, some three years after Otto was supposedly already dead.

Some of what Gabriele said, however, rang true or at least carried a degree of plausibility. She recalled that Rahn had a loyal bodyguard, whom I recognized by her description as the former barman from des Marronniers, Habdu, who had rescued the Grail hunter from the rising floodwaters during his descent into Fontanet. According to Gabriele, Rahn sent the Senegalese giant to intimidate the local priest in Ussat-les-Bains who had allegedly been stirring up the locals against him, accusing him of being a Nazi spy and a devil worshipper, both of which were probably true. Gabriele boasted that the priest had been so terrified he eventually apologized to Otto on his hands and knees, claiming that he had "seen the light." This still made her chuckle. She insisted Himmler would never have harmed Otto, whom she claimed in turn, had been totally behind the Black Order in everything they did. She made no mention of Otto Rahn's tour with the death's-head at Buchenwald, which came just after Kristallnacht, nor did she make any comment on his Jewish blood or his official resignation letter submitted a few months later. Claiming ignorance of any allegations concerning Rahn's less than Aryan ancestry, Gabriele insisted instead he had been forced to retire on account of "bronchial catarrh" from his chain smoking (80–100 a day) and the poor air in the camps that was hindering his attempts to complete work on his third and final book, "The Testament of Prometheus," whose missing manuscript she too expressed a great deal of curiosity in. Confirming the story that Martin Bormann was plotting to try to bring down Himmler at the time, she further drew my attention to the fact that

Fig. 16.3. Otto Rahn and his fiancée, Asta Baeschlin, pictured with her son by her first marriage.

Rahn had apparently been engaged to a young divorcée named Asta Baeschlin, who had broken off their engagement a month before his disappearance.

Apparently Otto Rahn had met Asta while vacationing in Lunberg and had gone as far as to announce his engagement to Himmler and his peers in the Black Order, presumably to allay continuing suspicion over his sexual orientation. Despite this announcement however, the marriage never took place, a factor that may well have contributed to his demise four weeks later. While Asta was still very much alive in 1998, she stubbornly refused to speak to me or respond to any of my many attempts to contact her. This was hardy surprising, given she was now a great-grandmother and presumably had no great desire to talk to researchers or camera crews about her prewar boyfriend in the SS.

In 1994, Asta Baeschlin issued the following statement to Reich historian Hans Jürgen Lange, her last word on the subject:

I was never engaged to Rahn, he just wanted everybody to believe that.... During my divorce in 1938 my son and I, together with a female servant, stayed during the summer in the Black Forest. By accident I met Rahn in a corner shop in the village. He told me about his books, and since I was quite interested in this matter he came to visit me a few times to tell me about his research. Not once did he touch me or attempt any overtures. On the contrary, he very much kept his distance, which suited me fine. Once he asked me if I intended to stay in Germany and if I would like to work on his research as well. I told him no, clearly. Rahn never once proposed to me. It seemed to me he would have liked a fictitious marriage, since he was not at all interested in me as a woman. In my opinion his true interest was with men. My suspicion grew when his friend Raymond Perrier came to visit him for some time. Rahn introduced me briefly to Perrier and after that I saw neither of them any more until Perrier left. I happened to be in the village and witnessed the pair saying farewell. Rahn cried his eyes out and apologised to me later for that. I regarded this scene as additional proof of my assumption. Later I understood that Rahn must have told his boss, Heinrich Himmler, also of an engagement—an unpleasant thing to have said. I presume he did it to camouflage his real tendency. I left at the end of August for Switzerland and sent Rahn a note that I wanted no further contact with him. (Hans Jurgen Lange, *Otto Rahn und die Suche nach dem Gral*, 1999)

"Nobody loved Otto, not Asta, not the French, perhaps not even his mother." Gabriele sighed, shaking her head. "Something must have happened to him that made him go looking for the Grail in the first place. You have to imagine why a young German would uproot himself and leave his home, friends, and family to go looking for something no one even believed existed. Something must have made him go to France, to Montségur, to learn French and Occitan, something that he kept to himself, that none of us will ever understand."

On September 1, 1937, Otto Rahn was implicated in a disciplinary hearing held for one of his black-garbed comrades, Karl Mahler of Arolsen, who was accused of "dishonorable conduct" in an investigation backed by Martin Bormann's private office. Bormann's staff had been engaged in gathering data to discredit the SS, which was threatening to become a virtual state within a state. It was impossible to know at this distance what Rahn's role may have been in this infraction, whether it involved the mistreatment of the prisoners or alleged homosexuality as Hans Jürgen Lange has suggested. In a signed declaration, Rahn was forced to swear off alcohol for two years and as punishment was stripped of his rank and reassigned to guard duty. According to both Suzanne Nelli and Christian Bernadac, Rahn had been forced to participate in the Nazi breeding program known as the *lebensborn* before being enrolled into a grueling exercise regime at Buchenwald designed to "toughen him up" for active military service. His former publisher, Albert von Haller, told me Otto was openly gay, insisting, perhaps a little too stridently, this had been the true cause of his downfall.

Gabriele, on the other hand, went out of her way to rebut these allegations, claiming Otto Rahn not only flirted with her but had spoken of Dachau in the most glowing terms and during his time there had paid particular attention to the planting of an extensive herb garden. Rahn had been very interested in naturopathy and herb lore and, according to Gabriele, saw his tour of duty as a chance to both creatively utilize the labor force and reeducate the prisoners, supervising, among other projects, the mass production of traditional gifts such as the *julleuchter*, a form of candleholder designed for the celebration of the Yuletide festivities that Wiligut-Weisthor hoped would one day supersede Christmas.

Dachau was not yet an extermination camp and only assumed those characteristics after Kristallnacht (November 9, 1938) when the genocidal persecution of the German Jews began in earnest. Despite Gabriele's claims to the contrary, what Rahn saw and experienced in the camp under the command of his homicidal superior, Theodor Eicke, must have left him chronically depressed.

He wrote repeatedly to Himmler's personal adjutant, Karl Wolff, asking to be released from his duties, but by now he had lost the ear of the reichsführer and his requests were ignored.

In a handwritten memo addressed to Karl Wolff, dated February 28, 1939, Otto asked to be allowed to leave the SS for "reasons so serious they can only be communicated orally." His discharge was granted by Himmler on March 17, penciling a single word in the margin—"*Ja*"—before initializing the request, which was backdated to February 22, although by then SS Obersturmführer Otto Wilhelm Rahn was in all likelihood already dead.

The story of Rahn's demise was already shadowy enough, but the tale of the two publishers only serves to further muddy the picture of his final days. One more example of the curious mirroring that seems to haunt every aspect of the affair.

"The last time I saw Rahn I was visiting the writer Kurt Eggars. Perhaps you have heard of him?" Albert von Haller, Otto Rahn's publisher sat blinking at me from his favorite armchair beside the hearth

Fig. 16.4. Otto Rahn's resignation letter.

Fig. 16.5. Albert von Haller, publisher of *Court of Lucifer*.

in the cluttered study of his home in Stuttgart. He was ninety-five years old and had recently written the libretto for a new opera about Eskimos. Still very active, he looked like a wizened old gnome out of a story by the Brothers Grimm, although in Rahn's day he must have been an imposing man, so imposing the young SS officer resorted to taking a full bevy of black garbed bodyguards to one of their meetings in a vain attempt to get Albert to pay his royalties.

"Rahn was always in financial difficulties," confided Albert. "The last time I saw him at Kurt's house, he looked tired and disheveled. His hair and clothes were a mess. He said he was on the run. On the run from the SS. My first instinct was to let him have my passport, which had a stamp for France so that perhaps he could escape across the border, but Kurt Eggers told me not to get involved. Rahn's downfall came as a result of a power struggle between Martin Bormann and the SS. Kurt knew the Gestapo would be watching him for sure."

According to Albert, Rahn's Luciferian buddy, Kurt, warned him the young Grail seeker was already under surveillance and that "when he is caught your passport will be found and then you'll be in it just like me!"

Over the years to come, I often wondered what 'it' was—and what Eggars really meant when he'd told Albert "you'll be in it, just like me." What were Rahn and Eggars caught up in? A scandal and an investigation for sure but had it come upon them because of their sexual orientation, Luciferian beliefs, occult practices, or Jewish blood? Or did they simply know too much?

"I understood," muttered Albert, averting his gaze, "and did nothing."

Albert's account stood in stark contrast to the testimony of Otto Vogelsang, the publisher of *Crusade against the Grail*, who told a very different story. Vogelsang claimed to have met with his former client a few days later on March 8 at the Hotel Zahringer in Freiburg. He insisted Rahn appeared "relaxed and happy" and seemed "confident about his future."

Otto Rahn left the hotel in Freiburg at approximately 11:00 p.m., apparently intending to travel back to Munich, although it must be assumed he made his way instead toward the French border. A postcard received shortly afterward by his friend and mentor Antonin Gadal in Ussat-les-Bains carries only four terse words: "I miss your country."

For some reason Rahn got off the bus at Zoll shortly before it reached the frontier. Perhaps they were stopping other vehicles up ahead and he knew he would be searched and sent back to the camp. He was an experienced mountaineer who could have easily made it across the border on foot. The mountains were little more than 66,500 feet high, a mere walk in the park for a man like him.

The last people to speak to him were the children of a Tyrolean farmer who saw a figure dressed in black emerge from the snowbound woods outside their cottage on the evening of March 13, 1939. The stranger had come to within a hundred feet of the house, stood still for a moment and looked at his golden watch. He had seemed to be in a hurry, pausing just long enough to ask the children if they knew the time. Then he turned and went down the valley toward the stream where they watered the cows. After that he seemed to disappear. As the shadows lengthened and a storm began to close in, the children's parents tried in vain to search for the mysterious hiker but were surprised to find that he had left no footprints in the snow.

"In mid March '39 by the Rechauerhof lay a meter of snow," explained Peter Maier, trudging uphill across a carpet of pine needles. "The next farmyard was an hour and a half away. He must have gone upstream, walking in the water so as not to leave any tracks. My brother

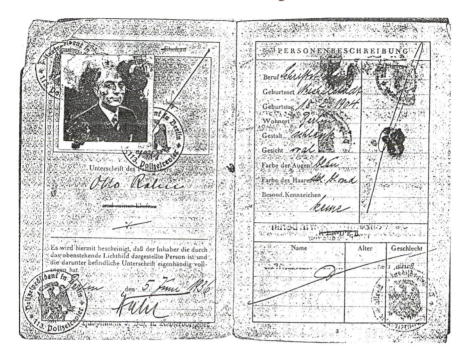

Fig. 16.6. Otto Rahn's water-damaged passport, retrieved from the corpse.

and I found him three months later when the spring thaw came, sitting just there under the tree, covered by his coat." Peter graciously pointed out the spot. The view was indeed breathtaking. Looking down one could see across two different valleys, as far as the frontier.

"We recognized him by his coat and hat. It was the man who had passed by our house. Next to his body lay two medicine bottles, one empty and the other half empty. He was identified by his passport, which was still in his breast pocket."

I don't know what was in those medicine bottles, but according to the subsequent police report filed in Zoll, the pills didn't kill him. He froze to death. The thirty-five-year-old German-Jewish Grail historian was buried at the base of the Kufstein where he lay until the end of the war when his body was moved to a plot in Darmstadt. For reasons that remain unclear, no formal death certificate was ever issued. Whether he was the victim of foul play or had voluntarily chosen to leave a world he

Fig. 16.7. The Meier farm.
Photo by Hamilton White.

saw disintegrating around him remains a matter of debate.

The fact that Wiligut-Weisthor was forced to retire from the SS that same month suggests that perhaps Rahn did discover something in the course of his travels, something that led to both men being abruptly silenced. Karl Wolff, Himmler's chief of personal staff who subsequently signed the deceased Grail historian's obituary in the *Volkische Beobachter*, would seem to have played a leading role in bringing about both Rahn and Wiligut-Weisthor's downfalls and the subsequent dismantling of the Ahnenerbe, the SS's prehistory department. The previous November, Wolff had paid a personal call on Wiligut-Weisthor's estranged wife, Malwinne, in Salzbug, taking the opportunity provided by the Anschluss, Germany's unification with Austria, to pull her husband's psychiatric records, which were subsequently dumped on Himmler's desktop, an action that effectively rendered the aging rune mage's continued presence in the SS untenable. One can only assume Wolff was acting in concert with a faction within the SS who were actively opposed to the Luciferian element that had taken root within the order.

Wiligut-Weisthor was too important to Himmler to be killed. Instead, he had been quietly sequestered and shuffled from one SS safe house to another throughout the war before dying on Gabriele's couch in the winter of '46. He was an eighty-year-old man with a history of psychiatric illness, whereas Rahn may have been more of a liability and—so the story goes—had to be eradicated and all trace of his research expunged from the face of the Earth.

Karl Wolff later became the Nazi ambassador to the Vatican and survived the war. He was granted immunity for his crimes by agreeing to testify against his former comrades at Nuremberg and later became well known as one of the principal interviewees and narrators of the BBC series *The World at War* (1973–1974), as well as playing an active role in discrediting the Hitler diaries for *Stern Magazine* and helping bring Klaus Barbie to justice in Paraguay. I was mercifully born too late to attend Nuremberg, but I did get to sit in on the libel trial in London's high court, which resulted in the downfall of British military-historian and Holocaust denier David Irving. Irving had consistently attacked the credibility of the experts introduced to counter his claims that a deliberate policy of mass extermination had never been practiced at Auschwitz or, by implication, the other camps, so when the barrister introduced Karl Wolff's testimony, he couldn't help quipping, "Surely you would consider the reichsführer's personal adjutant to be a credible witness, would you not?" Ignoring the polite murmur of laughter from the peanut gallery, Irving screwed up his eyes and remarked, "Well, it's a bit of a curate's egg, really . . ."

And the funny thing is I know exactly what he means. Only it isn't the slightest bit funny.

17
Aftermath

"There was a certain aftermath . . ."

Madame Nelli returned her gaze to the embers surging on the hearth. We were seated in the downstairs parlor at Maison Couquet where Maurice Magre and Déodat Roché had held the first neo-Cathar conferences in the spring of 1929. The fire had died down and for a moment I thought about putting on another log, but the hour had grown late.

"Something was set in motion back then," she said, "a seed planted." Suzanne Nelli relaxed and it was the first time I had seen her look content, eyes taking in the room and the memories it contained. She seemed particularly pleased by the sight of the round table and its famous yellow cloth.

"I take it you've read Greil Marcus's book *Lipstick Traces*?" I asked, checking to make sure we were still recording. Madame Nelli blinked, not following my train of thought. "He traces a line from Catharism via the dadaists, the surrealists, and the situationists to the modern counterculture," I explained. "He portrays the medieval heretics as a manifestation the same antinomian, negationist spirit as Sid Vicious and the Sex Pistols."

Suzanne Nelli sighed, shaking her head at the folly of it all. "There have been many, many different people drawn to this place, to the mountain, as if it were a beacon in the darkness. Otto Rahn was one of the first, but there were many that came after him: Umberto Eco; Paulo Coelho; Karl Oelbermann, the founder of the Wandervogel. They all stayed here at this auberge. There was even among us a black magician . . ." Her voice tailed off as an ember sparked on the hearth. Then she smiled, still lost in the immutable past.

"One day this black magician climbed on top of the chateau, his arms spread out like a cross atop the highest wall and he called upon his spirits. We were just sitting down about this table, waiting to be served, talking politely when suddenly the Prince of Saxe fell backward. You know the chairs here are sometimes . . . a few moments later it was my husband who fell backward. So we decided it wasn't normal, that it was the black magician exhibiting his powers. Perhaps he wanted to show he was more powerful than the Christian Cathars."

Her smile broadened into a laugh and just as suddenly she was serious again, that familiar baleful look returning to her dark eyes.

"There were a few faithful of Montségur, led by my husband and Joseph Mandement, who decided to celebrate the seven hundredth anniversary of the fall of the castle. You remember Mandement, of course? He was the one who reportedly threw Otto out of the cave. Anyway, he was the head of the Syndicate of the Initiative, which was in charge of the tourism in those days."

I nodded. The name was familiar to me. In fact I had already guessed that Mandement might have been the real culprit behind the esoteric graffiti, merely blaming Otto afterward as a convenient scapegoat. Given his interest in promoting tourism to the area he had both the motivation and the opportunity.

"It was 1944, so public gatherings were illegal. They might have been thrown into prison or maybe even sent to Germany. So Mandement went to see the commandant in Toulouse all by himself. Nobody wanted to go with him, but he kept a level head. The commandant told him there was no point in celebrating because soon the war would be over and the Berlin Philharmonic would come to mount a production of *Parsifal* at Montségur. So he left with nothing. But they decided to do it all the same. Seven or eight of them climbed the mountain. I can't remember all their names. It was cold. Well, it was the sixteenth of March. Someone read a poem. After that a plane was heard passing overhead. It's here that the myths and legends begin . . ."

So the plane had come after all. In Colonel Howard Buechner's 1991 account, *Emerald Cup, Ark of Gold*, the former Allied army surgeon claims Otto Skorzeny couldn't resist flying a victory lap over the celebrating neo-Cathars to show the Grail had been secured for the greater glory of Hitler's Reich—yet military records reliably place Skorzeny in Hungary on March 16, 1944.

"Maybe it was the command at Tours that sent a fighter plane to see if people were gathering at Montségur, to start a revolution, that kind of thing. It was said that there was someone behind the pilot, I don't know who. The plane circled above, making Celtic crosses." Suzanne paused, noticing the incredulous look in my eyes. "The Celtic cross is a cross centered in a circle. Why a Celtic cross? Because the origins of the Germans are Celtic. After the plane was sighted, they came down at full speed. They took the car and came here to eat a hearty dish of beans at Maison Couquet. That's a detail that proves the story is true."

Outside, a freezing mist was rolling in from the mountains. Leika IV stared past me into the encroaching darkness, ears quivering.

"I never knew what became of Rahn. Somebody told me that maybe he was on that plane."

Christian Bernadac believed the young explorer and occultist had escaped Germany by assuming the identity of his dead brother and it would have been reassuring to believe Otto had found his Grail and with it the secret of life eternal, although personally, I had come to suspect his remains were interred in the family plot in Darmstadt where they had been transferred after the war. In the absence of a death certificate, the only hard evidence I had to support this claim was a photocopy of the water-damaged passport found on the corpse and the body-bag tag from when the remains were moved from Zoll to Darmstadt.

Aftermath 327

Fig. 17.1. The tag from Rahn's body bag.
Photo by Hamilton White.

Fig. 17.2. The Rahn family plot in Darmstadt.

Of course, as Christian insisted, you would have to exhume the body and compare its DNA to a swab harvested from Ingeborgh to be absolutely certain. The only thing you can be sure of is that despite his many sins Otto Rahn died a martyr's death and hence deserves to sit among the elect of his unknown religion.

Standing beside the inconspicuous family plot in the vast central graveyard in Darmstadt, I said a prayer for Otto's soul.

Then, leaving him a bunch of twelve red roses and a blackbird feather I'd picked up from the floor of the grotto of Fontanet, I turned and walked back to the car.

18

The Three Mothers

Three sisters they are, of one mysterious household; and their paths are wide apart; but of their dominion there is no end . . .

THOMAS DE QUINCEY (1821)

Once upon a time, a young nobleman named Ignatio set out across Spain on his horse. On the way he met a Moor, a baptized Arab, and lured him into a discussion on the Virgin Mary. The Moor believed in the Immaculate Conception but contested the notion that her virginity could have survived intact after the birth of Christ. Ignatio took this as an insult to his faith and in typically violent terms sought immediate redress.

At that time, being the early sixteenth century, the chevaliers of Spain led an idle life around their sovereign and had lost the bravery and dignity of their ancestors. While demonstrating an excessive humility to their king and his favorites, they were rude and arrogant toward those they considered their inferiors, especially foreigners and people of a darker complexion. Ignatio had the outward appearance of a knight, hardy and provoking, dressed in a leather doublet, armed with both sword and pistol, his dark, receding hair curling from beneath the broad felt brim of his travel-stained hat, but his inward character was displayed by the murderous look in his eyes and is perhaps best summed up by an official document of the time, a claim brought by the Corrigidor of Guipozcoa in 1515 at the Episcopal tribunal of Pamplona in which the

Fig. 18.1. In the basilica of Montserrat.
Photo by Richard Stanley.

magistrate described the young nobleman as "treacherous, violent, and vindictive."

Accordingly the Moor was on his guard and beat off Ignatio's unprovoked attack before hightailing it, his Persian stallion easily outrunning the psychotic chevalier's long-suffering Spanish pony. As he watched the dark man's dust cloud dwindle across the flatlands, Ignatio asked himself if it was his duty or not to pursue his slanderer and kill him or at least die trying. In his soul and conscience, he could not resolve this dilemma so following an old superstitious tradition of chivalry he decided to rely on a sign, on this occasion the judgment of his horse. He freed the bridle and allowed his steed to choose its own path.

Before long he caught sight of a strange, jagged mountain range on the horizon and felt himself borne helplessly toward it. As he drew nearer to the gleaming white cliffs, the young chevalier noticed what looked like a monastery built on a plateau high above the clouds and tying up his faithful steed, he started up the winding stone steps toward the basilica. And so it was that the nobleman, Ignatius of Loyola, came without knowing it to the mountain of Montserrat and the temple of the Black Mother, *la Moreneta*, the "little dark one" of the Catalans. He spent the night meditating in the presence of the mysterious icon and later claimed to have been visited by "a blinding, celestial light" and a series of bizarre visions. "Something white resembling three keys of a clavichord or an organ" appeared to him and he immediately thought it was a manifestation of the Holy Trinity (Albert Ebneter, *Der Jesuitenorden*, 1982. Author's translation). Then the three shapes merged into the glowing body of a single luminous being and the young chevalier began to weep uncontrollably as he realized the error of his ways and all the harm he had caused to others during his worldly life. Later this miracle came to be known as the *gratia lacrymarum* or the "grace of tears" that marked the quest knight's spiritual metamorphosis. Then his luminous visitor took another form, becoming a huge, coiling rainbow-hued serpent whose beauty terrified him.

The Three Mothers   331

Fig. 18.2. Inside the basilica of the Black Mother.
Photo by Richard Stanley.

Laying down his weapons at the feet of Our Lady, the chevalier swore himself to her service as a defender of la Morenita's celestial kingdom.

In the fullness of time Ignatius of Loyola would become renowned as the founder of the Society of Jesus, the black-garbed warrior monks we call the Jesuits. Ignatius came down from the mountain to set off on his conquest of the "kingdom of the sky," sojourning for a while in a humid grotto at the foot of a cliff near Manresa, where he sought to cleanse himself by inflicting the most severe exercises of penitence on his suffering flesh. He would spend seven or eight hours every morning kneeling in prayer and sometimes fast and go without sleep for days on end. He would flagellate himself heavily and it was not uncommon that he would wound his chest with a stone.

One day he went so far he fell seriously ill and was carried unconscious into the house of a benefactor. The doctors gave him up for lost and some of the pious women began to beg the lady of the house to cede pieces of his clothing to them as relics. To satisfy their desires she opened the cupboard containing Ignatio's belongings, only to recoil in horror. Suspended within were neatly arranged the worst instruments of torture and mortification the mind could conceive; penitence belts in plaited steel threads, heavy chains, nails disposed in the form of a cross, and an undergarment bristling with iron tips. A typically medieval penchant for self-harm is reflected today in the barbed *cilice* worn by devout followers of Opus Dei, the order founded by another tortured soul who likewise found solace of sorts at Montserrat, Jose Maria Escriva, who, like Saint Ignatius, was posthumously canonized with unseemly haste. Yet there is more to this morbid sexual fetish than uninitiated eyes might readily discern. A method to its madness.

These are the spiritual exercises of the Jesuit order as laid down by its founder, Saint Ignatius of Loyola:

> He who practises them must, with the help of all his senses, undergo the experiences of Heaven and Hell, from sweet beatitude to devouring woe so that the difference between Good and Evil might imprint themselves forever on his soul. So that Evil is made tangible the spiritual exercises serve as a terrifying enactment of Hell. It must be represented in all its horror, full of the legions of the groaning damned . . .

Saint Ignatius codified this strange enactment into a series of precise points:

> The first key consists of looking with the imagination of the eyes at the length, width and depth of Hell and the immense fires of the abyss and the souls imprisoned in their burning bodies . . .

The second key consists of listening with the imagination of the ears to the lamentations, cries, vociferations and blasphemies which slander our lord and his saints . . .

The third key consists of breathing with the imagination of smell, the smoke, the sulphur, the mire and rot of Hell . . .

The fourth key consists of tasting with the imagination of taste, all things bitter, tears, sourness and the maggot of conscience . . .

The fifth key consists of touching with the imagination of touch the flames that burn the soul . . .

Then, and only then, is the candidate ready for Level Two.

There are many paths to enlightenment, as varied as the chemical elements that make up our material world and not all of them are as dismal as the one chosen by Ignatius, but it is a path nonetheless, a hard way perhaps, but the only one available to "those in whom a profound nature has been upheaved . . . by conspiracies from without and conspiracies from within . . . in whom the heart trembles and the brain rocks," for those who have come unwittingly into the domain of Our Lady of Darkness.

By the end of the century, I was a single man, burned out by prolonged exposure to the film industry and in a devil-may-care mood. My mother, Penny, expressed a growing desire to see all the places I told her about during her convalescence, and when she was strong enough I took her to meet the Mother of Darkness, Mater Tenebrarum, the Black Madonna of Montserrat. It was a pilgrimage I was keen to make, knowing in all likelihood it would be the last journey my mother and I would take together. Retracing Otto Rahn's steps from the autumn of 1932 when he acted on the Countess de Pujol Murat's advice and booked passage south to Montserrat, literally the "serrated mountain"— a second Grail mountain that was also a mountain of Venus, a spiritual twin and antithesis to Montségur. Here in the Benedictine monastery library, a facility housing possibly the most extensive collection of medieval manuscripts in the world, Otto Rahn had sought the final piece of

334   The Three Mothers

Fig. 18.3. Our Lady of Darkness—the Black Madonna of Montserrat.
Photo by Richard Stanley.

the puzzle that enthralled, obsessed, and ultimately consumed him—the key to spiritual tradition symbolized by the Grail, the mysterious life-giving font of the arcanum.

The subsequent report Rahn made to the Ahnenerbe SS in 1934 must have been striking, given the impression it made on the Reichsführer Heinrich Himmler, who felt compelled to visit the site in person. There is no doubt Himmler looked to the Jesuit Order as a model for the SS, to the extent that Hitler once referred to him as "my very own Ignatius." On October 21, 1940, Himmler was dispatched to Madrid to coordinate a meeting between Franco and Hitler at the border town of Hendaye. As soon as he had dealt with the necessary protocol and concluded the arrangements for the summit, Himmler put conventional politics aside and set out for Barcelona. The head of the SS was greeted with a triumphal arch of green laurel erected in his honor by Catalan nationalists in the Prat de Llobregat before making his way, accompanied by his personal adjutant Karl Wolff, to the holy mountain of Montserrat where Mater Tenebrarum waited to receive him. This

Fig. 18.4. Heinrich Himmler visits Montserrat—*La Vanguadia*, October 1940.

was surely an outcome the Countess de Pujol Murat could not have conceived, yet it was undoubtedly her advice that led the master of the Black Order to the site, not that it mattered to either her or Otto, for they were both one with the dust by then.

Just as another failed quest knight had come here in the early sixteenth century when Ignatio de Loyola, whose spiritual exercises were to provide a template for Himmler's SS, arrived in Montserrat after letting go of the reins of his horse and allowing his steed to choose its own way, Himmler was not the only martinet to have been drawn to the domain of the dark mother whose roll-call of unsavory courtiers across the centuries makes for alarming reading. Both Franco and Josemaria Escriva, the founder of Opus Dei, held Montserrat in high regard.

Fig. 18.5. An audience with Our Lady of Darkness.
Photo by Penny Miller.

My mother and I rode the cable car through the curling mists, joining the queue of pilgrims winding through the basilica, passing beneath an archway decorated by a seemingly incongruous mural depicting Salome clutching the severed head of John the Baptist to ascend a final flight of stairs and touch the globe in la Moreneta's extended hand. I closed my eyes and tried to pray, for my mother and the world, and if I wished for anything it was merely for the right thing to happen, for my ears to hear her whisper more clearly and my heart to know her mysteries more keenly.

The icon's ebony skin is a riddle older than Christ or the Torah, older even than recorded history. According to the guidebooks, the little dark one was found on the mountain in 888 CE, not long after the liberation of Barcelona from the Moors. She was apparently discovered by shepherds who were led by mysterious drifting lights to a grotto where the image of the Black Mother had been concealed by what the official texts describe as a "fleeing Gothic bishop," which frankly raises more questions than it answers. Apparently when repeated attempts to move the otherworldly icon to the nearest village, Manresa, were thwarted by violent electrical storms, it was decided to leave the image in situ and build the basilica around her so she might be venerated on the mountain where she belonged.

Over subsequent centuries, devotion to la Moreneta spread eastward with the Mediterranean conquests of the Catalan-Aragonese monarchy. Throughout their Italian territories there were over 150 churches dedicated to the Madonna of Montserrat. At a later period, the imperial dynasty in Spain consolidated the cult of the Black Mother in central Europe—in Bohemia and Austria, carrying her westward with the conquest of the New World. The Americas had close links with the little dark one from the very beginning, thanks to the presence at Columbus's side of a former hermit from the mountain, Bernat Boil, thus making her image the first "Christian" icon to officially cross the Atlantic. The first place the expedition made landfall was named in her honor, the remote, volcanic island of Montserrat and the first churches in Chile, Mexico, and Peru were dedicated to her, leading to her popular appellation—the Virgin of the New World.

That night I climbed alone to the summit of this second Grail mountain and sat beneath the stars, doing my best to still the babble of my inner voices and the countless unanswered questions that still confounded me. The basilica on the plateau below seemed as insignificant as a sandcastle and despite the hour I could see a light still blazing in the window of the Benedictine abbey library, some scholar working late on his translation, I supposed. Above the abbey, the white cliffs rose and rose, dwarfing the buildings and the icon they contained, the lights of Barcelona strewn like a handful of ineffectual glitter dust along the far horizon. According to the guidebook, the jagged rock formations are the result of a freak sedimentary deposit but seeing those stone spires by starlight left me in little doubt I was in the presence of giants, imprisoned behemoths, and impassive prehuman deities that had gazed mutely on infinity since time began.

In the beginning there was only the void and the eye in the void,

Fig. 18.6. Montserrat by starlight.
Photo by James "JB" Bourne.

the awareness the Egyptians called Set. The deity whose image is venerated on the magical mountain of Montserrat might have begun her journey as Au-Set, the seat of consciousness, the throne of her male counterpart Au Sar, the eye in the throne. As a woman conceives and begats life, so Au-Set symbolized the living embodiment of that primal awareness, much in the same manner the Hebrew Shekinah represents the installation, presence, or embodiment of divinity. The Greeks venerated Au-Set, the "consciousness embodied," as Isis and her counterpart Au-Sar as Osiris—also called Neb T-Chetta, Lord of Eternity. Her two daughters were Bast, the cat-faced one, and Neb Tet, the Lady of the Temple. Suffice to say, she was a radiant being and one of the nine original members of the grateful dead. They were not so much gods, these holy nine, as radiant aspects of the one God, for the Egyptian faith is in essence a heliocentric monotheism based around Ra, the sun god, who is the father of the other bright ones.

Some archaeologists have tried to argue the holy nine are descended from a quasi-mythological memory of an ancient hierarchical race who exerted a civilizing influence over the ancestors of dynastic Egypt. The Moors knew her homeland by another name, *al Khem*, or the Black Land. This epithet is thought by some to be an allusion to the rich, black, fertile soil of the Nile valley and by others as direct proof Egyptian civilization represented the finest flowering of African art and culture.

The science of Egypt, alchemy, came to be regarded by some as the dark art or the black art, just as the work of the Arab philosopher Geber was thought to be "gibberish" to uninitiated eyes, while only a select few recognized it as the secret language of algebra. The Arabic language is constructed so that many different meanings can be derived from tri-lateral root words and their variations. The writer and Eastern esoteric scholar Idries Shah Sayed insists that for *black*, we should read "wise." This confusion apparently arises from a play on two roots, FHM and FHHM, pronounced "fecham" and "facham," meaning "black" and "wise," respectively. The FHM root can also mean "knowledge" or "understanding," depending on context and pronunciation. Thus the so-called dark art is also the wise art, just as the black art is really the art of light.

I sat on the mountaintop and if I waited for a sign that night, none came. The gods of Montserrat were silent, as stone gods are prone to be, and the far Grail's beckoning light came no closer. Instead dawn arrived and I took breakfast at the monastery before attending morning mass with my mother and driving slowly back up north through the Pyrenees into the heartlands of old Occitania. I recall we stopped for a late, packed lunch in Montailou, a mountain-locked former Cathar enclave where Esclarmonde d'Alion once had her castle, a location familiar from the fourteenth century Inquisition register of Jacques Fournier, one of Otto's primary sources. Only a single briar-ridden wall remained of Esclarmonde's castle. A toothless old man seated in the town square told us the Cathars were gone now. Nothing remained. The only true mystery, he confided, was that sometimes the statue of the virgin moved by itself in the locked church at night.

The thought of that moving statue haunted me as we continued on our way, down through the white-capped valley of the Ariège by way

Fig. 18.7. Montaillou. Photo by Penny Miller.

of Ussat to Montségur and Madame Couquet's auberge, where the first fire of the season already smoldered on the hearth. Madame greeted us with open arms, looking somehow younger than when I saw her last. The old inn was the closest I had come to a real home over the years, and despite the language barrier, Madame Couquet struck up an instant rapport with my mother that was to become a lasting, almost intuitive bond. Strange and oddly reassuring as it was to see these two matriarchs together at the long table, the homecoming was not complete without a third mother, a replica of the Black Madonna I had purchased in Montserrat and presented now to Madame to watch over the auberge.

"Merci. It's very nice. But we already have one."

"What?"

"She says she's already got one."

"Thanks, Mom. I can . . . What d'you mean she's already got one?"

"Oui, oui!" Madame nodded, trying to explain in her heavily accented southern French.

"Notre Dame la Lumiere!"

"You mean another replica?"

"No. A real one."

And it was true . . .

The third mother had been there all along, hidden in plain sight in the tiny church opposite the auberge. To be fair, the chapel was kept carefully locked with only one mass performed every year on Lammas or Lughnasadh (August 1), the festival of the first fruits with a priest brought in from a neighboring village to perform the duties. Given a little help from Madame Couquet however, it didn't take me long to get the key.

And there she was. Beautiful, cryptic, proud, staring out from the dust of 300 years, since monks from Montserrat had first brought her from the far side of the mountains to symbolize their spiritual kinship with the hardy villagers of Montségur, explicitly linking the initiatory mountains in a way Otto Rahn had scarcely guessed at. Otto had spent enough time at Montserrat to familiarize himself with the Benedictine

Fig. 18.8. Our Lady of Montségur. Photo by Jason Stabler.

Fig. 18.9. Did you wonder what is behind the Black Madonna? The back of Notre Dame de Montségur's throne displays a cryptic lunar calendar. Photo by Jason Stabler.

library and draw on its medieval texts in his research, but in his haste to denigrate the Holy Roman faith responsible for the extermination of his beloved Cathars, he blinded himself to the common pagan roots that bound these sites together, roots that ran deeper than Christianity.

"My ancestors were witches and I am a heretic," wrote Otto Rahn and in his natural revulsion for the Inquisition and his hankering for the lost ideals of the troubadours, he missed what had been right under his nose all along. He derided the faith of Madame Couquet's father, who had given him lodging, and never set foot inside the church to catch sight of that all-important icon, the Black Mother who had been venerated in those mountains by one name or another since time out of mind. Perhaps in his haste to identify Montségur with the mythical Grail castle, he overlooked the fundamental contradiction of a heretical faith that viewed the material world as being inherently flawed having a material treasure to begin with. It was not in the nature of the Cathars to venerate relics in the manner of the Catholic Church, and the sight of the blood of Christ liquefying from the living rock tends to lose much of its superstitious charge if the attendant culture doesn't accept the existence or theological relevance of a flesh and blood messiah to begin with. As with the consistent conflation of the ancient Celts, the Druids, Beaker folk, and megalith builders of Stonehenge and Avebury into a single mythic culture by the modern New Agers, it was all too easy before the advent of reliable carbon dating and other techniques common to modern archaeology to misidentify the shrapnel of a dozen time periods as the residue of a single "old religion," and it transpires the caves of the Lombrives have been continuously inhabited since the end of the last ice age. It is my considered contention that Otto Wilhelm Rahn and Antonin Gadal did not find the Holy Grail or the mythical treasure of the Cathars, but rather the relics of a far older cult that had held those caverns sacred long years before Christ and his cup.

Before the Blessed Virgin Mary or the Black Madonna, before Kybele, or Cybele, or Sybil, she was known as Kubaba, the goddess of the caves, who was worshipped in grottos and on mountaintops since the dim-red dawn of creation and known to her adherents as the Great Mother—*Magna Mater* or *Meter Orie*, the "Mountain Mother," and by whose name we know the black stones that have been associated with her worship since timeless time: *meteorites*, quite literally the "stones of the Mountain Mother."

These ancient aerolites, fragments of the great outside that rained down through the jurassic mists of an antehuman Earth were sometimes referred to by our ancestors as Baetylus, Bethel, or Betyl stones and revered as hard, dark symbols of the gods themselves. The enigmatic epithet Betyl would seem to be derived from the Semitic *bet el*, or house of God, the name allegedly given by Jacob to the location near Haran where he slept with his head against a stone and experienced the dream of the ladder. Curiously this passage gives rise to the cryptic phrase the Abbe Berenger Sauniere engraved for his own peculiar reasons above the door of the church of Marie Madeleine in Rennes-le-Château—*Terribilis est locus iste*—quoting Genesis 28:17, "And he was afraid, and said, 'How terrible is this place! This is none other than the house of God, and this is the gate of heaven.'"

The stones that fell from heaven were venerated, not because of their extraterrestrial origin, which our ancestors could barely have guessed at, but because their alleged physical properties—the power to heal grave illness, protect against one's enemies, and grant the gift of prophecy—are so closely intertwined with the veneration of the Mother Goddess that the two are effectively one and the same. The ideograms for the Mountain Mother in the Hittite alphabet range from a lozenge or cube, a double-headed axe, a dove, a cup, a door or a gate—all images of the Goddess in Neolithic Europe. The very name Kubaba may betoken a cave or empty vessel, a wombspace, or possibly derive from *kube* or *kuba*, recalling at once the black meteoric cube of the Ka'bah, that was brought into Islam after Mohammed routed its original idolatrous worshippers out of Mecca.

It is said in pagan times, the seven priestesses of the Ka'bah circled the black stone naked as when the world was young. Today that practice is recalled in the Tawaf, the sevenfold counterclockwise circuit of the shrine, performed by all pilgrims to take the Hadj. The ancient ritual's roots almost certainly descend from the Sumerian goddess Inanna and her Babylonian equivalent Ishtar, who was supposed to have passed through the seven doors of death, or seven gateways, on her journey to the underworld, each successive gatekeeper demanding she remove a garment as tribute, until she finally stood naked before her elder sister Ereshkigal, Queen of the Great Earth, goddess of the underworld, a dance of death echoed in the later Christian myth of Salome and the dance of the seven veils. Ereshkigal is also known by the epithet *Allatu* (literally "the Goddess"), which is beyond question an earlier form of *Alilat*, *Allāt*, or *al-Lāt*, the deity identified by Herodotus in the fifth century BCE as the Goddess worshipped in Mecca before the coming of the prophet (peace and blessings be upon him) and the substitution and subsequent veneration of her patriarchal counterpart, Allah—essentially the goddess al-Lāt with a soft *t*. To this day the male servitors of the Ka'bah, whose veneration is not prescribed or even mentioned by the Quran, are known as the *sons of the Old Woman*; a term that hints at the practice's origins in lunar worship. In truth the epithet al-Lāt is used as either a name or title for multiple pre-Islamic Arabian deities described as being either the wife or daughter of Allah. *Elat* is used in some texts as the feminine form of the Semitic solar deity El or the *qaniyatu 'ilhm*—which may be translated as "the creatrix of the Gods" (Elohim), the Queen of Heaven, the Mother Goddess Asherah who is all but interchangeable with the Akkadian Ašratu, the Hittite Aserdu, and the Ugaritic Atirat, referred to in the Ba'al cycle by her full title, Lady Athirat of the Sea, She who walks upon the water or treads upon the waves, the bride of Anu, and the consort or feminine iteration of Yahweh, the god of Israel and Judah.

The lunar, feminine principal lies at the core of Hebrew mysticism, personified in the queen of the inner court who resides at the center of the kabbalistic conundrum known as the "Cube of Space," the literal crossroads of the four winds where the initial stepping down of the cosmic energy from the Ayn-Sof takes place via the thirty-two Nativot-Phaliot, or Wondrous Paths. Some kabbalists see the primal cosmic force, the unity of opposites that is the divine Ayn-Sof, as being synonymous with the *Shekinah*, a feminine Hebrew word signifying "divine presence" or the "presence of the Deity among its people."

The Cube of Space is the luminous Cube of Ayn Sof Au, whose "arms extend to infinity" and can be extrapolated from the three mothers—Alef, Mem, Shin—to form a complex map of cosmic energies and their functions in the manifestation of structure and consciousness in the universe. The cube is an internal mapping of the familiar outer mapping of the wheel of the zodiac, its inner dimensions symbolized by the four winds, or the houses of Taurus, Leo, Aquarius, and Scorpio. Just as de Quincey knew his three mothers by a single name, so the seventh seal at the center of the web and our very being, representing our own psyche perhaps, is the moon, the veritable eye of the needle. This Ur-Goddess at the core of creation, the Semitic Asherah, or al-Lāt of the Arabs has been commonly identified with the threefold lunar divinity codified by Robert Graves into the archetypes of virgin, mother, and crone, whereas in his introduction to the 2014 Penguin edition of *The Koran*, N. J. Dawood states the three mothers al-Lāt, al-Uzza, and Manat represent "the Sun, Venus and Fortune, respectively." The writer Alby Stone suggests the only heavenly bodies to be depicted regularly in early Mesopotamian art were a trinity of the Sun, the Moon, and Venus, tracing the roots of the names *al-Uzza* and *Manat* to an even more archaic source, betokening "strength" and "destiny." If the three daughters of Allah are personifications of natural phenomena, then al-Lāt / al-Latu / Ereshkigal is surely the earth, while the other two may well have stood for fire and water. Islamic oral tradition has it that initial iterations of the vision of the prophet (peace be upon him) endorsed the notion of the three mothers being creator deities although this was later disowned as a false teaching inspired by Satan (Mircea Eliade, *A History of Religious Ideas* [Chicago: University of Chicago Press, 1988], 3:68).

At Petra, the Nabateans venerated a four-sided stone named after al-Lāt (Arthur Cotterell, *Dictionary of World Mythology* [Oxford: Oxford University Press, 1998], 24), whose son Dusura is just another take on Tammuz / Dumuzi / Du'uzi, the green man, who dies only to be reborn every spring after six months in the underworld. The Sumerians called him Dumu-zi'abzu (faithful son of the abyssal waters) and believed that as in the later myth of Orpheus and Persephone, the goddess Ishtar/Inanna was forced to descend to the underworld to retrieve him. Her actions provoked the wrath of the gods and she was sentenced by the seven Anunnaki, the judges of the underworld, the hellacious counterparts of the Sebettu, the seven sages venerated by the Babylonians, and associated with the seven major cities that dominated their civilization.

Judaism identifies the Dome of the Rock on Temple Mount as the Eben Shettiyah, or stone of foundation, around which God built the world. Deep beneath the rock is a partly flooded cavity known to Muslims as Bir-el-Arweh, or the Well of Souls, and Jewish lore maintains that when David dug the foundations of the first temple he found the block that holds back the Abyss. When he tried to move the stone, the waters of the underworld burst forth mirroring a parallel tradition in Islam, which holds that when Mohammed (peace and blessings be upon him) cast down the idol that once stood in the sacred complex at Mecca, he unblocked an ancient well beneath the Ka'bah. The idol was said to resemble the body of a "black woman," a deity named Hubal, almost certainly another mask of Kubaba or Cybele, who was known to be venerated at that time in Phrygia. In truth, a Phrygian statue of Cybele "graven from a single meteoric aerolite" (Franz Cumont, *Oriental Religions in Roman Paganism* [Chicago: Open Court Publishing, 1911], 46–47) was apparently presented to Rome on 204 BCE by Attalus the king of Pessinus in Asia Minor. This dark goddess was known as Mater Idaea Deum and the ecstatic rites of her worship, while initially a little alien to the Roman temperament, seem to have caught on with the populace, who venerated her in the Phyrgianum, the vast temple that once stood on the site of the present-day Vatican. The high priest who presided over those frenzied rites was known as *Papus*, or father, the direct ancestor of the present-day pope. As her worship spread through the Empire, icons made in her image proliferated, painted black not because of the skin of the Egyptians, the dark alluvial soil of the Nile, or some obscure Arabic root word, but because the template on which she was based, the original statue that held sway over Rome, was hewn from a smooth black stone from another world. Behind the mask of patriarchal monotheism, the Goddess, the Grail, and the stones from the sky were one and the same all along.

Fig. 18.10. Who is really in charge here?

19

The Coming of the White Lady

I began my journey in the shadows, and completed it in the Light. . . . The scent of her whom I wish to liberate, mounts upwards to me. Long ago she was named Isis, queen of benevolent springs, come to me all you who labour and are heavy laden and I will comfort you. Others knew her as Magdalene with the celebrated vase of healing balm. The initiates knew her true name: Our Lady of the Cross . . . two times I.S., embalmer and embalmed, miraculous vessel of the eternal White Lady of Legend . . .

"LE SERPENT ROUGE" (UNKNOWN AUTHOR)

The years flew by and I found myself reluctant to return to the Grail castle for fear of what I might find. The last thing I wanted was to live to see the Cathar fortress reduced to theme-park status or the tiny village worn down by the influx of tourism that has eroded the character of so many other ancient and mysterious sites such as Stonehenge, Machu Picchu, or the great pyramids of Giza.

Fig. 19.1. Midnight at the Martyr's Memorial.
Photo by Richard Stanley.

The last time I had seen Madame Couquet, some seven years previously, she had been suffering from the early stages of cancer and the auberge had been closed to the public. I did not believe I would see her again and knew Madame's passing would mark the end of an era, severing the last direct link to the events that had taken place before the war. There seemed to be nothing left to find and nothing more to say on the subject and for a while I assumed the Rahn file was dormant, if not safely closed.

I found other projects, other adventures, and other relationships with which to distract myself, but the memory of the pog and the light at the top of the mountain stayed with me. I walked the world for close to a decade before I found I could no longer keep away and my worn boot heels bore me back to the high pastures. Time however had not only stood still in the village but, if anything, the clock seemed to have been turned miraculously backward. The grass looked greener on the Camp de Cremat and the trees grew taller and wilder in their profusion. Not one brick or tile had changed in my absence, the walls and roofs of the stone houses bearing a pleasingly uniform patina of age. Incredibly the auberge had not only reopened but business was quietly booming. Madame Couquet looked ten years younger, coping single-handedly with the influx of guests, still chopping wood, cooking, cleaning, and making all the beds as if she were half her age. She was delighted to see me, taking me firmly by the arm as if I hadn't been away more than a day or two and leading me back into the house. As I walked into the dining room all heads turned. One man started abruptly to his feet as if he had seen a ghost.

"But it is impossible! What are you doing here?"

I blinked, staring at him in confusion but the man was a complete stranger, a German tourist traveling with his wife.

"You are Richard Stanley! I see your documentary! I come all the way from Leipzig."

The other tourists gazed silently, and I realized that I had inadvertently become another link in the chain, a part of the story I had sought to tell. With the aid of my long-suffering director of photography, Immo Horn, I had finally succeeded in completing a feature-length documentation of the Rahn affair, *The Secret Glory* (2001), whose release to DVD had helped put Madame's auberge back on the map. Thanks to my research, both of Otto's books, *Crusade against the Grail* and *The Court of Lucifer*, had not only been brought back into print but had been translated for the first time into English and Russian and were now finding fans among the New Age and neo-pagan community who didn't seem to care the paperback editions they were leafing through were once compulsory reading at a certain level of promotion within the SS.

While the hardy, time-warped villagers had been friendly enough in the past I was nothing short of a hero now, embraced as a prodigal son and plied with food and drink at every turn. Where information had been guarded before, I found a new eagerness to finally tell all, to let me into the very heart of their secretive, utterly self-contained world. I did my best to catch up on the gossip. Madame Couquet told me that Madame Nelli had passed earlier that year and, with a flourish of hands, kept repeating the word *brulé* over and over again. I shook my head in confusion and looked to my traveling companion, a young Californian esoteric researcher named Ruby Amariah, whose French was marginally better than my own.

"I dunno." Miss Ruby shook her head, then, started to giggle. "Brulé? Do you think they made dessert out of her?"

"Oui, oui!" said Madame enthusiastically, mistakenly believing we had understood her. "Dans le château . . ."

"Ohh . . . I think they cremated her and scattered her ashes."

I nodded slowly. "That sounds like Suzie. She always wanted to be part of this place."

Returning to the holy mountain after all these years stirred up more than a few memories, but there was no time to pause now, not even for dinner, despite the smell of Madame's cassoulet simmering on the hearth. We were running late and there was only one place to be for sunset. Moreover the moon would be full that night and shortly after the witching hour it would be passing into full eclipse.

As we started up the narrow way from the Camp de Cremat my thoughts returned to Suzie Nelli and her little dog, Leika IV. Suzie's ashes had been scattered here alongside the dust of the Cathar martyrs, as someday might be my own. So many of the witnesses whose testimony had guided me along that pathless trail lived now only in my memory. Christian Bernadac, Paul Ladame, Guy Puysegur, Albert von

The Coming of the White Lady   353

Fig. 19.2. *Les Anciens*—Montségur graveyard by moonlight.
Photo by Richard Stanley.

Haller, Professor Symmonds, Gabriele—all—gone. I had begun this quest in the hope of finding the secret of life eternal but here I was, almost two decades later, more fully mortal than before.

I caught my breath as I reached the summit, still not really knowing why I was there. I had spent countless nights on this mountain and while the memory of those dawns, fiery dusks, and clear, cold stars would never leave me, nothing had occurred since the evening of that long-ago electrical storm to make me suspect the castle was anything more than just another ruin, albeit one with a unique and tragic past. Surely the Grail castle could hold no surprises for me, not after all these years, yet the sense of weird anticipation only mounted as we climbed,

Fig. 19.3. Toad Mother.
Photo by Richard Stanley.

like a constant low-level alarm, urging me onward and upward over the darkening boulders.

Bats flurried playfully about us and the shadowy foliage was alive with rustlings, barks, grunts, and slitherings as the night animals went about their furtive business. Halfway up the incline we passed the largest toad I have ever seen, a monstrous yellow ochre beast with a disturbingly humanoid face and bloated torso, crashing heavily through the undergrowth as it hopped uphill toward the waiting castle, eagerly hurrying toward some secret assignation of its own.

As the light faded from the day, I reacquainted myself with the castle's weird dimensions and the embrasures artfully cut into its walls.

**Fig. 19.4. The keep.
Photo by Richard Stanley.**

Ruby's "spider sense" kept drawing her back to the long vertical slit that communicates between the rear wall of the courtyard and the donjon keep, an area I had previously identified as the citadel's acoustic focus. As midnight approached it became increasingly difficult to shake the sensation we were not the only ones in the courtyard. I kept catching shadows moving out of the corners of my eyes but told myself it was just a trick of the clouds and the moon, not dissimilar to what I had glimpsed on the night of the storm.

Miss Ruby was increasingly on edge and although the night was warm she couldn't help but suppress a shudder, insisting she was "picking up the impression" of a screaming woman in the shadows near the castle gate. I stood staring into the blackness for a moment and although the young psychic claimed the apparition was shrieking and thrashing, I saw and heard nothing, nor did I honestly believe her words. In all

356   The Coming of the White Lady

Fig. 19.5. The vigil—Montségur by moonlight.
Photo by Richard Stanley.

likelihood I figured whatever she sensed was merely a projection of her own fears, although the rather chilling thought did occur that perhaps she had somehow caught a glimpse of Cat shortly before we fled the castle seventeen years ago.

As the moon began to go into eclipse we made our way around the side of the fortress to the tower room. The atmosphere seemed strangely charged, a cloud of flying ants swarming above the battlement and bats circling inquisitively about us, flitting every which way in the gloom. I mounted the wooden steps, realizing the full moon was directly in line

The Coming of the White Lady 357

Fig. 19.6. Just another shadow in Shadowland.
Photo by Richard Stanley.

Fig. 19.7. Moon portal. Photo by Richard Stanley.

with the embrasure in the far wall of the chamber, a perfect beam of silvery luminescence splitting the dark.

"Look at the moon!"

Ruby was pointing and we both stood as if turned to stone, seeing the rim of the moon darkened by a crimson penumbra, the shadow of the world spreading like a stain across its face.

I stared, gaping, feeling the short hair rise on the back of my neck.

Just then the wind changed direction. The night breeze that had been whirling down from the Pic de Saint Barthélemy only moments before lulled and I felt an incongruously warm wind gust against my face that seemed to be blowing from out of the tower itself. I took a step toward the source of the wind, catching a sweet, half-familiar smell, an intoxicating blend of wet grass and rosebay. A faint hint of almonds. At that moment all the cows in the fields beneath the castle began to low at once and I paused remembering the sounds I'd heard on the night of the storm. I glanced back, nervously meeting Ruby's eyes. The sound of the cattle was so outlandish she began to giggle only to fall silent as we heard the crunch of footsteps approaching from what seemed like the direction of the courtyard.

"Someone's coming," whispered Ruby.

At first I thought it was a stray tourist and waited for them to step around the corner of the tower yet no figure appeared on the narrow wooden stairway and the path below remained utterly silent.

"What's the matter with me?" I thought. Over the past ten years I had spent countless nights on this mountain without the faintest shadow of disquiet, but now I felt my skin prickling. I turned, seeing a pale shape before me in the gloom and realized to my astonishment there was a young woman standing only a few feet away from us on the far side of the chamber. I narrowed my eyes but it wasn't a trick of the light. And she wasn't a ghost. She was a living flesh and blood human being. At first I tried to tell myself she was some kind of Wiccan priestess whom we had inadvertently surprised in the midst of a secret nocturnal ritual, but then I remembered there was only one entrance to the chamber and no way this figure could have climbed those wooden steps or gotten past Ruby and myself. My mind reeled as I tried to come to terms with the fact that the woman who stood before us had seemingly just stepped through solid rock, as if the wall of the tower room wasn't really there.

And no, I wasn't stoned. Nor am I much of a drinker.

I could see her long red hair haloed in the luminescence pouring through the embrasure, an otherworldly incandescence edged with pink or violet. Her tresses were worked into what appeared to be three long braids swept back from her high forehead and her proud, aristocratic face, muscular limbs, and pale, statuesque torso seemed to glow as if sculpted from living moonlight.

I recalled the stories about how the castle's defenders, the sons and daughters of Belisama or the children of Luna were said to have smeared their skin with a phosphorescent pigment in order to throw terror into

Fig. 19.8. The coming of the White Lady.
Sketch by Richard Stanley.

the hearts of the Christian crusaders, but this was no mere war paint. The figure who stood before us in the north-facing tower of the Grail castle seemed to glow from within as if her very flesh were made of light and about her shoulders she wore a mantle of shadows.

Ruby trembled, placing one hand against the stone wall, her hair fluttering as the warm, unearthly wind eddied crazily about us, too stunned and frightened to move, the moment expanding effortlessly upon itself. I took a half step toward the glowing figure, my rational mind still putting up a struggle. I knew this place was capable of some pretty edgy natural phenomena. During the electrical storm the twisting lightning bolts had resembled a huge fiery hand reaching into the keep and I recalled feeling that same warm wind back then and catching that subtle familiar smell.

In the summer of 1998, I had seen the tower's east-facing embrasures channel the first faint rays of the rising sun into sanguine beams that had drawn a weird, shifting pattern on the walls of the chamber. If the castle's architects were capable of such almost superhuman ingenuity then surely, I reasoned, the singular, vertical slit that communicated with the courtyard might be capable of capturing and funneling the moonlight into some sort of three-dimensional hologram, channeling the wind even.

Even if the woman who materialized before us had been a medieval hologram it would have stretched credibility, but the figure that strode out of the shadows of the tower room as the moon went into eclipse on the night of August 27, 2007, had weight and mass and I heard the loose pebbles crunch on the flagstones beneath her feet as she approached.

I took off my hat and bowed, instinctively placing one hand to my chest, thumb at right angles to my palm. I think I was too afraid at first to meet her gaze but as she narrowed the gap between us, I dimly recognized her regalia. Those high calfskin boots, the curious, braided belt or girdle criss-crossed about her pale midriff, the short sword or long knife that rode in its scabbard against her left thigh and that hooded mantle that floated about her shoulders seemed so deeply familiar it was as if I had finally come home. Or to my senses.

For a moment our gaze met, the old certainties of my life in the twenty-first century crumbling around me as I realized who she was. The look she gave me was fathomless and immense. Standing before me was the proud, ferocious chatelaine of the castle—the immortal na Esclarmonda, the light of the world, the illegitimate daughter of Roger Ramon the redheaded Count of Foix, a woman who was at once a creature of the flesh and a figure equated in popular tradition with the queen of the Elves, a real human being, and the living embodiment of magic, the avatar of an all but forgotten Ibero-Celtic warrior deity or something even older, a force that had inhabited these mountains since the chilly winds of the ice age.

And she welcomed me.

It was like waking from a dream. There was no way in hell the matrix could ever reassert itself after something like that. It was as if I'd finally been forgiven, for what I don't know, handed the "get out of jail free" card I'd been waiting for all along. I finally understood what Otto and the countess had seen here and put a face to the force that set this quest in motion. I had seen something of the divine in every one of my partners, in all the women I had been privileged to love, like moonlight shining through cloud, spirit refracted through matter, yet here was the naked face of the Goddess, the quintessence of all I loved and she shone with an incandescence so fierce I scarcely dared to look at her for fear I might cease to exist. In a sudden flash of illumination, I was afforded a glimpse of the endless passage of humanity through the mists of time, of radiance and of valor. Just as the black stone of the nigredo gives way to the whitened final substance of the great work, so I had passed from the realm of the Black Mother into the kingdom of the White Lady.

For a moment I stood transfixed, suspended between worlds, between dream and waking, reality and its reflection, past and present. Then bowing, I fell to my knees before the guardian of the Grail and wept like a child.

I had not cried actual tears in more years than I could remember, yet I wept now not out of sadness but out of gratitude and joy, out of the sure knowledge that it was true. Na Esclarmonda lives—and if she lives then perhaps Merlin still sleeps in a stone somewhere, just as Arthur waits in Avalon. Na Esclarmonda had been born more than seven centuries ago, but she was younger than I was, the "living incarnation of youth and freedom" in the words of the poet, Maurice Magre. I couldn't tell if she had stepped across the threshold into our world or whether we had been drawn into hers. She seemed solid enough but perhaps I and all the others who had been drawn to her magic mountain were merely reliving or reexperiencing something that had already happened hundreds of years ago, somehow recorded in the crystalline structure of the rocks and now replaying itself through the wetware of our nervous systems. Was I reexperiencing someone else's prerecorded memories or were they my own, the perception of some other quantum version of myself, caught up in events that either took place in the distant past or were still taking place now in another time stream?

Stephen Hawking admitted to the theoretical possibility of time travel although he stipulated such an operation would require a Faraday cage not dissimilar to the grid formed by the castle walls, a superconductor, not dissimilar to those blessed black stones in my pocket, and more energy than your average A-bomb. Granted this feat may be beyond the limits of our current technology, but what if such a thing was known to the sorcerer scientists of the past, a knowledge the Inquisition deliberately sought to suppress? What if the Cathar perfecti really had found a way to transcend the cycles of time, to bridge the abyss of seven centuries and transmit the flame of their unknown faith to future generations? What if the dark energy beloved of our contemporary physicists turned out to be synonymous with spiritual energy, the raw soul fire that served as wax to Montségur's taper? For a while I didn't seem to know which time period I really belonged to, nor could I tell exactly how long the audience in the tower room lasted. As if in a dream the encounter seemed to take place outside of time, but in all likelihood only lasted as long as it took for the shadow of the Earth to cross the face of the moon.

I saw her make a sign with her hand before turning away. That familiar bittersweet smell filled my nostrils as the quality of the light in the tower room subtly changed. In accounts of Marian apparitions, such as those reported at Lourdes or Fatima, they refer to this rather intoxicating aroma as the "smell of sanctity" but it may be a common side effect of ultradimensional intrusions into our paradigm, like the hint of ultraviolet that seemed to halo the Lady when she met my gaze. That blessed smell, like roses or icing sugar, exists at one extreme of our olfactory spectrum, just as hydrogen sulphide, the fire and brimstone associated with demonic apparitions, lies at the other pole, marking the outermost edges of human perception. As the connection faded, na Esclarmonda wordlessly withdrew, passing clear through the rear wall of the keep. I don't think she even knew she was walking through a wall. She simply stepped through a doorway that didn't exist in our paradigm and as before, Ruby and I heard her receding footsteps for a few seconds after she was gone as if she were physically traversing a passageway between worlds. Then the cows began to low again and I realized we were alone.

I staggered out of the chamber to find Miss Ruby standing motionless at the top of the narrow wooden stairway, eyes turned toward the bellowing farm animals in the field beneath the castle.

"Tell me that isn't happening . . ."

I followed her gaze, noticing that the cattle had arranged themselves into a perfect circle. I'd seen crop circles before, of course, but this was something different. This was a cow circle. I muttered an incoherent curse, then began to giggle, feeling a crazy sense of elation.

"Could be electromagnetic spillage from the keep, I guess."

"What are you talking about?"

"EMP." According to research conducted by scientists using Google Earth, cows and sheep have a tendency to align themselves according to the Earth's magnetic fields. Kinda like iron filings."

"You're kidding me?"

"All I'm saying is maybe they're reacting to what just happened in the tower room. Same deal as the way our hair stood up in there or the way our compass needles always seem to be a little off. A bona fide anomaly."

Just then a light came on in a farmhouse at the edge of the village and an angry French woman with a flashlight started up the hill to see why her cattle were kicking up such a fuss.

"Allez!" she yelled, jabbing at the lowing animals with her flashlight until the circle began to break up and the beasts reluctantly went back to their grazing.

"You think this happens often?"

"So what did happen back there? In the tower, I mean."

"That . . . I . . . I'm gonna have to think about that a li'l longer."

"You saw her too, right?"

"Yeah. I don't know who or what she was but after this I don't think anything is ever going to be the same again."

I turned my eyes toward the heavens but it had already begun to cloud over. The moon was lost from sight. "Funny thing is it felt like I already knew her. I didn't just see her. I remembered her."

I felt different, changed by what I had seen as if roused from a long sleep, yet that process was not so much an act of awakening as an act of anamnesis, of remembering, which implied there had to be something to remember. The Sufi scholar Idries Shah Sayed describes the initiatory flash of Revelation as being akin to photography. Not until one of the stages has been attained is the "photographic plate" fixed. The experience itself "fixes" what has already been exposed and developed.

The next morning I drew a picture of the woman we had seen in the tower on a pad and showed it to Madame Couquet, using an English/French dictionary to laboriously translate what had happened. Madame smiled, nodding as she got the gist. "Ah oui. Les anciens." She didn't seem particularly surprised, taking the encounter to be a good omen, which I suppose it was.

Goofy as this may sound, Miss Ruby's attempts to sleep after returning from the mountaintop were troubled by a recurring dream. She recalled being in a cave overlooking a steep, glacial valley. There was some kind of ancient altar illuminated by a beam of light that fell through a cleft in the rocks and a group of "dead old men" were standing behind her all trying to talk at once. Coming, as it did, within twenty-four hours of our first encounter with the folkloric White Lady, I decided to take a leap of faith and drove south.

USSAT-LES-BAINS, SUMMER 2007

Although it was high summer, Ussat retained the desolate air of a ghost town. As we trolled through its silent, shuttered streets I couldn't help but feel the population was hiding from the daylight like denizens of some European *Salem's Lot*. We stopped at the only store still open and while I was inquiring after cigarettes, a very old lady approached Ruby, trying to tell her something in French. She kept giggling and touching her hair whispering, "Jolie, Jolie," until we both got a little spooked and decided to make ourselves scarce.

"I think she was trying to measure my neck," muttered Miss Ruby uneasily.

It was a bit of a climb to the Bethlehem Grotto. I was first shown the site a good decade ago by the late Christian Bernadac. Monsieur Bernadac had always distrusted Otto and his mentor Antonin Gadal and had done his best over the years to expose their links with both the Nazi party and the Coca-Cola company. Since I first set foot on the path, a fence and metal gate had appeared, bearing no less than three separate locks. The barrier made access to the grotto trickier than anticipated and marred the natural beauty of the site.

It came as little surprise that Miss Ruby had been dreaming of the Bethlehem Grotto. In her vision the dead old men had been standing a little higher than her and we observed the floor of the cave had been recently dug away as if someone was excavating the site. Judging by the fresh wax on the altar and beneath the pentagram it was clear the shrine had been recently used, probably on the night of the eclipse. I understood now who that crude portrait scrawled within the pentagram was supposed to represent, as well as why it had seemed so familiar to me. After all these years only part of her countenance still remained, one eye and the edge of her mouth. Beneath it I found, on closer inspection, a single, smudgy word scrawled in that familiar wilting hand—"traum . . ."

"Now where are we going?"

Miss Ruby followed me as I started back down the path from the cave, feeling as if I was lost in a mirror maze whose reflective avenues, bordered with hieroglyphic columns, ended at the gateway of a phantom temple.

"To get some answers."

I paused at the base of the trail, feeling a vague prickly sensation on the back of my neck. The last time I visited the area Antonin Gadal's house had been boarded up, but it was evidently now in the hands of new owners. There was a fresh coat of paint on the walls and through the open shutters I could see the rear rooms had been converted to hold rows of military-style bunk beds. The front room had become an office, the wall above the desk adorned with a photograph of Montségur and a flag bearing the Occitan cross.

"Hang on just a moment . . ."

My voice tailed off as a jeep pulled to a halt behind us, precluding any chance of escape.

"Don't look but I think we're busted," muttered Miss Ruby as a bunch of stern-faced men piled out of the vehicle. They were dressed in identical black sweatshirts, each bearing a tiny red Montségur decal on the left breast above the heart, depicting the geometric shape of the castle.

"Bonjour. I . . . uhh . . ."

For a moment my French deserted me. Then I recognized one of the newcomers at more or less the same moment he recognized me. "What are you doing here?" It was Christian Koenig, the former museum curator from Tarascon who had first told me about the Graal Pyrenean back in the '90s. He had shaved his beard, which made him look years younger but there was no doubt he was the same man. He seemed baffled and not a little uneasy to see me, doubtless assuming I had come to steal more of his treasures.

"I . . ."

I decided to brazen it out. There was nothing left but to tell the truth.

"I know this may sound strange but this young lady from California has been having recurrent dreams that she described to me in some detail. She saw herself in a cave with a bunch of old dead dudes all trying to talk at once, trying to tell her something important. It sounded like the Bethlehem Grotto, so I figured I'd take her up there to see if her dreams were on the money. Which they were."

"But how did you get in? What about the gate?"

"We climbed over the wall."

Christian emitted a long-suffering sigh, on the verge of finally losing his cool.

"Listen, I'm better informed about what's going on around here than last time. We've seen the lady."

Christian turned in a semicircle, trying to take this on board. I figured na Esclarmonda was the one he really took his orders from and had gone over his head, relying on higher management to see us through. In the end he had no choice but to invite us in for another cup of chai.

The meteoric relic removed from the caves by Otto Rahn and Antonin Gadal rested on a shelf in the former minister of tourism's study. I had heard so much about the blessed thing over the years it seemed somehow anticlimactic to finally see it with my own eyes and to touch its hard, dark surface. Above the relic hung a portrait of the White Lady, bequeathed to Christian by an old woman he said was now "one with the spirit." The painting showed na Esclarmonda much as I remembered her, standing atop a rock formation overlooking the Blanque River, arms outstretched, her face a blur of light.

Something ancient was awakening here in the mountains. We could all agree on that. A 700-year-old prophecy was working its way out and this time I could only pray the forces that secretly manipulated human affairs chose their foot soldiers more carefully. Last time the White Lady appeared, to Otto Rahn, Maurice Magre, and the countess, the world was poised on the brink of an apocalypse. I prayed that wasn't the case now. Christian seemed unperturbed, suggesting the White Lady had always been there and it was only human consciousness that waxed and ebbed over the passage of centuries. Just as a ship traveling on a canal has to wait until the water is raised in a lock before sailing on to the next level, so the seeker's consciousness has to be raised in order to pass through the gate, he suggested, to enter her kingdom, that mysterious otherworld that exists outside the cycles of time.

"Yet change is coming," agreed Christian calmly. "In fact, change is the only certainty. The weather changes. The land changes and its creatures also change. It is not for us to know the ways of the world to come, only to safeguard what has been handed down to us and disentangle and make clear what we can for those who come after."

I listened, feeling strangely empty, wondering if this was really the end of the quest or just the beginning. I wanted a cigarette but knew Christian's neo-Cathar ways frowned on such an unhealthy indulgence. Christian had recently taken over Gadal's ramshackle gingerbread gothic villa and, since the closure of the museum, had been doing a bit of digging on his own. In fact, he had just returned from the grotto of Fontanet that very morning with his fellow brothers and was keen to show us his findings.

"This thing we disentangle is the heart of life."

Fetching an old shoebox, Christian happily showed us its dusty contents. Among the prized pieces was a shard of pottery showing a human outline standing in a pentagram, arms outstretched.

Although I was not a member of the order, I had passed through all its initiations as if I had been led toward a destiny already singled out for me. Seeing the light at the top of the mountain and those bleeding stones, the first real physical evidence of the unknown, had been enough to keep me hooked but after the visitation the night before I could no longer deny the reality of the supernatural. It was as if the events had been deliberately contrived, with Ruby as eyewitness, to make certain I didn't have any hope of explaining them away. Had a mythological figure stepped through a solid wall into my life while I was on my own, I might have rationalized it as an acid flashback or temporary insanity, but given the circumstances, I had no such recourse. A shared hallucination was the only thing that sprang to mind, but what the hell is a shared hallucination when you get down to it and how can you possibly distinguish such a thing from so-called real life? There was no point in trying to explain myself to my family or to my colleagues back in London. I'd had close friends and family members tell me they had seen UFOs or the living presence of Christ or the blessed virgin before and knew all too well how impossible it was to take that kind of thing on board unless you've experienced it for yourself. Extraordinary claims demand extraordinary evidence and given our programming it is only natural that we reject secondhand reports of marvels and miracles. This is the nature of the initiatory process, the essence of gnosis, which demands firsthand experience of the mysteries. The written word and even the most heartfelt teachings and testimonies can only take us so far. Ultimately the ego that acts as gatekeeper to the unconscious shrugs them off in order to maintain the existing status quo of what we take to be reality. We are, all of us, in this manner, our own personal jailers, trapped by the arrogant assumption we already know everything there is to know about creation and that we are somehow in control of our lives. Magic, if we desired it somewhat as children, is generally perceived as simply not being relevant to adult life. If you keep banging on about it, people will just start checking their texts or, if they really care about your well-being, might politely suggest you see an analyst.

Miss Ruby was right. Nothing would be the same after this. Nor could it be. The change within me was permanent. The things I had

Fig. 19.9. The Graal Pyrenean.
Photos by Remei and Joseph.

seen could not be unseen, nor the knowledge unlearned. I was no Cathar perfecti, not even an initiated credente. I was neither a pacifist, nor a vegetarian, and the thought of a celibate, monastic lifestyle just never appealed. Yet the veil had been lifted, just enough to stop me from turning my back on the holy mountain and returning to the waking world where gods, sacred treasures, and sorceresses weren't supposed to exist. Na Esclarmonda must have known that by allowing me that glimpse into her otherworld she would only draw me further in, just as Otto had been drawn in before me, as helpless as a moth to a flame.

Had the moon been full the night Otto climbed that mountain on the German-French border? Did he think perhaps he was finally going home?

EPILOGUE

Portal into Summer
Montségur June 21, 2015

> *Any sufficiently advanced technology is indistinguishable from magic.*
>
> — ARTHUR C. CLARKE (1917–2008)

It had been raining for weeks on end, day after day of cold wind and gray skies. Still, even in these wretched conditions, the last of the faithful gathered as usual on the morning of the summer solstice to view the annual solar phenomena in the tower room. The ranks of the onlookers had thinned since I first witnessed these curious lights in 1998. The neo-Nazis we'd nicknamed the "boy scouts" had all grown up, gotten jobs, gotten married, gone to jail, or died. Today's turnout amounted to an assortment of some forty-odd pilgrims from Argentina, England, Norway, and Germany huddled in the predawn dark, praying the clouds would part long enough for the castle to do its thing. A television crew from Toulouse was conducting vox-pop interviews, asking the onlookers if they were there for religious or spiritual reasons, but no one seemed capable of giving a straightforward answer. Fair enough. Most folks just looked cold and sleepy.

Finally, the clouds parted as if on cue, affording the assembly a brief glimpse of the marvel they had come to witness. At approximately 6:05 a.m., the disc of the sun appeared above the horizon and the first rays began to enter the east-facing embrasures in the lower chamber of the donjon keep, marking out rectangles of light on the inner surfaces of the slits in the far wall.

I stood in silence, taking in the spectral display, doing my best to still the flurry of memories stirred by the light show. After reaching an apogee at approximately 6:20 a.m., the lights began to fade and the crowd broke up. I was among the last to leave, reluctant as ever to start back down the mountain, but the wind was still rising and smelled of snow. I wanted to believe the Cathar prophecy would be borne out, that after seven centuries the laurel would turn green again, but looking about myself at the deserted tower room I couldn't help but wonder if I was really all that was left. The last of the faithful.

Fig. E.1. The last of the faithful—neo-Cathar sympathizers gather at Montségur to mark the anniversary of the castle's fall, despite inclement weather, March 16, 2016. Photo by Richard Stanley.

Fig. E.2. Neo-Cathars at the Martyr's Memorial.
Photo by Richard Stanley.

On October 16, 2016, a group of Holy Roman prelates led by the bishop of Pamiers, Jean-Marc Eychenne, took the first steps toward reconciliation with the Cathar Church by issuing a carefully worded apology for the genocidal campaign against Occitania. They were met at the church of Montségur by an estimated 1,500 Cathar sympathizers, many of them bearing sprigs of green laurel—a vital step toward the rehabilitation and revival of the old religion.

I live alone with my books now in a stone-walled cottage at the base of the mountain, having long since fled the homage of the world. I have devoted my life to defending the castle and safeguarding its secrets, as those who came before me have done. What little time I have, I spend in meditation and study, translating, copying, and organizing the surviving texts and scraps of data that have come down to us, trying to disentangle the truth or what remains of it for those who come after.

Fig. E.3. The time of prophecy—October 16, 2016, a group of Holy Roman prelates issue a carefully worded apology. Many feel the apology for "commtting acts contrary to the gospels and fighting fire with fire" did not go far enough, implying the Cathars started the conflict. The pope and the Dominican Order were both invited but refused to attend. Photos by Richard Stanley.

Portal into Summer 375

Fig. E.4. Madame Couquet hears the official apology, October 16, 2016.
Photo by Richard Stanley.

Fig. E.5. The Roman prelates.
Photo by Richard Stanley.

Fig. E.6. Christian Koenig at the Martyr's Memorial.
Photo by Richard Stanley.

Fig. E.7. Montségur abides.
Photo by Hamilton White.

Fig. E.8. Telling the tale.
Photo by Hamilton White.

I repeat the names of the martyrs every March 16 on the field of the stake and tell the story to those who need to hear it. Thanks to diligent and tireless research, the identities of three quarters of the combatants who took part in that final ten-month siege are known to us now (appendix 3) and it is my fancy that the castle likes it when the stories of its heroes and their deeds are repeated, that the shadows draw more closely about me and the moonlight burns more brightly on the walls of the keep where I spend so many of my nights.

Under the influence of the divine flame, my old life was consumed and a new one conjured like a phoenix from its ashes. On the whole I don't miss the "real" world. It seems like a dream at best, at other times like a vaguely remembered nightmare. When I am forced to leave the Zone on one mission or another, I am always grateful to return, counting each day here as a blessing.

The people of the book, the adherents of the three great monotheisms, insist the evil and pain in this world is all part of "God's plan," but while pain might ennoble man, as William Peter Blatty rightly points out, "does pain ennoble a caterpillar?" Children and animals are innocent. Why should they suffer and die? The creator of this world (God, Yahweh, Jehovah, Allah, or what you will) either does not exist or is quite clearly insane and does not necessarily love us, nor mean the best for us. Although this force has the power to torture our physical bodies, kill us, or even burn us to ashes, it has no power over our immortal souls, which the Cathar perfecti believed were part of the true, good God and hence eternal. It is scarcely surprising these heretical ideas took root and found sustenance in the Dark Ages when life was, by all accounts, nasty, brutish, and short. In order to hide the truth from us, the perfecti taught that an illusory veil had been drawn over our eyes and that another, better kingdom exists beyond all this—our true homeland.

As in many initiatory faiths and mystery schools, the Cathar adepts suggested what we think of as the real world is in fact little more than a dream or fiction—the realm of maya. We are in truth asleep and in the hands of a dangerous black magician who has usurped creation. Yet this seemingly malign force, which deliberately manipulates and misleads us (known as Rex Mundi, or the king of the Earth, to the Cathars), cannot be infallible, otherwise you would not be reading this. The all-seeing eye is not all-powerful but tries to deceive the children of the kingdom into believing so. And if the designer of the prison program is fallible, then it can be beaten. That is the true meaning of the first law of magic: as above, so below. "Gods" are only enlightened mortals; hence, mortals might, through the piecing together of seemingly dissociated information accumulated over successive generations, someday regain the key to their secret. Until then we shall certainly not stop searching. The Cathar perfecti allegedly knew how to pass from the delusional prison world into the peaceful kingdom while still alive through an act of direct initiation, the consolamentum, but this tradition, a secret sign or a form of laying on of hands passed from initiate to initiate like a spiritual game of tag said to date back to the proto-Christianity of John the Baptist and the Essenes, was presumed to have been extinguished when the last true adept was burned at the stake in 1321. Unless the ancient spiritual masters can reach across time, their latter-day descendants are forced to either assimilate what they can from the few surviving documents and direct personal experience of the mysteries or seek eventual posthumous transcendence through multiple involuntary incarnations.

In the close to ten years since I made my home in Montségur, I have become the only de facto English-speaking mountain guide in the area—somebody has to be, I guess—and in the summertime I have my hands full, there being no shortage of seekers to shepherd. Close to 100,000 make their way to the castle gates every season. Only a fraction have the slightest inkling of what this place really is but they are drawn to it nonetheless, looking for something that can't be contained in words. In all truth a great many of them are pretty damaged by the time they reach me. You usually have to be, on some level, to go looking for something as ineffable as a Grail.

In the winters, human traffic on the mountain drops off to nothing, there being none foolhardy enough to make it past the Mountain of Fear, the Rock of Shadows, and the Forest of Toads. Even the eternally energetic Madame Couquet retreats to lower altitudes, staying with her nephews and nieces in Foix from January through to April when Our Lady of the Snows is abroad in the land and the col becomes all but impassable to twenty-first century vehicles. During these months, my only companion is my black cat, Doozy—named after the heroine of Fritz Laing's *Doktor Mabuse, Der Spieler* (1922)—la Comtesse Dusie von Told—as I figured Montségur needed a mysterious countess in residence. I am never really alone though, just as I am never bored. The seclusion is a Goddess-given opportunity to practice my art and hone my craft, the knowledge being its own reward and solace.

I do not know what purpose na Esclarmonda ultimately has in mind for us, but her continued patronage and protection is validation enough, that and the privilege of knowing I can return to her kingdom whenever I wish. Christian was right when he said she was always there and always will be. She is there now. Her hand is making a sign to show she has not forgotten us, that like ourselves she is eternal. Na Esclarmonda manifested herself in these mountains to show that humanity must strive toward perfection and I have sworn my life, my soul, and my sword to her. When the time comes to abandon this tunic of flesh, I have no doubt she will set me high among her legions—or at the very least find me a permanent position on the castle staff.

Most folk find it hard to fathom why someone like myself would choose to abjure the world, its twenty-first-century conveniences and comforts, to deliberately live as a quasi-medieval hermit in an environment where the only heating is provided by a wood fire and the most reliable form of transport is still the horse. Outsiders do not understand that I am, above all, happy here although I do not advocate a wholesale retreat into a new dark age, there being things I still hold dear about contemporary civilization, namely digital cameras, dentistry, anesthesia, analgesics, smallpox and polio vaccine, nor should I wish to see a return to tribalism, feudalism, racism, sexism, and all the other "isms" beloved of our ancestors.

Fig. E.9. The view from the pog. Photo by Maxim Spektor.

Fig. E.10. At home in the Zone. Photo by Maxim Spektor.

I cannot agree with Otto Rahn and Baron Julius Evola's "revolt against the modern world," nor can I condone the methods by which they sought to achieve their ends. The sons and daughters of the Goddess, the neo-Cathars and neo-pagans of the days to come, the children of Belisama, Cybele, or Gaia if you prefer, must reserve the right to choose their own future, to discard the shackles of patriarchal monotheism and materialism while retaining for their own all that art, culture, and pure science has to offer, the liberatory potential of the technosphere, genetic engineering, and the space program. As free princes of this postindustrial wasteland, cast up and left to flap like fish on the steel beach of the anthropocene, it is our right as much as a necessity to call to our aid all the knowledge of the ancients, the true treasure of the ages, the magical science and mystical disciplines of our forgotten forefathers. We must reattune ourselves to the Earth Mother's subtle rhythms, to the old ways of hill and stream while simultaneously demanding a new technology, an implosive technology that transcends explosive nuclear energy, a hardware that embraces the power of quarks, of quasars, and quantum universes. Maybe we can make it to the next level but it ain't easy, as Gilgamesh found out. We are nothing more than an energy wave, a frequency after all. Perhaps it's possible to change channels? Christ, like na Esclarmonda or the prophet Elijah, is said to have entered alive into the kingdom of heaven.

Other ascended masters are rumored to have existed over the centuries and possibly continue to exert an influence over human affairs, guiding us in the ongoing struggle to liberate our consciousness by whatever means available.

Someday this war is going to end. Someday the ceaseless chafing of Spirit against matter, the endless dispute between light and darkness, over who created whom will finally be resolved, and until then, if we are judged at all, we will be judged according to which force we give allegiance to—the vengeful god of the earth, the demiurge of the material world, or the other gods that exist beyond all this, whose names no human tongue can pronounce, the messengers of spirit and the true kingdom of heaven.

A bird circled high above the castle, and as I stepped out of the tower room the cold wind abruptly lulled. For a moment the world was silent. Then, I felt a warm breath against my face, gentle as a sigh, redolent with the smell of sap and rosebay.

And, just like that, summer began.

Fig. E.11. The light of the world. Photo by Richard Stanley.

APPENDIX 1

Otto Rahn

Life of the Grail Hunter

1904	Born February 18, Michelstadt, Germany. Father: Karl Rahn; Mother: Clara Margaret Hamburger.
1910	School, Bingen on Rhine.
1922	Reheprüfung, Gießen.
1924	Diploma, Universities of Gießen and Fribourg.
1924/29	Studies philology, specializing in literary history.
1929	Doctoral thesis, "The Research of Master Kyot of Wolfram von Eschenbach."
1930	Economic crisis in Germany. Works as substitute teacher, cinema usher, salesman, proofreader, translator, and movie extra; becomes fluent in French.
1931	Arrives in Montségur after sojourning in Paris, takes over lease of Hotel des Marronniers in Ussat-les-Bains.
1932	Linked to the Polaires in two articles in *La Dépêche de Toulouse*.
1932	Declared bankrupt by the commercial court in Foix, obliged to leave France.
1933	Joins Association of German Writers. Adolf Hitler comes to power (Jan. 30); publication of first book *Crusade against the Grail*.

1936	Joins SS in Weisthor cell, visits Iceland.
1937	Publication of second book, *The Court of Lucifer*, Himmler personally buys 100 copies.
1938	Certificate of Aryanism demanded.
1939	Asks to leave SS (Feb. 28); invites Weisthor and Himmler to wedding; dies in a mountain storm (March 13). Resignation officially accepted (March 17).
Present Day	Revered by neo-Cathars, Rosicrucian spiritualists, and Masons; young Germans have built a monument to Otto Rahn's memory, near Marbourg, made from stones taken from Montségur.

THE UNKNOWN RAHN

Unpublished manuscripts by Otto Rahn, currently in the custody of his niece, Ingeborgh Roemer-Rahn include:

- "Count Saint Germain: Magician or Charlatan?"
- "Endless Xmas" (SS Yuletide play)
- "The Ratcatcher of Hamlyn" (a play in verse)
- "Conradin, the Last Howenstauffen" (historic play)
- "Michelle Listens to the Sea Wind Whistle," or "The Life of Our Blue Boy"
- "Freedom Lane" (a play about Arnold Winkelreid)
- "Field of Honour, Field of Work"
- "Til Eunspiegal" (a radio play for Jugen station)
- "Carl the Great"
- "Egil the Sklader"
- "Emmanuel Glockenkraut" (the story of Walter Tyrolf)
- "Graf Rigoletto" (a sketch)
- "The Enderle of Ketsch"
- "Lauren" (90-page manuscript)
- "A Friend of Humanity: The 130th Death Day of Johan Gotfried Herder"

"Hans Sachs: The Shoemaker and Poet" (a story in pictures)

"The Search for the Grail: A Journey through Montsalvach's Mountains, Caves, and Backgrounds" (radio script)

"Minne, Mani, and Graal" (radio script)

"What Happened to Me in the Pyrenean Cave" (radio script)

APPENDIX 2

Chronology of the Last Crusade

1155   Birth of Esclarmonde de Foix, daughter of Cecilia Trencavel and Roger Bernard I, the lord of the mountainous Ariège.

1156   An ecclesiastical council in the town of Albi condemns the aberrant beliefs of the southerners, giving rise to the name by whence the heresy is defined—the "heretics" are referred to as Cathars.

1160   Birth of Esclarmonde de Foix's younger brother, Raimond Drut, son and successor to Roger Bernard I. Raimond will grow up to become the hero of the south, known to his people as "Raimond the Beloved."

1167   The Council of Saint Felix de Caraman, the first official gathering of the heads of the Cathar Church, is presided over by Papa Nicetas who travels from Lombardy bringing with him the Book of the Seven Seals (also referred to as the lost Gospel of Saint John, or the Book of Nicetas). The first four Cathar bishoprics are set up in Toulouse, Carcassonne, Agen, and Albi.

1175   Esclarmonde de Foix marries Jourdain II of Isle Jourdain, Vicomte de Gimoez. Their children include Bernard,

	Guillamette, Olive, Othon de Terride, and Bertrand, Baron de Launac.
1184	Birth of Raymond Roger Trencavel, future viscount of Béziers, Carcassonne, Albi, and Razes.
1187	Raimond Drut woos Ettienette de Penautier, more commonly known as Loba, the she-wolf of Cabaret. Adhering to the custom of their time, however, they marry according to the dictates of their station. Loba marries Jourdain of Cabaret, the name of her castle becomes synonymous with the great gatherings of minstrels, mummers, and acrobats who flock to her court.
1188	Death of Roger Bernard I; Raymond Drut succeeds his father as the comte de Foix.
1189	Raimond Drut marries the Countess Phillipa to secure a treaty with the Aragonese house of Montcade.
1198	The election of Pope Innocent III, who later launches the Albigensian crusade.
1202	The death of Jourdain II. Now widowed, Esclarmonde de Foix embarks on a thirty-year apostolacy, she leagues the barons of the Pyrenees against the authority of the patriarchal Roman pontiff and the local tyranny of the abbeys. Along with her sister-in-law, Philippa, she founds a spiritual retreat in the high mountains at Dun, which functions as a home for aged perfecti and a girls' school.
1203	**January:** Raimond Drut makes a pact with Arnaud, viscount of Castelbon, to join possessions. Raimond's cousin, Count Ermengol VIII of Urgell and Bernard de Villemur, bishop of Urgell, see this as a potential threat and declare war.
	February: Raimond Drut and Arnaud de Castelbon are overcome and captured.
	September: King Pedro II of Aragón intervenes, wishing to spare Raimond Drut and Arnaud in order to aid the ambitious regent in his plans to conquer the Languedoc for Greater Catalonia.

1204 Birth of Pierre Roger de Mirepoix, a cousin of Raimond de Pereilha (Seigneur of Montségur and a vassal of Raimond Drut), who claims direct descendency from Belisama the moon goddess and will later become a key figure in the defense of the pog and the foundation of the Sons and Daughters of Belisama, the most radical of all Cathar sects. Raimond Drut attends a ceremony in Fanjeaux in which his sister Esclarmonde de Foix is confirmed by the Cathar bishop Guilhabert de Castres as a high priestess of their faith. Along with three other women of high rank, Aude de Fanjeaux, Fays de Durfort, and Raymonde de Saint-Germain, she receives the Cathar sacrament, the consolamentum.

1205 While hunting a wolf in the high pastures of the Ariège, Raimond Drut spends the night at a remote convent and impregnates the abbess who gives birth to illegitimate twins, Esclarmonde and Loup de Foix. Ensconced at the family's Pamiers estate, Esclarmonde de Foix experiences a presentiment of the coming apocalypse and advises Raimond de Pereilha, the Seigneur of Montségur, to refortify the old ruins on the summit of the pog and stock the cisterns and granaries for a coming siege.

1206 The Spaniard, Domingo de Guzman, sees a fireball fall from the sky and proclaiming it to be a miracle founds a monastery at Prouille.

1207 Esclarmonde de Foix attends the conference of Pamiers, the last attempt at peaceful debate between the Cathars and the Holy Roman Church, which is represented by Domingo de Guzman. When Esclarmonde attempts to address the assembly, she is ordered to "return to her spinning" by the patriarchal Roman prelates.

1208 Pope Innocent III dispatches apostolic legates to Toulouse to set an example. Their first victim, magistrate Pierre Maurand, is interrogated, convicted of heresy, and condemned to death. The elderly Maurand recants and is forced to walk barefoot from the prison to the church of Saint Sernin between the bishop of Toulouse and one of the legates who beats him unmercifully with rods. His property and possessions are confiscated; he is forced to scourge himself and wander the streets naked for forty days before being exiled. The outraged public retaliates and one of the legates, Pierre de Castelnau, is murdered while crossing the river near Fourques. This event provides a pretext for a military campaign against Occitania.

March 10: Pope Innocent III issues a call to arms summoning all Christian nations to launch a crusade against the south. Simon de Montfort, a fortuneless soldier of noble birth, master tactician, and a ruthless administrator of conquered lands, is placed in overall military command of the crusade.

1209 The onset of the Albigensian Crusade. An army of crusaders gathers in Lyon and marches south toward Provence. They are joined by Arnaud-Amaury, a fanatical papal legate who is granted titular leadership as spiritual advisor in the "holy" campaign. Raymond of Toulouse seeks to reconcile with the church and pledges to expel the Cathars from his lands. The crusaders march to Montpellier and Roger de Trencavel, the young prince of Carcassonne, demands an audience with Arnaud-Amaury in order to "surrender to the Church," but Amaury refuses to receive him. Knowing his lands are to be attacked, Trencavel returns to Carcassonne to organize his defenses, taking with him most of the Jewish population of Béziers to whom he grants safe passage. Some of the Jews stay in Béziers to their detriment.

Early July: Simon de Montfort captures the hilltop village of Servian, east of Béziers.

July 21: The crusaders reach Béziers and demand that

the Cathars in the population be handed over. This is refused even by the Roman Catholics of the town.

July 22: The defenders launch a sortie that is closely pursued back through the gate by the crusaders. Once inside the walls, the crusaders seize Béziers within an hour and begin a mass slaughter of Catholics and Cathars, alike. Accounts vary as to the number slaughtered (10,000 to 20,000, with just over 200 estimated to have been Cathars). The massacre frightens many other towns into surrendering. Guiraud de Pépieux, lord of a small estate between Carcassonne and Minerve, rallies to the crusaders' camp after the fall of Béziers. Later, he revolts, captures Puysegur castle, and takes two of the knights left to guard the fortress prisoner. By the time de Montfort arrives with aid, Guiraud has mutilated his prisoners, cutting off their faces before abandoning them and departing for Minerve.

August 1: The crusader army arrives before the walls of Carcassonne. This fortified city sits above the Aude River, which it relies on for its water supply. The Trencavels are vassals to King Pedro II of Aragón, who is also the brother-in-law of Raymond VI de Toulouse. King Pedro comes in person to Carcassonne in an attempt to mediate, but Arnaud-Amaury refuses to give any quarter. A fierce siege ensues with both sides employing trebuchet and mangonel rotating-beam artillery.

August 7: The capture of two fauborgs outside the walls of Carcassonne effectively cuts off the defenders' access to the river. Thirst and spreading disease force Roger de Trencavel to seek negotiations for surrender. While supposedly under safe-conduct, Roger de Trencavel V is taken prisoner, an act pinpointed by some modern historians as the death of the age of chivalry.

August 15: Carcassonne surrenders. De Montfort's

crusaders do not conduct a massacre, but force the residents to depart the walled city, "taking nothing but their sins." Roger de Trencavel's wife and young son (Raymond-Roger IV) take refuge with Raimond Drut, the comte de Foix. The towns of Castelnaudary, Fanjeaux, Montréal, Limoux, Castres, Albi, and Lombers surrender without any real fight, leaving the way clear for the crusaders to attack Raimond's holdings in Mirepoix, Foix, and Saverdun. Some towns including Castres, Lombers, and Montréal revolt against the occupying army. Cathars and faidits (lords dispossessed of their lands) take refuge in Minerve, Termes, and Cabaret, launching counterattacks against the crusaders. Simon de Montfort seeks suzerain status over Carcassonne, Albi, Béziers, and the Razès area. The comtes de Nevers and Saint-Pol return to their northern domains after the fall of Carcassonne, but the duc de Bourgogne remains in the area, looting at will.

September: Simon de Montfort and the duc de Bourgogne attack Lastours, a city nine miles north of Carcassonne, where Pierre-Roger de Cabaret (Loba's brother-in-law and a vassal of the Trencavels) is harboring many of the fleeing Cathars. Lastours-Cabaret is a system of four castles—Cabaret being the residence of Loba and her husband, Jourdain II; Lastours the main citadel structure; and the other two being simple towers close enough to provide cover for one another. Loba's brother-in-law manages to take de Montfort's lieutenant (and cousin), Bouchard de Marly, lord of Saissac, captive.

October: The duc de Bourgogne publicly burns two Cathars before heading for home rather than face the onset of a bleak winter in a troubled land.

November 10: The betrayed twenty-five-year-old prince Roger de Trencavel conveniently perishes in the dungeons of occupied Carcassonne.

December: Simon de Montfort is recognized by Innocent III as a direct vassal of the Roman church and presses his claim for suzerainship over all Occitania. King Pedro II of Aragón places the fiefdoms of Querigut and Usson under Raimond Drut's protection. The dead prince's heir, Raymond Roger de Trencavel II, officially becomes a ward of Raimond Drut.

1210 A mass uprising takes place against the Catholic clergy in Chartres. Several properties belonging to the church come under siege and are plundered. Those responsible are excommunicated and a sentence of anathema pronounced against the city. A fire deliberately started in a settlement on the banks of the Eure by an unnamed priest destroys "nearly all the houses of the blasphemers." The devastation stretches up to the cloister of Notre Dame, yet the houses within the cloister are not touched, leading to even "greater anger of disorder and envy" among the citizens. During the winter the bloodthirsty zealot, Arnaud-Amaury, is installed as the archbishop of the strategically vital port of Narbonne. The costal town is to become a major entry for crusaders' supplies and additional men. Reinforcements come from Anjou, Frisia, Lorraine, Bavaris, Gascony, Champagne, Brittany, Flanders, Normandy, Aquitaine, and numerous parts of Europe.

March: De Montfort captures Bram after a three-day siege and orders the blinding and mutilation of over 100 captives, cutting off their faces in reprisal for the treatment received by his own men at Castle Puysegur. He leaves only one man with one eyeball to guide the walking wounded to Pierre-Roger de Cabaret at Lastours to serve as a graphic illustration of his intentions.

June: De Montfort lays siege to the fortress of Minerve, constructing the most powerful catapult in military history.

The siege engine destroys the staircase to the secure well supplying the castle.

June 27: Some of the besieged inhabitants of Minerve make a night sortie and set fire to the machine, which they have nicknamed Malvoisine, they believe has destroyed their well.

July 22: Thirst forces Minerve to surrender. Arnaud-Amaury refuses any negotiated terms. Three women of the town agree to convert and are spared. Some 140 Cathars, who refuse to abjure their faith, die at the stake in the first mass burning of the crusade.

August: De Montfort begins his siege of Termes (whose lord is a devout Cathar) but is hampered by Pierre-Roger de Cabaret's raids, which seriously damage the wooden siege engines. In another attack, de Cabaret decimates de Montfort's rearguard and mutilates those he captures as a response to what de Montfort did to his captives at Bram.

December: Termes surrenders after the defenders run out of water. The lord of Termes is consigned to the dungeons of Carcassonne where he eventually dies. By Christmas, the Court of Love has fallen and Puivert, Coustassa, Minerve, and Termes have all come under crusader occupation.

1211 **January:** Arnaud-Amaury accuses several prominent citizens of heresy and when Raymond VI, the lord of Toulouse, refuses to prosecute them, Amaury again excommunicates him. King Pedro II is present when Amaury presents his ultimatum to Raymond VI and expresses his resentment at the zealot's outrageous demands. Raymond VI de Toulouse is encouraged by the Aragónese king's support and begins to organize a coalition of his neighboring lords including the comte de Comminges and Raimond Drut, the comte de Foix, whose fiefdoms are threatened by de Montfort's land grabbing.

March: With the arrival of a new host of crusaders from northern France de Montfort is able to threaten Pierre-Roger de Cabarat's formidable Lastours-Cabaret defense complex. Loba is forced to flee and Pierre-Roger agrees to free Bouchard and surrender his fortresses in exchange for some land in Béziers.

May: De Montfort seizes Lavaur, the castle of Aimery de Montréal, a lord who had revolted against him. Aimery and his knights are hung and 300 to 400 Cathars burned. Aimery's sister, Giralda de Laurac, is reportedly turned over to be abused by de Montfort's soldiers before being thrown into a well and stoned to death. During de Montfort's attack on Lavaur, the comte de Foix, Raimond Drut, and the comte de Comminges manage to engage and briefly hold off a massive host of Teutonic knights from Germany that arrive at the eleventh hour to reinforce the murderous crusaders. The fortress of Montferrand is surrendered by Raymond VI de Toulouse's brother, Beaudouin, who joins the ranks of the crusaders as he turns over his castle, Bruniquel, to de Montfort.

Early June: The fortress of Cassès is swiftly taken by the crusaders and about fifty Cathars are burned.

June 15: De Montfort, reinforced by a large Teutonic contingent, lays siege to Toulouse. The formidable walled city is reinforced by warriors under the command of the comte de Comminges and Raimond Drut, the comte de Foix.

June 29: After repeated sorties from within the city, de Montfort is forced to lift the siege and pull back to replenish his ranks.

September: Raymond VI de Toulouse and Raimond Drut press home their advantage, leading a sizable force (possibly about 10,000) to besiege de Montfort at Castelnaudary. Raimond Drut engages a relief force, led by Bouchard de Marly, on the road to Castelnaudary. De Montfort abandons the defense of Castelnaudary to assist. His arrival turns the tide of the battle and leads to the defeat of Raimond's army. However, de Montfort is not strong enough to prevent Raimond Drut's escape and the subsequent seizure of Castelnaudary by Raymond VI de Toulouse who is able to recapture about sixty fortresses or towns held by de Montfort's crusaders.

In the autumn of 1211 Raymond VI de Toulouse and Raimond Drut try unsuccessfully to retake Cabaret.

1212 **April:** De Montfort is reinforced, enabling him to conquer Quercy, Agenais, and Comminges. Guy de Montfort, Simon's brother, unsuccessfully lays siege to Montségur.

July 16: King Pedro II achieves an epic victory over the Almoravid sultan at Las Navas de Tolsa, effectively driving the last of the Moors from the subcontinent. Meanwhile Pierre Maurand, the first victim of the Crusade, returns from his exile in the Holy Land. He is immediately reelected magistrate in Toulouse and the town's increasingly desperate citizens appeal to King Pedro II for aid.

1213 Simon de Montfort lays siege to Montségur, again unsuccessfully.

September: King Pedro II leads an army to Toulouse in response to de Montfort's aggression. He besieges Muret, one of the castles held by de Montfort's troops, and Raimond Drut and the comte de Comminges immediately join him.

September 11: The lord of Toulouse is on his way to Muret with a large siege train when de Montfort returns to reinforce the besieged garrison.

September 12: King Pedro II launches a dawn assault on the castle that is quickly repelled. His attack is followed by a daring sortie by de Montfort that forces the Catalan monarch's army to engage in an unexpected melée. Ignoring Raimond Drut's advice not to face de Montfort on open ground, King Pedro II of Aragón is killed in the action and his army panics. De Montfort wins a decisive victory. Occitania's fate as an independent nation is sealed.

1214 Pope Innocent III appoints a new legate to replace Arnaud-Amaury.

April: Raimond Drut and the comte de Comminges submit to the new legate. Raymond VI de Toulouse is helpless to put up any further resistance. He flees to England and the pope proclaims that Toulouse is to be ceded as a fief to the king of France, Philippe II. Philippe II's fortunes have been recently bolstered by his victories over the English king John I's attempted invasion of southwest France, and then over the German emperor Otto IV at the battle of Bouvines (July 27, 1214) in northeastern France, freeing the French monarch to consider acquiring the regions to the south of his principal domain.

November: Simon de Montfort advances to the northern borders of Languedoc and into Périgord, taking some castles along the Dordogne River. The region is the territory of Bernard de Casnac, a bold Cathar military leader. Domme castle, a former Cathar stronghold, is abandoned before de Montfort arrives. Next, he takes possession of the auspiciously named Montfort castle, which has also been left deserted before the approach of the crusaders.

De Montfort continues along the Dordogne to the fortified castles of Castlenaud and Beynac, each on opposite sides of the river, only a short distance apart. Finding Castlenaud empty, de Montfort places a garrison in it before proceeding to Beynac where he attempts to demolish the fortifications while taking care not to harm the locals who are under the protection of the king of France. The Dordogne operations will mark the northern limit of the Albigensian wars.

1215 Early in the year, Bernard de Cazenac seizes back Castelnaudary and kills the garrison left behind by de

Montfort who conducts a swift expedition back into Périgord, recapturing the castles and killing all the Cathar defenders. Bernard de Cazenac avoids capture and continues to engage the crusaders' flanks. On his return de Montfort and his son Amaury cut a deal with Bernard d'Alion who will later become the lord of Usson.

May: King Philippe II sends his son, Prince Louis (future Louis VIII), to accompany de Montfort when the latter enters Toulouse.

November: Raymond VI de Toulouse and Raimond Drut travel to Rome to appear before the Fourth Lateran Council. The pope confirms de Montfort's right to Toulouse although the rights of Raymond VI de Toulouse's eldest son, eighteen-year-old Raymond VII to Provence, are not affected. However, Raimond's ward, the ten-year-old Raymond Trencavel, son of the deceased Raimond Roger de Trencavel, is disinherited.

In Toulouse, the Order of the Black Friars is founded by Domingo de Guzman. The black-robed Dominicans are to become the principal architects and administrators of the Inquisition. Death of Pierre Vidal, noted troubadour and one-time wooer of Loba, the she-wolf of Carcassonne.

1216 **April:** De Montfort pays homage to Philippe in Paris, ceding his conquests to the French sovereign. Resentment rises in the Languedoc region, which welcomes the return of Raymond VI de Toulouse and his nineteen-year-old son, Raymond VII, at the port of Marseilles. Avignon, which is within the domain of the comte de Provence and a dependent of the German emperor, rallys to their side and contributes troops for the capture of Beaucaire where de Montfort has installed some troops under Lambert de Thury regardless of the fact that the Provence fortress is outside his rightful lands.

May: Raymond VII besieges the French garrison at

Beaucaire. His father, Raymond VI de Toulouse, seeks reinforcements from Aragon. Simon de Montfort rushes to relieve the town.

July: Death of Pope Innocent III, election of Honorius III. Order of Black Friars confirmed.

August: De Montfort surrenders Beaucaire, his first major defeat. Immediately after, de Montfort puts down another revolt at his capital city of Toulouse. Following this, he goes to fight in Bigorre and meets another defeat at Lourdes in the Hautes-Pyrenees, which marks the western limit of the crusade.

1217 De Montfort leads a campaign against the county of Foix, laying siege to the lands of Raimond Drut. He captures Montgrenier and his campaign reaches the Corbières area as far as the Drôme Valley. Meanwhile, Raymond VII leads a large Aragonese host across the Pyrenees.

September 13: Raymond VII's force liberates Toulouse. De Montfort returns and attempts a siege.

1218 **June 21:** During the siege of Toulouse, Simon de Montfort's brother Guy is wounded by a crossbow bolt. When Simon goes to his aid he is struck and killed by a rock fired from a rotating-beam artillery machine reportedly crewed by women. The death of de Montfort dramatically changes the nature of the crusade as there is no noble ready or available to take his place as leader. The new pope, Honorius III, asks the king of France to assist Simon's twenty-six-year-old son and heir, Amaury de Montfort. Philippe II Auguste sends Prince Louis for a second time and the Cathar refuge of Belcaire comes under renewed siege. However, Louis's expedition is very circumspect and his father waits for the confusion in the Lauguedoc to settle down before making a decisive move.

December: Vowing to avenge his father, Amauray de Montfort lays siege to Marmande.

1219	Raymond VII de Toulouse and Raimond Drut succeed in defeating a huge army of northern French knights at Baziège.

June 3: Prince Louis reinforces Amaury de Montfort, forcing the capitulation of Marmande and the entire population (possibly 5,000 men, women, and children) are massacred.

June 16: Amaury and Prince Louis march on Toulouse, briefly renewing the siege. Prince Louis abruptly withdraws and returns to northern France, leaving Amaury de Montfort to suffer a series of defeats as one crusader garrison after another surrenders to Raymond VII and Raimond Drut. |
| **1220** | Raymond VII and Raimond Drut reliberate Castelnaudary. During the attack, Guy de Montfort (Simon's younger son), is killed. This time, Amaury de Montfort is unable to recapture the town despite an eight-month siege lasting til March 1221. |
| **1221** | **February:** Raymond IV and Raimond Drut recapture Montréal. During the attack, the local lord, Alain de Rouey, who killed Pedro II of Aragón at the battle of Muret, is mortally wounded. The nearby village of Fanjeaux has now become a crusader stronghold and is attacked and burnt by Raimond Drut. As Raimond and his comrades recapture their lands, Catharism resurfaces and many Catholic priests, friars, and prelates are forced to flee. |
| **1222** | Death of Domingo de Guzman. Amaury de Montfort and Raymond VII offer sovereignty of Toulouse to Philippe II Auguste, who refuses it.

July: Raymond VI de Toulouse dies and is denied a Christian burial by the church. His son, Raymond VII, succeeds him as the comte de Provence and rightful lord of all Occitania. The fiefdom of Alet is handed over to Raimond Drut by Father Boston. While Raimond the Beloved is proclaimed as a hero and the savior of the south, his reputation |

is blackened by the church and wild rumors are spread by the monks of Mercus abbey claiming that his bastard daughter, Esclarmonde, is a witch.

1223 Death of Phillippe August, the king of France. His successor, Louis VIII initially remains remote from any strong support of Amaury de Montfort.

March 27: Raimond Drut dies of wounds received relieving the siege of Mirepoix. He is succeeded by his son Roger Bernard. The castles of Montségur and Usson are granted to his seventeen-year-old daughter Esclarmonde as part of her dowry.

1224 **January:** Amaury de Montfort abandons Carcassonne and retreats to northern France. He offers the conquered lands to the new French monarch, Louis VIII. Eighteen-year-old Raymond-Roger IV de Trencavel returns from exile and enters his father's former capital city. At this point, the crusade seems to have failed and Arnaud-Amaury dies a bitter and disillusioned man. King Louis VIII is ready to expand the royal domain and accepts Amaury de Montfort's offer. However, Pope Honorius III (not eager to have a stronger French presence in the Languedoc) has to be persuaded by the bishops in southern France to continue supporting the crusade. Domingo de Guzman is canonized as Saint Dominic and Raimond Drut's orphaned daughter is proclaimed by some to be the saint of another "unknown religion"—the second Esclarmonde. Her older sister Caecilie is forced to marry Bernard of Comminges to protect herself from the rising storm.

1225 The resurgent Cathar Church calls a general assembly at Pieusse. A new Cathar bishopric is established in Razes. Raymond VII de Toulouse is excommunicated when he attends the Council of Bourges (November–December 1225).

1226 **June 6:** As a fief of the German emperor, Avignon refuses to open its gates to the king of France. A three-month siege ensues.

June 16: Carcassonne surrenders to Louis VIII.

September 12: Avignon capitulates and Toulouse prepares to resist alone.

November 8: King Louis VIII dies in Auvergne as he is returning to northern France. His seneschal, Humbert de Beaujeu, continues the crusade. Blanche de Castille, the regent for her son Louis IX, confirms Beaujeu's position.

1227 The death of Pope Honorius III leads to the election of Pope Gregory VIII. Labécède is besieged by Humbert de Beaujeu and the bishops of Narbonne and Toulouse; the entire town is reportedly massacred.

1228 Guy de Montfort, brother of Simon de Montfort, and uncle to Amaury, returns to the Languedoc and is killed besieging Vareilles in January 1228. Toulouse is starved in the summer.

November: Bernard and Oliver de Termes are surrounded. Blanche de Castille agrees to recognize Raymond VII as the legitimate owner of the county of Toulouse (and vassal of France) if he marries his only daughter, Jeanne (nine years old), to her son, Alphonse of Poitiers (also nine and brother to the young Louis).

1229 **April 12:** Raymond VII agrees to Blanche's terms and agrees to fight the Cathar heresy, to return all church property, to demolish the defenses of Toulouse, and to turn over all his castles as well as pay damages. Raymond VII is imprisoned and his wife is expelled from Toulouse. This marks the end of independence in the Languedoc. The Inquisition is established in Toulouse with a brief to root out and destroy the "heresy" by whatever means available.

1232 Guilhabert de Castries requests that Montségur become the center of the Cathar Church and the treasures of their faith are taken there for safekeeping, including the Book of the Seven Seals and, allegedly, the Grail itself. After taking refuge in the chateau of Albedun in the Corbières, de Castries asks Raimond de Pereilha to allow the faithful to live at Montségur. De Castries and the heretical bishop of Agen, Tento I, move their sees to the pog. Both subsequently disappear from recorded history.

1233 Pope Gregory IX supports the Dominican-run Inquisition, allowing it limitless powers to torture and burn heretics at the stake.

April: The Inquisition is established in the Languedoc. Cathars are ruthlessly sought out. Many resist or take refuge in the castles of Fenouillèdes and Montségur. Sick, eldery, and even exhumed bodies are burned. The Inquisition's gruesome excesses incite revolts in Narbonne, Cordes, Carcassonne, Albi, and Toulouse.

1234 Pierre Roger de Mirepoix arrives at Montségur, marries Raimond de Pereilha's daughter, Phillipa, and is effectively placed in charge of the castle garrison.

1235 Popular uprisings against the Inquisition occur in many areas of former Occitania. The Dominicans are expelled from Toulouse. An inquisitor is thrown into the river Tarn at Albi. At Cordes, three inquisitors are thrown down a 100-foot well to their deaths, allegedly in reprisal for the murder of Dame Gerauda. By autumn, the Inquisition had been run out of Toulouse, Albi, and Narbonne.

1236 The Inquisitors return to Toulouse. Esclarmonde the bastard marries Bernard d'Alion to secure a vital treaty and safeguard the supply lines to Montségur.

1237 Raimond de Pereilha, the lord of Montségur, is accused of heresy. The Dominican friars initiate their inquests in Castelbo, leading to the imprisonment of forty-five heretics and the customary exhumation and burning of their dead co-sectarians. With the Inquisition operating in Catalonia and Aragon, many of the remaining Cathars are forced to flee to Lombardy.

Chronology of the Last Crusade

1240   Raymond-Roger IV de Trencavel leads a final revolt from the Corbieres region, raising an army, and liberating Limoux, Alet, and Montreal.

Esclarmonde dons armor to fight alongside her twin brother, Loup, who has become the head of the resistance in the mountains. Raymond-Roger IV de Trencavel is defeated at Carcassonne and forced to begin negotiations in Montréal after thirty-four days of siege. He retires to Aragón with the remnant of his army. Meanwhile, the French army, under Jehan de Beaumont, enters the Fenouillèdes.

November 16: Peyrepertuse, the largest of the Cathar fortresses, surrenders to Beaumont after a three-day siege.

1241   Louis IX orders Raymond VII to destroy Montségur. A reluctant siege ensues. The defenders, dubbed the children of Belisama by Pierre Roger de Mirepoix, prevail.

At Hautpoul, the parfait, Guilhelm d'Airons, miraculously heals the wounds of the Catharists with his outstretched hands. The death of Pope Gregory IX is followed by the election and sudden death of his successor Pope Celestin IV.

1242   **May:** Raymond VII de Toulouse obtains support from the kings of Castile, Aragón, Navarre, and England and revolts against Louis IX. Simultaneously, the English king, Henry III, invades southwestern France, initiating the Saintonge War. Meanwhile, a courier brings a letter to Montségur from a clandestine Cathar, Raymond d'Alfaro, the bailiff at Avignonet. The letter informs Pierre Roger de Mirepoix that the chief Inquisitors of Toulouse, Etienne de Saint-Thibery and Guillaume-Arnaud, will be arriving in Avignonet within the next few days. Pierre Roger de Mirepoix quickly descends from Montségur with his knights and at Gaja-la-Selve they recruit a small force of men armed with hatchets and cudgels.

May 28: On the eve of the Feast of Ascension, the raiding party from Montségur position themselves in a copse of trees known as Antioch Wood on the outskirts of Avignonet where they are met by Guillaume-Raymond Golairan, one of Alfaro's men, who informs de Mirepoix that he has personally ensured the black Dominicans are lodged in the central chamber of the castle keep. The knights Guillaume de Lahille, Bernard de Saint-Martin, and Guillaume de Balaguire lead the force into Avignonet. The raiders are allowed to slip into the castle and are guided to the quarters where the Inquisitors are sleeping. Some of the Inquisitors and approximately ten friars attempt to take refuge in the chapel and are duly cut down. After the massacre is complete, their clothes, funds, and belongings are looted and the Inquisition registers are carefully searched out and set on fire.

July: Louis IX defeats King Henry III at Saints and at Taillebourg. Raymond VII de Toulouse's allies fall away as they see the French king preparing for a massive campaign into the Languedoc.

1243 January: Raymond VII de Toulouse is compelled to submit to the French king. Though Louis IX pardons Raymond VII, the Roman Catholic Church does not and he remains excommunicated. Montségur is dubbed the Synagogue of Satan by the Council of Béziers, who elect to destroy the Cathar stronghold at all costs. The siege of Montségur begins in earnest. Raimond de Pereilha, Esclarmonde d'Alion, and the castle's 500 inhabitants, including the garrison of 150 men-at-arms under de Mirepoix and some 15 knights, stand alone against an army of 10,000 under the command of Hugues des Arcis, seneschal of Carcassonne, and Pierre Amiel, the archbishop of Narbonne. The siege continues throughout the winter with battles fought every day. The election of Pope Innocent IV helps stabilize the Holy Roman Church's hold over Europe.

1244 **January:** Brilliant young inventor Bertrand de la Vacalarie breaks through the crusader lines and succeeds in building a siege engine within the castle walls, effectively prolonging the stand off for another two months.

March 1: Basque mercenaries, led by shepherds from Camon, scale the sheer side of the pog under the cover of darkness and penetrate the Ers tower, forcing the posterns and bringing the keep within range of ballista fire. A sortie lead by de Mirepoix fails to dislodge the mercenaries from the barbican. Most of the remaining able bodied men die this night. Only a promise to surrender on the following morning prevents a general massacre.

March 2: Ceasefire negotiations begin with Pierre Roger de Mirepoix's brother-in-law, Raimond d'Aniort, acting as an intermediary between the head of the castle garrison and Hugues des Arcis. The defenders are given a fifteen-day truce in which to prepare themselves, the men-at-arms are granted an amnesty, and the convictions against the knights who took part in the Avignonet massacre are waived. During the ceasefire, the castle's treasures, including the Book of the Seven Seals, are allegedly smuggled to safety.

March 15: The priestess Rixende de Tell and the priest Betrand Marty preside over a ceremony within the castle walls to mark the spring equinox and the Cathar feast day of Bema. Several of the men-at-arms convert to Catharism at the last moment and take the consolamentum, choosing to die on the fire rather than lay down their arms and walk away.

March 16: Approximately 225 perfecti are burned alive, including Rixende de Tell, Bertrand Marty, Corba de Pereilha, and her daughter, Esclarmonde de Pereilha. The remains of Esclarmonde d'Alion (also known as Esclarmonde the bastard, or Esclarmonde de Montségur) are never found.

1245 Guy de Levis is placed in charge of Montségur. He installs guards equipped with hounds trained to hunt down those heretics who still feel compelled to return to the ruins of the castle when the moon is full. The job of clearing the thorn bushes from the side of the pog and hunting down the remaining fugitives is entrusted to Bernard Espinasser, the "Thorn Cutter." The Cathar Church is dismantled and its last leaders flee to Lombardy.

1249 Raymond VII assists the Inquisition in an effort to clear his name and cooperates in the burning of some people at the stake in Agen. He dies shortly afterward as he is preparing to join Louis IX on the seventh crusade. Jeanne, his daughter, becomes comtess de Toulouse.

1250 According to the Summa of the Inquisitor Rainerius Sacchoni, the number of surviving Cathar perfecti in the old churches of Albi, Toulouse, Carcassonne, and Agen stands at barely 200. In contrast, the Cathar perfecti in Italy, including those of the exiled church of northern France, number approximately 2,550.

1253 Fall of Puilaurens.

1255 The final military action in the forty-five-year crusade is the siege of the small Cathar fortress of Quéribus. Louis IX requests that the seneschal of Carcassonne, Pierre d'Auteuil, finish off this last bastion of resistance and take the castle from Chabert de Barbaira.

August: Quéribus falls to the crusaders.

1258 Bernard d'Alion is publicly burned in the town square in Perpignan.

1262 Pierre Roger de Mirepoix dies in exile in northern Spain.

1271 Death of Alphonse de Poitiers and Jeanne de Toulouse without issue. Toulouse passes to the French crown. Occitania technically ceases to exist.

1311 Pierre Authié, the first Cathar perfecti to return to Montségur in an attempt to revive the faith in the area after the fall of the castle, is condemned and publicly burned.

1318 Bishop-Inquisitor Jacques Fournier conducts the first of his hearings at Montaillou. His Inquisition register will serve as the primary source for many latter-day historians such as Otto Rahn and Emmanuel Le Roy Ladurie.

1321 The last known Languedoc perfecti, Guilhelm Bélibaste, is burned alive at Villerouge-Termenes. The chain of direct initiation is broken. The last mass burning of Cathars takes place in Carcassonne.

APPENDIX 3

Cathars of Montségur

The Martyred and Their Legacy

A PARTIAL ROLL CALL OF THE CATHAR MARTYRS KNOWN TO HAVE PERISHED IN THE FINAL DAYS OF THE SIEGE OF MONTSÉGUR

Sons of Belisama: Knights, Sergeants, and Faidits

Knight Jourdain du Mas: Consolamentum under special circumstances in February 1244. He was in a coma after being struck by a stone missile and could not consciously acknowledge the procedure before dying.

Knight Betrand de Bardenac: Consolamentum before dying "after Noel 1243."

Sergeant Bernard Rouain: Consolamentum at death from wounds on February 21, 1244.

Sergeant Bernard de Carcassonne: Consolamentum at death on February 26, 1244.

Pierre Ferrer: Catalan bailiff of Pierre-Roger Mirepoix, consolamentum at death from wounds on March 1, 1244.

Sergeant Guillaume D'aragon: Participant in the Avignonet assassinations, killed at an undetermined date.

The Faithful: Perfecti and Credentes

Approximately 225 martyrs perished on the Camp de Cremat on March 16, 1244. Surviving inquisition documents record only sixty-three of them by their names and ranks:

Raymond Agulher: Perfect at Tarascon in 1204 and present at Montségur from 1234

Guilleme Aicart: Resident at Montségur from 1234 with his wife and three sons; consolamentum on the night of March 13

Pons Ais: Perfect present at Montségur from the start of the siege where he served as a miller Pierre Arau: Perfect

Bernard D'Auvezines: Perfect

Raymonde Barbe: From Mas Saintes-Puelles, sister of perfect

Raymond du Mas: Aka, Raymond de Na Rica

Raymond De Belvis: Crossbowman from Arnaud and seigneur of Usson; arrived at Montségur circa May–June 1243; consolamentum on March 13

Arnaud De Bensa: From Lavelanet, sergeant, wounded end of February 1244, consolamentum on March 4

Etienee Boutarra: Perfect

Bresilhac: Dispossesed knight from Caihavel; present at Montségur from 1236; consolamentum on March 13

Pons Capelle: From Gaja; perfect; arrived at Montségur circa 1242 with his son, a sergeant

Guidraude De Caraman: Perfect

Arnaud Des Casses: Knight and seigneur of Casses; believer since 1220; perfect before 1243

Clamens: Present at the seige; circa March 13, 1244, named as having transfered church treasury into the custody of Pierre Roger de Mirepoix; presumably a Cathar perfect

Jean De Combel: Knight from Laurac; believed to have accepted consolamentum during the truce

Saissa De Congost: From seigniorial family at Puivert; perfecta from 1240; householder on Montségur

Raymonde De Cuq: Sister or cousin of Berenger, the seigneur of Lavelanet; perfecta at Lauran in 1230; lived with Corba de Pereilha at Montségur

Guillaume Dejean: Perfect from Tarabel; ordained deacon at Montségur

Guillaume Delpech: Sergeant; arrived to reinforce Montségur May 21, 1243; consolamentum on March 13

Arnaud Domergue: From Laroque d' Olmes; sergeant residing at Montségur since 1236 with wife; consolamentum on March 13

Bruna Domergue: Wife of Sergeant Arnaud Domergue; consolamentum March 13

Rixende Donat: From Toulouse; perfecta

India de Fanjeaux: Lady from the Lahille branch of Fanjeaux; perfecta in 1227 and householder on Montségur

Guillaume Garnier: Cowherd from d'Odars near Lanta; believer since 1230; sergeant at Montségur in 1243; consolamentum on March 13

Arnaud-Raymond Gauti: Knight from Soreze and Durfort; believer in 1237

Bernard Guilhem: Perfect

Raymond Isarn: Brother of Etienne; perfect

Guillaume D'Issus: Knight and co-seigneur of Montgaillard in Lauragais, believer in 1230; present at Montségur since 1243 and reported burnt

Jean de Lagarde: Condemned by the Inquisition in Moisac in 1233; escaped to Montségur; burnt

Bruna de Lahille: Sister of Guillaume; believer in 1234; perfecta at Montségur in 1240

Guillaume de Lahille: Dispossesed knight from Laurac; defender of Castelnaudary against Amaury de Montfort in 1219–1220;

one of the Ers of the massacre of the Inquisitors at Avignonet; at Montségur from 1240; seriously wounded February 26, 1244; consolamentum on March 13

Limoux (Limos): Perfect at Montségur

Raymond de Marseillan: Dispossessed knight from Laurac; believer in 1232; consolamentum on March 13

Bertrand Marty: From Tarabel; Cathar bishop at Toulouse and head of the Cathar Church at the time of the seige; known to be at Montségur in 1232 and reported burnt

Guillelme Marty: From Montferrier; baker at Montségur; perfect

Pierre du Mas: From Mas Saintes-Puelles; perfect in 1229 and reported present at Montségur in March 1244; probably executed

Maurina (Maury): Perfecta

Braida de Montserver: Related to Arnaud-Roger de Mirepoix; believer in 1227; consolamentum during a grave illness in 1229 at Limoux; arrived as perfecta at Montségur in 1240

Arsende Narbona: Wife of sergeant Pons Narbona; consolamentum on March 13

Guillaume Narbona: Rider to knight Raymond de Marseillan and brother of Pons Narbona; consolamentum on March 13

Pons Narbona: From Carol and Cerdagne; sergeant; consolamentum with his wife on March 13

Raymond de Niort: Perfecta from Belesta; arrived clandestinely at Montségur in October 1243 with a letter from the Cathars of Cremona in Italy

Arnauld D'Orlhac: From Lavaur

Corba de Pereilha: Wife of Raimond de Pereilha; believer; consolamentum with her daughter on March 13

Esclarmonde de Pereilha: Daughter of Raimond and Corba de Pereilha; consolamentum with her mother on March 13; subsequently burnt on March 16, 1244

Peronne: Perfecta; arrived at Montségur in 1237

Guillaume Peyre: Sergeant; agent of Raimond de Pereilha; perfect;

with Clamens, consigned the Cathar treasury at Montségur to Pierre Roger de Mirepoix on March 13, 1244

Guillaume Raou: Perfect

Alazais Raseire: From Bram or district; captured at Montségur and returned for execution by fire at Bram

Jean Rey: From Saint-Paul-Cap-de-Joux; courier; arrived at Montségur on January 1, 1244, bearing a letter from the Cathars of Cremona; consolamentum March 13

Pierre Robert: From Mirepoix; merchant; believer since 1209; arrived at Montségur 1236; consolamentum March 13

Martin Roland: Brother of sergeant Bernard de Joucou and uncle of the Narbona brothers; believer in Lavelanet in 1232; perfect at Montségur in 1240

Bernard de Saint-Martin: Dispossessed knight from Laurac; one of the leaders of the massacre of the Inquisitors at Avignonet; believed to have received consolamentum with the mercenary knights Guillaume de Lahill and Brezihac de Cailhavel on March 13; burned on March 16

Raymond de Saint-Martin: Perfect and deacon

Pierre Sirven: Perfect; assistant to Cathar Bishop Bertrand Marty

Taparel: Perfect

Rixende de Telle (Teilh): Mother superior of the perfecta at Montségur during the siege

Arnaud Teuly: From Limoux; arrived at Montségur before Feberuary 14; consolamentum March 13

Raymond de Tournebouix: Sergeant; consolamentum March 13: subsequently burnt on March 16

Marquesia Unaud of Lanta: Seamstress to the Cathars at Montségur; believer since 1224; ordained perfecta at Montségur in 1234

Ermengarde D'Ussat: Believer at Montségur from 1240; consolamentum on March 16

THE ROSE OF MONTSÉGUR

Le Poème de la Rose de Montségur
Anonymous oral tradition

Le secret de la Rose vaut bien quelques épines
Ne plains pas tes efforts, sache courber l'échine
Ne sois jamais la proie du découragement
Rien ne vient ni avant ni après que son temps
Et pour la retrouver il faudra sept cents ans
N'oublie pas Compagnon, la Rose est ta compagne
Et non une ennemie, une plaie, un fardeau,
Si elle t'a piqué, arpente la montagne
Car pour toujours ami, elle y est Cartugo.
Poitevin le maçon m'a parlé d'une rose
Rose toujours fermée, rose jamais éclose
Cachée à Montségur, et que tous les quatre ans
On peut au mois de mai découvrir simplement
Pour cela il te faut ami, dès le réveil
Te tenir au mitan du Temple du Soleil
Tu tourneras ton corps face à l'ultime étoile
Quand le Soleil levant fera s'enfuir le voile
De la nuit, mon ami, prends alors ton compas
Prends aussi ton équerre, ton fil et n'oublie pas
De chasser de ton cœur les ennuis, la rancune
Sois serein face au ciel afin qu'Isis la Brune
Puisse enlever pour toi les voiles de la nuit.

Author's translation

The Secret of the Rose is well worth a few thorns
Do not spare any effort, know how to bow your head
Never fall prey to discouragement
Nothing comes before or after its time
And to find it will take seven hundred years
Don't forget, good companion, the Rose is your true companion
And not an enemy, a plague or a burden,
If she has stung you, then walk the mountain
Because my eternal friend, she is Cartugo.*
Poitevin the mason told me about a rose
A rose that was always closed, a rose that never bloomed
Hidden in Montségur, and every four years
In May we can discover its secret very simply
All you need to do is wake up early, my friend
Stand in the middle of the Temple of the Sun
And turn your body to face the last star
When the rising sun chases away the veil
Of night, then take your compass, good friend
And take your square and your line and don't forget
To drive from your heart all troubles and resentment
Be serene in front of the sky so Isis the Dark One
Can lift from you the veils of the night.

---

*Etymologically obscure; possibly a reference to a mountain in the Catalan Pyrenees.

APPENDIX 4

The Holy Grail in the *Nottingham Evening Post*

A 1931 article from the *Nottingham Evening Post* details how the engineer Monsieur Arnaud planned to retrieve the mythical treasure of Montségur. The text reads:

The Holy Grail—Search in Castle Ruins for Famous Relic Believed Hidden in Underground Passage

The Holy Grail, famed in Arthurian legend and the object of the quest on the part of the knights of the round table, is believed to be hidden in a ruined castle in the south of France.

M Arnaud, a French engineer in charge of hydro electric development work in the Ariége department of the Midi, who has made a life study of the Albigenses or Catharist heretics famed in the south of France in the 12th and 13th centuries, is convinced that the Holy Grail was hidden by them in the historic ruins of the chateau de Montségur, near Foix.

The Holy Grail, according to legend, was last discovered in a medieval English castle by some knights.

It subsequently disappeared from England and was said to have been hidden in a secret place.

The quest for the Grail and the adventure of the knights of the round table is famous in English literature and is also reflected in many memorable French and German works, both ancient and modern.

The origin and nature of the Holy Grail is founded in complete mystery. According to one story, the Holy Grail is the chalice used by Christ at the last supper, and in which Joseph of Arimathea collected the heart blood of the Christ at the foot of the cross of Calvary.

200 Burned Alive at Stake

The Albigenses or Catharist heretics came into conflict with the Pope who declared a crusade against them. They maintained that Christ was not God, but a great archangel who was next in power to the Almighty, and it was on this account that he was titled as the son of God. This doctrine, amplified by other beliefs, details of which were hidden by the last surviving heretics at Montségur, gained great popularity throughout the Midi, especially in Languedoc, and numerous priests and bishops accepted the new religion.

The end of the Catharist religion came in 1213 when 200 Catharists, the last remaining hand of the heretic army, after a valiant stand, surrendered in the chateau de Montségur to the opposing army. Before they did so, however, it is claimed that they concealed in the subterranean vaults of the hill the Catharist Bible, the Holy Grail, and other important treasures in their possession.

After their surrender the 200 Catharists were tied together at a common stake at the foot of the hill leading to the castle and burned alive by an immense bonfire, which was built especially for the purpose.

M Arnaud, the French engineer, who is making his investigations independently among the ruins at Montségur, recently discovered a very thick stone wall behind some rocks. This he believes marks the entrance to the subetarranean passages beneath the castle itself.

The work of clearing the ruins and making an entrance to these passages will be a long and difficult one, but M Arnaud is confident that his theories regarding the Catharists will justify the continuance of his task and lead to important discoveries.

French press comment on the report that a modern search is in progress for the Holy Grail states, "The world of learning will await the results with curiosity."

Bibliography

Angebert, Jean-Michel. *The Occult and the Third Reich*. New York: Macmillan, 1974. First published in French as *Hitler et la tradition Cathare*.

Baigent, Michael, Richard Leigh, and Henry Lincoln. *The Holy Blood and the Holy Grail*. UK: Jonathan Cape, 1982.

Bernadac, Christian. *Le mystère Otto Rahn: le Graal et Montségur: du catharisme au nazisme* [The Otto Rahn mystery: from Catharism to nazism]. Paris: Éditions France-Empire, 1978.

Birks, Walter, and R. A. Gilbert. *The Treasure of Montségur*. Wellingborough, UK: Crucible, 1987.

Botiva, Zam [Cesar Accomani]. *Asia Mysteriosa: The Oracle of Astral Force as a Means of Communication with the Little Lights of the Orient*. UK: Polair Publishing, 2012. First published in French in 1930.

Brennon, Anne. *Le Vrai Visage du Catharisme*. Portet-sur-Garonne: Loubatieres, 1988.

Buechner, Howard. *Emerald Cup, Ark of Gold*. Metairie, LA: Thunderbird Press, 1991.

Cooke, Ivan. *Thy Kingdom Come*. London: Wright & Brown, 1933. Republished as *The Return of Arthur Conan Doyle*. UK: White Eagle Publishing Trust, 1956.

Doumayrou, Guy-René. *Géographie Sidérale*. Paris: Union Générale D'Editions, 1975.

Duvernoy, Jean. *Le Dossier de Montségur: Interrogatoires d'inquisition 1242–1247*. Toulouse: Pérégrinateur Éditeur, 1998.

Ebneter, Albert. *Der Jesuitenorden*. Zürich: Benziger Verlag, 1982.

Evola, Julius. *Pagan Imperialism*. UK: Gornahoor Press, 2017. First published as *Imperialismo Pagano* (Italian) in 1928.

———. *Revolt against the Modern World: Politics, Religion, and Social Order in the Kali Yuga*. Rochester, VT: Inner Traditions, 1995. First published in Italian as *Rivolta contro il mondo moderno* in 1934.

Gadal, Antonin. *On the Path to the Holy Grail*. Haarlem: Rozekruis Pers, 2006.

Godwin, Joscelyn. *Arktos: The Polar Myth in Science, Symbolism and Nazi Survival*. London: Thames and Hudson, 1993.

Goodrick-Clarke, Nicholas. *Black Sun: Aryan Cults, Esoteric Nazism and the Politics of Identity*. New York: New York University Press, 2001.

———. *The Occult Roots of Nazism*. New York: New York University Press, 1985.

Graddon, Nigel. *Otto Rahn & the Quest for the Holy Grail*. Kempton, IL: Adventures Unlimited Press, 2008.

Guirdham, Arthur. *The Cathars and Reincarnation*. London: Theosophical Publishing House, 1978.

———. *The Great Heresy*. Jersey: Neville Spearman, 1977.

Hüser, Karl. *Wewelsburg: Kult und Terrorstätte der SS*. Paderborn: Verlag Bonifatius, 1982.

Kerr, Philip. *Berlin Noir: The Pale Criminal*. London: Penguin Books, 1990.

Ladame, Paul Alexis. *The Mirages of Munich, or Europe Hypnotised*. Lausanne: Éditions Luce Wilquin, 1989.

———. *La Quete Du Graal, or Europe United*. Lausanne: Éditions Luce Wilquin, 1991.

Ladurie, Emmanuel Le Roy. *Montaillou: The Promised Land of Error*. New York: Random House, 1979. First published as *Montaillou, village occitan de 1294 à 1324* (Editions Gallimard, 1975).

Lange, Hans Jürgen. *Otto Rahn und die Suche nach dem Gral*. Germany: Arun Verlag, 1999.

———. *Weisthor: Himmlers Rasputin und Seine Erben*. Germany: Arun Verlag, 1998.

Levenda, Peter. *Unholy Alliance*. New York: Avon Books, 1995.

Magre, Maurice. *Le sang de Toulouse: Histoire des Albigeois du XIIe siècle* [The blood of Toulouse]. Paris: Fasquelle, 1931.

———. *Magiciens et illuminés*. Paris: Bibliothèque-Charpentier, 1930. English translation published as *The Return of the Magi* (Philip Allan, 1931).

Markale, Jean. *Montségur and the Mystery of the Cathars*. Rochester, VT: Inner Traditions, 2003. First published in French as *Montségur et l'énigme cathare* (Paris: Éditions Pygmalion/Gérard Watelet, 1986).

Maurin, Krystel. *Les Esclarmonde: La femme et la feminite dans l'imaginaire du Catharisme*. Toulouse: Privat, 1995.

Merrifield, Jeff. *The Perfect Heretics: Cathars and Catharism*. Lyme Regis, Dorsett: Enabler Publications, 1995.

Moore, R. I. *The Formation of a Persecuting Society*. New York: Blackwell, 1987.

Moulis, Adelin. *Croyances, superstitions, observancese en Comté de Foix*. Toulouse: Éditions Loubatières, 1995.

Nelli, René. *Les Cathares*. Paris: Hachette, 1981.

Oldenbourg, Zoe. *Massacre at Montségur*. Marlboro Books, 1990. First published in French as *Le bûcher de Montségur* (Librairie Gallimard, 1959).

O'Shea, Stephen. *The Perfect Heresy*. London: Profile Books, 2000.

Pagels, Elaine. *The Gnostic Gospels*. New York: Random House, 1979.

Peyrat, Napoleon. *Histoires des Albigeois: les Albigeois et l'inquisition*. Paris: Librairie Internationale, 1870.

Rahn, Otto. *Crusade against the Grail*. Rochester, VT: Inner Traditions, 2006. First published in German as *Kreuzzug Gegen den Gral* (Freiburg: Urban Verlag, 1933).

Richards, Jeffrey. *Sex, Dissidence and Damnation: Minority Groups in the Middle Ages*. London: Routledge, 1991.

Roché, Dèodat. *Ancient Gnosis and Modern Thought*. Narbonne: Sociéte du Souvenir et des Études Cathares, 1906.

Roquebert, Michel. *L' Epopée Cathare*. 5 vols. Paris: Perrin, 1970–89.

Runciman, Steven. *The Medieval Manichee*. Cambridge: Cambridge University Press, 1991.

Saunders, Tracy. *Wellspring: The Grail, the Reich and the Man in the Black Hat*. N.p.: Priscillan Press, 2023.

Shirley, Janet. *The Song of the Cathar Wars: A History of the Albigensian Crusade*. Aldershot, UK: Scolar Press, 1996.

Stein, Walter Johannes. *The Ninth Century and the Holy Grail*. Forest Row, UK: Temple Lodge Publishing, 1988.

Stoyanov, Yuri. *The Other God*. New Haven, CT: Yale University Press, 2000.

Strayer, Joseph R. *The Albigensian Crusades*. Ann Arbor: University of Michigan Press, 1971.

von Eschenbach, Wolfram. *Parzival*. Ca. 1200–1210. Available at Project Gutenberg (website).

Weis, René. *The Yellow Cross*. New York: Vintage Books, 2000.

Index

absinthe, Rahn and, 126
Accomani, Cesar. *See also* Fille, Mario
   about, 160, 163
   Fille and, 163, 165–67
   in founding of Polaires, 165
   Grace Cooke and, 172–75
   Lady Doyle and, 172
   magic applied to the art of singing and, 178
   mission to master the red rays and, 177
   oracle and, 165–67
   on the order, 167
   Parisian sessions, 165–66
   resignation from Brotherhood, 181, 184
   as Zam Bhotiva, 160, 167, 174, 176–77
Agharta, 163–65, 179, 306, 307, 308
Ahnenpass, 235–37
Albigensian crusade, 105, 387, 389
Albigensians, 6–7
alchemy, 297, 339
alignment, sun and moon, 254
al-Lat, 347
altar of Fontanet, 277
Amariah, Ruby, 352, 355–58, 363–67
Ancient and Mystical Order Rosae Crucis (AMORC), 171, 299
Andreae, Johann Valentin, 299
Arctic Circle, Rahn journey, 303–5
Ark of the Covenant, 10, 64, 194
Arnaud-Amaury, 37–38, 393
Arthur Conan Doyle's Book of the Beyond (Cooke), 176
Asia Mysteriosa, 160–61, 167
Au-Set, 339
Avignonet massacre, 47–48

Baeschlin, Asta, 315–16
ballista ammunition, 3
bankruptcy, Rahn, 202
Bélibaste, Guilhelm, 57–59, 93
Bernadac, Christian, 122–26, 141, 209, 326
Bernadac, Paul, 124, 125–26, 129–32
Bethlehem Grotto
   about, 138–40
   ancient altar, 257

422 Index

Mandement and, 141, 325
photo, 139
return to, 366–67
Ruby dream and, 366–67
stone pentagram, 140, 292
Bhotiva, Zam, 160, 167, 174, 176–77
Black Glove, 245, 249
Black Madonna of Montserrat
　about, 333
　author at, xiv
　churches dedicated to, 337
　photo, 334
　replica, 341
Black Mother, basilica, 206, 330, 331, 337
Black Order, 131, 210–11, 222, 225, 228, 305, 314–15
black stones, 280–82, 285–86, 287, 291, 344–45
Black Sun (Schloss Wewelsburg), 218, 219
Blanchard, Victor, 185–86
bleeding stones, 278–83, 295, 300, 309, 369
bon Marburg, Konrad, 82
Book of Love (Book of the Seven Seals), 28, 55, 181
Book of Half-Open Lotuses, The (Magre), 91
Bormann, Martin, 314, 317, 319
Bouan grotto, 121, 125
Bourne, JB, 110–11, 114, 272–74, 279
Bram, 38–39, 392, 393
Buechner, Colonel Howard
　about, 11–12
　on Arctic cavern discovery, 306–7
　fantasy, 12–13
　Holy Grail and, 12–13, 272
　the pog and, 66

on Pyrenean Grail, 307
Rahn as imprisoned, 73–74
Rahn as still alive and, 65
on valley skirmish, 62–66
Carcassonne
　abandonment of, 400
　metaphysical enlightenment and, 29
　Spring 1998, 235–43
　surrender, 390–91
　survivors of siege, 39
Castelnau, Pierre de, 35
Cathar Church
　establishment in the south, 201
　foundation document of, 28
　gathering of heads of, 386
　head of, 46
　resurgence, 400
Cathar faith
　about, 278
　asceticism and, 27
　belief system, 27, 28
　as driven underground, 27
　after fall of Montségur castle, 53
Catharism, 5, 6, 31, 50, 57, 91, 246
Cathar perfecti, 159, 240, 362, 378
Cathars
　Christ as prophet and, 288
　Druids and, 83
　fate of (drawing), 41
　first understanding of, 22
　goodness and evil and, 27
　Lucifer and, 117–19
　mass burning of, 40–41
　of Montségur, 408–12
　term usage, 5–6
Caussou, Arthur, 55–57
Cavalcanti, Guido, 201
cave paintings, 69–70

caves of Ussat
  Gadal claim of ownership, 126
  Gadal with relics from, 269
  Graal blazon, 141–43
  journey to, 122
  Koenig on, 267
  Rahn desire to return, 204
  Rahn exploration of, 127, 131–32
  silence and darkness of, 143–44
Chambon, Fabrice, 104
chivalry, 25–26
chronology of last crusade, 386–407
chronology of life, Otto Rahn, 383–84
CIA, 150, 191
Coca-Cola Europe, 150, 151, 293
Collins, Andy, 286
Colum, 187–89
consolamentum, 28, 50
Cooke, Grace
  about, 158
  Accomani and, 172–75
  channeling Sir Arthur, 158–60, 174–75
  disembodied Cathar adepts and, 180
  founding of British chapter of Polaires, 184
  "mysterious illness," 180
  na Esclarmonda and, 181
  photo, 173
  Polaires and, 177–78
  séances, 174–75
Cooke, Ivan, 173, 175–77
"Count Sainte Germaine: Magician or Charlatan" (Rahn), 80
Couquet, Aimeé. *See also* Maison Couquet
  about, xi, 62
  death of, 350
  hearing official apology (photo), 375
  Laffont and, 66–68

Oelbermann and, 134
Our Lady of Montségur and, 341
photo, 63
revisiting, 351
Court of Lucifer, The (Rahn)
  about, 211
  companion in caves, 137
  edition discrepancies, 239
  final passage, 304
  Goethe and, 223
  illustrated, 211
  on looking for divinity, 201
  lump of amber, 79–80
  Nazi propaganda, 237
  on *Parzival* names, 182–83
  promotion of, 211–12
  three manuscripts and, 290
CRC, 297–98
crown of Lucifer, 105, 107
Crusade against the Grail (Rahn)
  about, 205–6
  data compiled for, 105
  first edition (photo), 207
  inscription on fly leaf, 193
  manuscript, 290
  Otto Rahn at work on (photo), 202
  signed copy, 198
  Wiligut and, 223
Cube of Space, 345–65

Dachau, 11–12, 74, 135, 150, 317
d'Alion, Bernard, 53
d'Alveydre, Saint-Yves, 164–65
Dante, 141, 169, 201, 294
Dawn of Magic, The (Pauwels and Bergier), 10
death story, Rahn
  body tag (photo), 327
  death certificate and, 321–22

Hotel Zahringer and, 320
Maier family and, 320–21, 322
as martyr's death, 327
passport from corpse and, 321
von Haller and, 318–20
Zoll and, 320, 321
de Bourgogne, duc, 391
de Castries, Guilhabert, 46, 401–2
de Cazenac, Bernard, 396–97
Dee, Mike, 8, 11, 16–17, 21, 60–62, 72
de Guzman, Domingo, 33, 388
de Laurac, Giralda, 40
de la Vacalarie, Bertrand, 48
de Massabrac, Alzeu, 51
de Mirepoix, Pierre Roger (the Peacock)
about, 47
birth of, 388
concealing heretics, 52
death of, 406
fate of, 52
Inquisitors of Toulouse and, 403
phosphorescent paint and, 254–55
de Montfort, Guy, 42, 398
de Montfort, Simon
about, 36–37
death of, 42
Giralda and, 40
illustrated, 36
mass burning of Cathars and, 40–41
Montségur siege and, 395–96
warfare, 40, 389–96
de Pereilha, Esclarmonde, 411
de Pereilha, Raimon, 51, 402
de Pujol Murat, Countess Miryanne
about, 92
Lordat ruins and, 155, 159
as mentor, 119, 239
Montségur and, 94
na Esclarmonda and, 180–81

picnicking with the Polaires, 159
as Polaires spiritual figurehead, 171
time of prophecy and, 92–93
de Toulouse, Raymond VII, 397–404, 406
de Trencavel, Raimond Roger, 37, 387
de Trencavel II, Roger, 43–44
de Troyes, Chrétien, 85, 86
Devil's Bridge, 280, 282–85
Devil's Lake (Lac du Diable)
about, 15, 109
Ariègeois drawn to, 114
author at, 114–16
author at edge of (photo), 116
location of, 113
as mouth of hell, 113
photo, 110
pilgrimage to, 113
Rahn at, 105
reflections in (photo), 111
visit to, 108–19
Di Mambro, Joseph, 262, 263
Doctrine of the Two Principles, The (Nelli), 98
Doinel, Jules, 93
Dome of the Rock, 347
Donat, Rixende, 50, 410
Doyle, Lady, 172, 175, 176
Doyle, Sir Arthur Conan, 156–58, 171
Drut, Raimond, 43–44, 45, 117, 386, 387, 394, 396, 400
du Champigny, Henri Meslin, 168

Eggers, Kurt, 212, 319
eglise, 70, 71, 122
Egypt, 339
"emerald cup," 12
Emerald Cup, Ark of Gold (Buechner), 11, 306, 326

Ereshkigal, 345
Escher, Joachim, 225, 228
Esclarmonda statue, 117, 240
Esclarmonde, second (Esclarmonde the bastard), 44–46, 52, 113, 402
Esclarmonde de d'Alion, 52
Esclarmonde de Foix. *See also* na Esclarmonda
  about, 29–30, 31
  conference attendance, 388
  illustrated, 31
  Montségur stewardship, 46
  pilgrimage to Montségur, 34
  postcard images, 32
  second (Esclarmonde the bastard), 44–46, 52, 113, 402
  skull, 54
Esclarmonde de Montségur, 52
Esclarmonde de Pereilha, 50, 52
Esclarmonde the bastard, 45, 52, 113, 402
Evola, Julius, 207–8
Externsteine, 311–12
extraordinary claims, 369

faidits, 47
Fama Fraternitatis, 296
Fanck, Arnold, 89
"fear, the," 230
feast of Mary Magdalene, 37, 41
feminine principle, 345–46
Fille, Mario. *See also* Accomani, Cesar
  about, 161
  in founding of Polaires, 161–63, 165
  Giuliano and, 161–63, 165
  oracle and, 165–67
  on the order, 167
  Parisian sessions, 165–66
  workings of the oracle and, 186

Fleischmann, Herbert, 289
Foix castle, 30
Forest of Toads, 45, 379
Formisano, Ciro. *See* Kremmerz, Giuliano
Fornier, Jacques, 57, 340, 407
French Wood Gas Company, 65
Fulcanelli, 266, 289
funding, Rahn, 135, 209

Gadal, Antonin
  about, 97
  caves of Ussat and, 126
  correspondence with Rahn, 204–7
  Graal Pyrenean and, 269–70
  home of, 259–61
  Hotel des Marronniers and, 129
  Koenig on, 267–69
  photo, 97, 127
  Rahn and, 126–29, 135
  with relics from the caves (photo), 269
  as second father, 151
  Wolff and, 136
Galaad memorial
  about, 257–59
  photo, 258
  plaque, 258
Gate of the Gods, 18, 99, 106
Geheimnis Tibet ("Secret Tibet"), 314
Giuliano, Padre, 161–63, 165, 168
Gnostic mass, 93
"goose foot," 254
Graal blazon, 141–43
Graal Pyrenean, 269–70, 288, 307, 370
graffiti, cave. *See also* Grotto de Lombrives
  about, 146
  illustration detail, 148

Mandement and, 325
Rahn and, 146–47
Grail family, 30
GRAME (Groupe de Recherches Archéologique de Montségur et Environs), 55, 104, 246
Great White Brotherhood, 163, 179
Grebe, Hans, 205
Green Order, 262
Grotto de Lombrives
  author (photo), 145
  cathedral, 138, 146, 147
  descent into, 145–46
  graffiti, 146–48
  grail hunter photo, 149
  Rahn and Gadal (photo), 144
  Rahn in, 138
grotto of Fontanet
  about, 274–75
  altar, 277
  author in (photo), 276, 277
  black stones, 280–82, 285–86, 287, 291
  Devil's Bridge, 280, 282–85
  Otto Rahn visit to, 275
  photo, 276, 277
  river, 280
  standing stones near, 275
Guardian of the Grail, 30
Guyot of Provence, 86

HAARP (High Frequency Active Auroral Research Program), 289
Habdu, 137, 314
Hall of the Dead (Schloss Wewelsburg), 218, 223, 229
"hand of God," 72
Hawking, Stephen, 362
Heinrichdorf, Wolff, 212–13

hexenkeller (torture chamber), 217
Himmler, Heinrich
  Black Order, 131, 210–11, 222, 225, 228, 305, 314–15
  with daughter Gudrun (photo), 312
  genealogy research, 232
  genetic engineering experiments, 237–38
  head of SS role, 218
  Macher dispatch to the castle, 227–28
  overflying the pog, 66
  pledges to, 238
  Race and Settlement Office (RUSHA), 313
  Rahn reporting to, 209–10
  signature on Totenkopf ring, 222–23
  surrender, 228
  visiting Montserrat, 335–36
  Wiligut and, 220–21
Hitler, Adolf, 9–10, 12, 129, 186, 281
Hitler dictatorship, 150, 225, 233, 311–12, 313
Hollow Earth, 307, 308
Holy Grail
  about, xii
  as book or tablet, 87–88
  Buechner and, 12
  Catholic use, 87
  contact with, 146–47
  crown of Lucifer, 105, 107
  knowledge of, 2
  as Luciferian symbol, 118
  in *Nottingham Evening Post*, 415–17
  path of, 88
  as spiritual current, 142
  as Stone, 87
  as symbol, 86–87
  taken before fall, 55
  von Eschenbach portrayal, 87

holy trinity, 110
Horn, Immo, 72, 81, 110, 145, 216, 280–86, 293, 304–5
Hotel, Zahringer, Freiburg, 320
Hotel des Marronniers
   about, 129
   as "her inn," 151
   location (postcard), 128
   now derelict, 259
   postcard depiction, 131
   Rahn management, 135, 151
   securing lease of, 129

Iceland
   author journey to, 302–8
   cave mouth, 305
   Mount Krafla, 302, 305, 308
   pictoglyphs, 305
   Rahn and, 303–5
   subterranean warm water lake, 306, 308
   weather of, 302–3
Ignatius of Loyola
   background, 328–30
   Black Mother basilica and, 330–31
   self-harm and, 332
   as Society of Jesus founder, 331
   spiritual exercises, 332–33
Irving, David, 323

Jacolliot, Louis, 307
Jouret, Luc, 262, 263

Kali Yuga, 93
Kasdan, Lawrence, 11, 13
keep (Montségur)
   author at, 16–21
   electromagnetic field within, 20
   photo, 355
   songs of praise sung in, 181
   storm and, 72
   summer solstice, 246–54
King Pedro II, 42
Knightly, Cat, 8–9, 16–22, 60–64, 68–69, 194, 266, 356
Koenig, Christian
   about, 261, 266
   artifacts, 273
   on the caves, 267
   on change, 368
   on Gadal, 267–69
   on the Grail, 267–68
   home, 272
   home, break-in, 300–301
   at Martyr's Memorial, 376
   meeting with, 265–72
   on meteoric artifacts, 269–70
   photo, 265
   revisiting Bethlehem Grotto and, 366–68
   on unofficial digs, 268–69
Kremmerz, Giuliano
   about, 168–69
   as Fille initiator, 169–70
   as "Kremm-Erz," 170
   matriarchy and, 170
   photo, 169
   transmission of underground stream, 169
Kubaba, 343–44

la Bouiche (subterranean river), 125
Ladame, Paul Alexis
   about, 195
   "the fear" and, 230
   first meeting with Rahn, 196
   initiation (photo), 199
   Magre and, 199

Montségur recollections, 199
"One of My Little Pals," 201
as PAL, 297
as Rahn friend, 197–201, 234–35
on Rahn's death, 234
recall of events, 295–96
on relationship with Rahn, 232–33
signed copy of *Crusade against the Grail*, 198
in *Westfront*, 197
at work (photo), 196
Lady in the Hood, 69
Laffont, Antoine, 66–68
Lake of the Trout (Lac des Truit), 109
"land mines," 40
"land of the Cathars," 6
la Reboule, 67
last crusade, 35–40
last crusade, chronology, 386–407
"Lauren" (Rahn), 80
Lavaur castle, 39–40, 394
Lectorium Rosicrucianum (LR), 204, 257, 271, 295
Les Catharisme (Roché), 140
Lesètre, Monseigneur, 168
Lewis, Harvey Spencer, 299
lightning, 18–19, 61
Light of China, The (Magre), 91
Little People, 305
Lucifer, 117, 144, 213, 235
Lux-Europa Filmgesellschaft, 89

Macher, Heinz, 227–28
Magre, Maurice
  about, 45, 90–91
  countess introduction, 92–93
  first meeting with Rahn, 91–92
  Grail fellowship, 97
  inner circle, 96–97
  Languedocian heresy and, 92
  photo, 91
  as poet laureate of Catharism, 91
  publications, 91–92
  view of Catharism, 98
Mahler, Karl, 317
Maier family, 320–21, 322
Maison Couquet. *See also* Couquet, Aimeé
  about, 62
  autumn, 1998, 272–74
  incubatory role, 94–96
  Madame Nelli at, 324–25
  photo, 63
  Rahn at, 94
  reopening of, 351
Mandement, Joseph, 141–43, 144, 325
map, quest, 125
Marty, Bertrand (Bishop), 50, 51, 405, 411
Martyr's Memorial, 102, 350, 373, 376
Mater Idaea Deum, 347–48
Maurand, Pierre, 35
meteorites, 271, 280, 344
Miller, Penny (author's mother), 308–9
Minerve, 40–41, 390, 392–93
"miracle of Fanjeaux," 33
Montaillou, 340
Montréal-de-Sos castle, 141, 142
Montségur
  about, 8
  battlefield (photo), 67
  isolation of, 14
  Mountain of Fear, 15, 45, 379
  1944 skirmish, 66–69
  postcards from, 95
  Rahn arrival in, 96
  return to, 352–54

Rock of Shadows, 15, 379
Rock of Witches, 15
underground reservoir, 54–55
village (photo), 14
village ruins (photo), 104
Montségur castle
  about, 15
  anniversary of fall (photo), 372
  author's travel group at, 16–22
  Belisenna (goddess) and, 248
  building of, 34–35
  capitulation, 50–51
  as castle of the Grail, 14
  countess de Pujol Murat and, 94
  deaths at, 54
  defenders of, 48–49
  east-facing embrasures, 360
  fall of, 15, 120–21
  given to de Levis family, 53
  ground plane, 246
  initial excavations, 261–62
  the keep, 20, 72, 181, 246–54, 355
  legend, 21
  midwinter (photo), 195
  Munsalvaesche link, 93–94, 207
  natural phenomenon, 360
  orientation, 103, 246
  period of grave, 49–50
  photo, xii, 9, 16, 192, 376
  procession, 244–46
  Rahn initial visit to, 178–79
  raiding party from, 47–48
  rebuilding of, 53
  siege of 1244, 48–52, 246
  siege survivors, 15–16
  stewardship, 46
  summer solstice, 244–55
  sun and moon alignment, 254
  surrender negotiations, 49
  treasures, 46–47, 49–50, 107
  walls as Faraday cage, 20
  winter solstice, 255
Montségur graveyard, 353
Montserrat, 206, 337–39, 340. *See also* Black Madonna of Montserrat
Montserrat, basilica, 329
Morenci Cross, 58
Mounié, Marius, 103
"Mountain Mother," 344
Mountain of Fear, 15, 45, 379
Mount Krafla, 302, 305, 308
Munsalvaesche, 87, 93–94, 207

Nadi astrology, 183
na Esclarmonda
  author and, 362–63, 367, 370
  calling divinities, 114
  channeling of, 240–41
  Cooke, Grace and, 181
  de Pujol Murat and, 117, 180–81
  Domingo and, 33
  as guardian of the Grail, 111, 240
  as light of the world, 361, 382
  materialization of, 360–62, 380
  on Opera poster, 243
  patronage and protection, 379–80
  under stewardship of, 46
  tomb, attempt to location, 178
Nazi breeding program (lebensborn), 317
Nazi mysteries, 10, 13
Nelli, René, 98, 238–39
Nelli, Suzanne
  death of, 352
  death of husband, 235
  as head of Centre for Cathar Studies, 96, 237
  la Comtesse and, 241–42

at Maison Couquet, 324–25
on Otto Rahn, 237
photo, 97
on Rahn as military envoy, 104
Rivail and, 239–40
Nerother Bund, 133–35
Nicetas, "Papa," 29
Ninth Century and the Holy Grail, The (Stein), 87
Nottingham Evening Post, Holy Grail in, 415–17

obituary, Rahn, 234
Occitania
  about, 23
  code of chivalry and, 25–26
  as democracy, 25
  equal rights and, 25
  fall to crusaders, 35–43
  folk music, 70
  Jews and Muslims, 23–24
  military campaign against, 35–36
  mountainous heartland, 43
  tradition of feminine divine and, 25
  universities, 23–24
Occult and the Third Reich, The (Angebert), 10
Odin, René, 181–82, 186
Oelbermann, Karl, 134
Oelbermann, Robert, 133–34
Olympic Games (1936), 230–32
"One of My Little Pals" (Ladame), 201
Operation Smile, 232
Opus Dei, 332, 336
Order of the Black Friars, 397, 398
Ordo Templi Orientis (OTO), 93, 263, 265
Ornolac grotto, xiii, 71, 122, 152
"Orpheus: A Journey to Hell and Beyond" (Rahn), 79–80, 290–91
Our Lady of Darkness, 333, 336. *See also* Black Madonna of Montserrat
Our Lady of Montségur, 341–43
Oxbrow, Mark, 286–87

PAL, 297
Paraire, Pierre, 57
Parzival (Eschenbach), 80–87
passport, Otto Rahn, 321
pentagram (Bethlehem Grotto)
  about, 292–93
  author and, 292–95
  depression size, 294–95
  face in, 294–95
  image of hope, 294
  Karl Rinderknecht and, 295
Perceval, the Story of the Grail (de Troyes), 85
Perrier, Raymond, 89, 150
Peyrat, Napoleon, 121
Phillipe, Andre, 155–56
pog
  about, xii
  ballista ammunition, 3
  map of the quest, 2
  overflown by Luftwaffe plane, 66
  photo, 61
  as sacred centre, 179
  skeletons recovered from, 53, 54
  view from (photo), 380
Polaires
  about, 154
  Accomani departure, 181, 184
  AMORC and, 171
  Asia Mysteriosa and, 161
  de Pujol Murat and, 159
  FUDOSI and, 171, 185
  Grace Cooke and, 177–78

Index

grand masters, 168–71
insignia, 166
lodge, 167
Lordat excavations and, 178
mission to master the red rays, 177
origins, 161–63
Rahn and, 154–55
rules and rituals, 166
Pole Star, 166
Pope Innocent III
  apostolic legates and, 35
  call to arms, 389
  death of, 398
  dispatching of apostolic legates, 388–89
  election of, 387
  heretics and, 31
  illustrated, 34
  punitive military campaign, 35
postcards (Rahn), 128, 129, 130
prism diagram, 250
Puivert castle, 26
Puységur, Guy, 190–93, 194

Queen of the Elves, 30
quest map, 125

Race and Settlement Office (RUSHA), 313
Rahn, Clara, 77, 78, 132, 151
Rahn, Karl, 75, 77, 78
Rahn, Otto (images)
  Ahnenpass, 236
  with brother, 76, 77, 79
  drawing, 1, 64
  with friend (1928), 88
  going to school with brother, 79
  with mother Clara, 132
  photo, 74, 191, 310
  playing with family dog, 80
  in Rahn family album, 77
  school days, 78
  sketch ("One of My Little Pals"), 201
  at work on first book, 202
Rahn, Otto Wilhelm
  about, 74–75
  brother's death and, 78
  death of, 147
  death story, 318–21
  as enigma, 237
  as imprisoned in Dachau, 73–74
  Ingeborgh description of, 78
  interest in stories and legends, 81–82
  life chronology, 383–84
  obituary, 234
  resignation letter, 318
  room at Maison Couquet, 64
  sexual orientation, 89, 150, 210
  as still alive, 65, 73
  stone dove of Montségur and, 56
  surviving personal effects, 79
  unpublished manuscripts, 384–85
Rahn, Rudolph, 150–51
Rahn family album, 77
Rahn family plot, Darmstadt, 326, 327
Rausch, Albert, 83, 89
Ravenscroft, Trevor, 10–11
Renewed Order of the Solar Temple (ROTS), 262
Rennes-le-Château, 194–95
resignation letter, Rahn, 318
Return of the Magi (Magre), 92
Return of Sir Arthur Conan Doyle, The (Cooke), 173
Rex Mundi, 378
Rinderknecht, Karl, 295
Rivail, Hippolyte, 239–40

Roché, Déodat
  about, 100
  apron, 100
  conferences with, 239
  in gate of Montségur fortress (photo), 99
  Grail as spiritual current, 142
  initiation, 100
  Mithras figure and, 140
  Montréal-de-Sos castle and, 142
  photo, 99
  principle titles, 101
  Rahn and, 103–5
  Society of Memory and, 100–101, 102
  Society of Remembrance, 238
Rock of Shadows, 15, 379
Roemer-Rahn, Ingeborgh, 75, 78, 79, 80, 205
Roerich, Nicholas and Helena, 164
Rose-Croix, 185–86, 298
Rosenkreutz, Christian, 296, 297–99
Rose of Montségur, The, 413–14
Rosicrucian manifestos, 298–99
Rosicrucian Order, 296–300

Sandy, Isabelle, 202
Schloss Wewelsburg
  architectural plans, 215
  Bartel's redesign, 225–26
  Black Sun, 218, 219
  defaced SS runes, 216
  Grail chamber, 223–25
  guard post, 216
  Hall of the Dead, 218, 223, 229
  Hall of the Supreme Leadership, 218
  lightning bolts, 13
  looting, 228
  North Tower, 217
  photo, 215
  Rahn's Grail transport to, 227
  torture chambers, 217
Schloss Wildenburg, 80–81
Schwabenland, 303, 304
Secret Glory, The, 286, 292, 351
Set, 339
Shambhala, 164, 300, 307
shepherd encounter, 111–13
"Shepherdess song," 266
Skorzeny, Otto, 12, 13, 62, 65–66
"smell of sanctity," 363
Society of Jesus, 331
Society of Memory, 100–101, 102
Society of Remembrance, 238
Sovereign Order of the Solar Temple (OTS), 262, 264
Spear of Longinus, 10
Spear of Destiny, The (Ravenscroft), 10
Spiritualist Association of Great Britian (SAGB), 155, 156, 160
SS order castle. See Schloss Wewelsburg
standing stones, 275
Stein, Walter Johannes, 10, 87
Stella Polaris, 187
stone dove of Montségur, 55–56
stone pots, 55–56
stones (meteorite), 269–71, 344
Stones from the Sky, 257
summer solstice, at Montségur
  Black Glove and, 245, 249
  east-facing embrasures, 246
  fiery rectangles, 251
  at the keep (6:05-6:09 a.m.), 247
  at the keep (6:10 a.m.), 248
  at the keep (6:13 a.m.), 249
  at the keep (6:14 a.m.), 250
  at the keep (6:15 a.m.), 251
  at the keep (6:16 a.m.), 252
  at the keep (6:25 a.m.), 253

photo, 245
prism and, 249–50
procession, 244–46
scene of, 249
watching, 249–53
Switzerland and Quebec slaughter, 263–64
Symmonds, Graham, 194

Tabachnik, Michael, 264
Tabor, the
  about, 109–10
  author on summit (photo), 112
  forests of (photo), 112
  heretics fleeing across, 120–21
  lakes of, 109
  view from (photo), 119
Tawaf, 345
terminology, this book, 5–7
"The Testament of Prometheus: A Journey to Hell and Beyond" (Rahn), 305–6, 314
three mothers, 328–48
Throne of Gods, 17, 69
Thy Kingdom Come (Cooke), 175–76, 181
"tomb stone," 311
Totenkopf ring, 222–23

Un Oracle Kabbalistique (Fille and Odin), 186
unpublished manuscripts, 384–85
Ussat-les-Bains. *See also* Hotel des Marronniers
  about, 256–57
  Gadal house, 259–61
  Galaad memorial and, 257–59
  photo, 273
  Rahn settlement in, 122
  summer, 207, 365

Vidal, Pierre, 48–49
von Eschenbach, Wolfram
  contact with Grail and, 146–47
  Grail portrayal, 87
  guardians of the Grail and, 287
  Guyot of Provence and, 86
  Kyot and, 86, 90, 105
  Munsalvaesche and, 87, 93–94, 207
  Parzival inspiration, 83
  poem contents, 84–85
  quest narrative, 86
  Schloss Wildenburg and, 80
  source for Grail myth, 85–86
von Haller, Albert, 318–20
von Sievers, Wolfram, 226, 227

wandering birds (Wandervogel), 82–83
Wandervogel, 132, 133
Westphalia, 214, 311, 312
Wewelsburg, 214
White, Hamilton, xi–xiv
White Eagle Lodge, 155, 184
White Lady, the (author meeting). *See also* na Esclarmonda
  as dream, 361
  initiatory flash of revelation and, 364
  Madame Couquet and, 364
  materialization of, 360–61
  Ruby and, 363–64, 365
  sign with hand, 363
  sketch, 359
  "smell of sanctity," 363
  ultraviolet, 363
  welcoming of, 361
Why I Am a Buddhist (Magre), 91
Wiligut-Weisthor, Karl Maria
  about, 219–20
  in army, 220

in asylum, 220
Crusade against the Grail and, 223
death of, 323
forced retirement, 322
Himmler and, 220
as "Himmler's Rasputin," 222
photo, 221
prophecy, 218–19
Rahn and, 223–25
rune image (photo), 221
Totenkopf ring, 222–23
Winckler-Dechend, Gabriele
about, 312–13
on Asta Baeschlin, 316
on "bronchial catarrh," 314
on Dachau, 317
on Habdu, 313–14
on Himmler and Rahn, 314
at premier of Tibetan documentary, 313–14
Rahn relationship, 313
Wiligut-Weisthor death and, 323
Wolff, Nat
about, 135
assumed names, 136–37
Bethlehem Grotto and, 138
Gadal and, 136
as "Karl," 136
as Nazi fifth columnist, 135
Rahn and, 135–36
wooden book of Montségur, 182–84

You-Kantor, 168

Zoll, 320, 321
Zone, the, xi, 278, 381